Math for All

Math for All

Differentiating Instruction, Grades K–2

Linda Dacey &
Rebeka Eston Salemi

Math Solutions Publications
Sausalito, CA

TO OUR GRANDCHILDREN

LINDA:
Benjamin, Brianna, James, Liam,
Lucas, Madelyn, Nicholas, Quinn, and Téa

BECKY:
Macy, Samantha, and Savanna

We wish them mathematics classrooms
that honor and nurture their ways of thinking.

Math Solutions Publications
A division of
Marilyn Burns Education Associates
150 Gate 5 Road, Suite 101
Sausalito, CA 94965
www.mathsolutions.com

Library of Congress Cataloging-in-Publication Data

Dacey, Linda Schulman, 1949–
   Math for all. Differentiating instruction, grades K/2 / Linda Dacey and Rebeka Eston Salemi.
      p. cm.
   Includes bibliographical references and index.
   ISBN-13: 978-0-941355-77-3 (alk. paper)
   ISBN-10: 0-941355-77-2 (alk. paper)
   1. Mathematics—Study and teaching (Primary) I. Salemi, Rebeka Eston. II. Title. III. Title: Differentiating instruction, grades K/2.
QA11.2.D329 2007
372.7′049—dc22

                                                                                          2007014894

Editor: Toby Gordon
Production: Melissa L. Inglis
Cover design: Jan Streitburger
Interior design: Joni Doherty Design
Composition: ICC Macmillan Inc.

Printed in the United States of America on acid-free paper
11 10 09 08   ML   2 3 4 5

A Message from Marilyn Burns

We at Math Solutions Professional Development believe that teaching math well calls for increasing our understanding of the math we teach, seeking deeper insights into how children learn mathematics, and refining our lessons to best promote students' learning.

Math Solutions Publications shares classroom-tested lessons and teaching expertise from our faculty of Math Solutions Inservice instructors as well as from other respected math educators. Our publications are part of the nationwide effort we've made since 1984 that now includes

- more than five hundred face-to-face inservice programs each year for teachers and administrators in districts across the country;
- annually publishing professional development books, now totaling more than sixty titles and spanning the teaching of all math topics in kindergarten through grade 8;
- four series of videotapes for teachers, plus a videotape for parents, that show math lessons taught in actual classrooms;
- on-site visits to schools to help refine teaching strategies and assess student learning; and
- free online support, including grade-level lessons, book reviews, inservice information, and district feedback, all in our quarterly *Math Solutions Online Newsletter*.

For information about all of the products and services we have available, please visit our website at *www.mathsolutions.com.* You can also contact us to discuss math professional development needs by calling (800) 868-9092 or by sending an email to *info@mathsolutions.com.*

We're always eager for your feedback and interested in learning about your particular needs. We look forward to hearing from you.

Math Solutions®
PUBLICATIONS

Contents

Preface

*T*he idea for this book began four years ago when we started to think about how few ideas related to differentiating instruction were integrated into the mathematics education literature. Our previous two books, *Growing Mathematical Ideas in Kindergarten* (1999) and *Show and Tell: Representing and Communicating Ideas in K–2 Classrooms* (2002) had provided glimpses into classrooms where differing individual needs were met, but we had not given explicit attention to this aspect of teaching. We felt strongly that a book focused on differentiating instruction in mathematics was needed.

To more effectively reach teachers' specific grade-level needs, our idea for one book grew into a two-book series, one for grades K–2 and the other for grades 3–5. Jayne Bamford Lynch agreed to collaborate on the upper elementary volume. There is significant overlap between the two books, though each is tailored to its particular grade span. The classroom vignettes differ, of course, as well as most of the teacher reflections and some teaching strategies and techniques. Sometimes particular stories and reflections were relevant across the grade levels and we made only those changes necessary for the intended audience.

Trends and buzzwords come and go in education, but the need for differentiated instruction is constant. Our students deserve to have their individual learning needs met in their classrooms. Throughout the book we suggest that teaching this way is a career-long goal, one part of our professional journey. We know that this is true for us, and we are eager to share our current thinking with you.

—LINDA DACEY
—REBEKA ESTON SALEMI

Acknowledgments

*T*his book features stories and student work from a number of classrooms. Numerous colleagues, workshop participants, children, and parents have informed our work. We are profoundly thankful for their insights, time, and contributions. We are particularly grateful to the Massachusetts students and teachers in public schools in Cambridge, Lincoln, Melrose, Peabody, Somerville, and Tyngsboro.

Linda would like to acknowledge Lesley University and the Russell Foundation for their generous support of her work. She is also indebted to the many teachers who have opened their classrooms to her. Becky remains grateful to students, parents, colleagues, and administrators in the Lincoln Public Schools who have been so supportive of her, and her work, over so many years. In particular, the rewards of being able to work and learn with colleagues such as Rachel Scheff, Kathy O'Connell, and Debbie Carpenito are rare and wonderful gifts. Together, we would like to express appreciation for Jayne Bamford Lynch who helped shape this work. Finally, our families and our friends fuel our spirits and we are always thankful for their patience, flexibility, and love.

We thank our editor, Toby Gordon, for her interest and guidance in this project from its earliest inception, and Marilyn Burns for her direction and support. Thank you, too, to Joan Carlson and Melissa Inglis and the many other talented people we have encountered at Math Solutions Publications.

Chapter 1
Thinking About Differentiation

*T*his year Erin, a kindergarten teacher, has a student whose mathematical ability far exceeds any student she has ever taught before. Erin feels as if she is constantly working to challenge this student without using activities that the child will be exploring in future grades. She wants to provide the child with work that relates to what the other students are doing, but at a more sophisticated level. Erin finds this situation particularly difficult. Though she has a strong background in early childhood education, she has never been taught how to teach more complex mathematical skills. She worries that she is not serving this child well.

Kim, a second-grade teacher, is most concerned about a student who consistently needs additional instruction and modeling. The child has difficulty explaining his thinking or making connections among problems and ideas. Often, he is just beginning to understand one concept when the class is ready to move on to another one. He is starting to say he doesn't like math. Kim recognizes that the student does better when he works one-on-one with an adult, but an additional adult is not often available and she is trying to meet the needs of all of her students. Kim would like to help this child be more successful, but just isn't sure what to do.

Christa, a first-grade teacher, worries about a child who joined the classroom in November. The student is just learning English and Christa has noticed that the child often isn't able to concentrate for more than five minutes at a time. The child is able to focus longer when the class is using Unifix cubes to represent numbers or is building patterns, but much of the current content work is related to story problems. Christa isn't sure if the problem is rooted in learning a new language, a result of the child's level of attention, or caused by difficulty with understanding mathematics. She wonders if she should do a unit on geometry and not focus so much on word problems for awhile.

These three teachers are like most teachers of young children. They want to provide for the needs of all of their students. They want to recognize the unique gifts and developmental readiness each child brings to the classroom community. These teachers also realize that addressing the variety of abilities, interests, cultures, and learning styles in their classrooms is a challenging task.

Variations in student learning have always existed in classrooms, but some have only been given recent attention. For example, our understanding of intelligence has broadened with Howard Gardner's theory of multiple intelligences (Gardner 2000). Teachers are now more conscious of some of the different strengths among students and find ways to tap into those strengths in the classroom.

Brain research has given us further insight into the learning process; for example, it has shown us that there is an explicit link between our emotional states and our ability to learn (Jensen 2005, Sprenger 2002). Having a sense of control and being able to make choices typically contributes to increased interest and positive attitudes. So we can think of providing choice, and thus, control, as creating a healthier learning environment.

At the same time that we are gaining these insights, the diversity of learning needs in classrooms is growing. The number of English language learners (ELLs) in our schools is increasing dramatically. Classroom teachers need to know ways to help these students learn content, while they are also learning English.

Different values and cultures create different learning patterns among children and different expectations for classroom interactions. In addition, our inclusive classrooms contain a broader spectrum of special education needs and the number of children with identified or perceived special learning needs is growing. On a regular basis, classroom teachers need to adapt plans to include and effectively instruct the range of needs students present.

How can teachers meet the growing diversity of learning needs in their classrooms? Further, how do teachers meet this challenge in the midst of increasing pressures to master specified content? Differentiated instruction—instruction designed to meet differing learners' needs—is clearly required. By adapting classroom practices to help more students be successful, teachers are able to both honor individual students and to increase the likelihood that curricular outcomes will be met.

This book takes the approach that differentiated mathematics instruction is most successful when teachers:

- believe that all students have the capacity to succeed at learning mathematics;
- recognize that multiple perspectives are necessary to build important mathematical ideas and that diverse thinking is an essential and valued resource in their classrooms;
- know and understand mathematics and are confident in their abilities to teach mathematical ideas;
- are intentional about curricular choices; that is, they think carefully about what students need to learn and how that learning will be best supported;
- develop strong mathematical learning communities in their classrooms;
- focus assessment on gathering evidence that can inform instruction and provide a variety of ways for students to demonstrate what they know; and
- support each other in their efforts to create and sustain this type of instruction.

We like to think about differentiation as a lens through which we can examine our teaching and our students' learning more closely, a way to become even more aware of the best ways to ensure that our students will be successful learners. Looking at differentiation through such a lens requires us to develop new skills and to become more adept at:

- identifying important mathematical skills and concepts;
- assessing what students know, what interests them, and how they learn best;
- creating diverse tasks through which students can build understanding and demonstrate what they know;
- designing and modifying tasks to meet students' needs;
- providing students with choices to make; and
- managing different activities taking place simultaneously.

Many teachers find that thinking about ways to differentiate literacy instruction comes somewhat naturally, while differentiation in mathematics seems more demanding or challenging. As one teacher put it, "Do we have to differentiate in math, too? I can do this in reading, but it's too hard in math! I mean in reading, there are so many books to choose from that focus on different interests and that are written for a variety of reading levels." While we recognize that many teachers may feel this way, there are important reasons to differentiate in mathematics.

There are several indications that we are not yet teaching mathematics in an effective manner, in a way designed to meet a variety of needs. Results of international tests show U.S. students do not perform as well as students in many other countries at a time when more mathematical skill is needed for professional success and economic security. There continues to be a gap in achievement for our African American, Native American, and Hispanic students. Finally, we are a country in which many people describe themselves as math phobic and others have no problem publicly announcing that they failed mathematics in high school.

In response to these indicators, educators continue to wrestle with the development and implementation of approaches for teaching mathematics more effectively. The scope of the mathematics curriculum continues to broaden and deepen. There are shifts in emphasis. For example, current trends stress the importance of algebra and, as a result, the elementary curriculum is shifting its focus to include early algebraic thinking. The way we teach math has changed, requiring students to communicate their mathematical thinking, to solve more complex problems, and to conceptually understand the mathematical procedures they perform. And, all of this is happening at a time when our national agenda is clear that "no child is to be left behind."

Even though teachers strive to reach all of their students, learners' needs are ever increasing and more complex to attend to in the multifaceted arenas of our classrooms. Considering the ways differentiation can assist us in meeting our goals is essential. Carol Tomlinson, a leader in the field of differentiated instruction, identifies three areas in which teachers can adapt their curriculum: *content, process,* and *product* (Tomlinson 1999, 2003a, 2003b). Teachers must identify the content students are to learn and then judge its appropriateness to make initial decisions about differentiation. The first step in this task is to read the local, state, or national standards for mathematics. A more in-depth analysis asks teachers to be aware of the "big ideas" in mathematics and then to connect the identified standards to these ideas. A decision to adapt content should be based on what teachers know about their students' readiness. Thus, the teacher needs to be aware of or to determine what students already know. Taking time to pre-assess students is essential to differentiated instruction. Based on this information, teachers can then decide the level of content that students can investigate and the pace at which they can do so.

Differentiation Within a Unit

Let's consider second graders who are beginning a unit on estimation and measurement. One of the standards of this content area is that students be able to estimate measures of length. The classroom teacher knows that a big idea in measurement is the relationship between the number of units and the relative size of those units. Understanding that one foot is longer than eight inches is confusing or counterintuitive for many children. They are swayed by the greater number and lose sight of the size of the unit. This teacher recognizes that young children need considerable exposure to different units of measure to comprehend this inverse relationship. She wants all of her students to build preliminary concepts related to this idea, even if it's as simple as recognizing that it will take fewer giant steps than baby steps to walk the length of the classroom. The teacher decides to incorporate this big idea into the estimation process, but first, she wants to informally pre-assess her students. She wants to capture an initial perspective on their thinking, a benchmark to which she can compare later.

She'll launch the unit by asking students to estimate the length of an object using different units of measure. The activity will allow her to get a feel for her students' common understanding and to identify those students who may need more or less support in this area. She'll observe her students carefully as they work and make anecdotal records. She'll be able to use these data to inform her planning of the subsequent lessons.

She asks students to get out their math journals and pencils and gather around the art table. She shows them a craft stick and asks, "How could we measure the length of this table in craft sticks?"

"We could get a bunch and line them up," offers Sandra.

"We could use one and keep putting it down," suggests Mark.

"We could measure the stick with a ruler. You use a ruler to measure length," explains Lynne.

Already, the teacher is seeing variation in the students' thinking. Sandra's suggestion of repeated units is at a more concrete level than Mark's notion of iteration. Lynne is already thinking about the use of a measurement tool, though the teacher wonders what Lynne really means. Does Lynne realize that she can measure without a ruler as long as she uses a uniform unit? Might Lynne realize that if she finds that the craft stick is about four inches long, she can count by fours as she places the sticks end to end? The teacher makes a note to follow up on this with Lynne, but decides not to delay the start of the activity in order to do so now.

Next the teacher asks the children to imagine using one of these methods to estimate how many craft sticks it will take to measure the length of the table. She tells the students to "Look at the craft stick on the table and think about how many you would need to measure this whole length. Without talking to anyone, I want you to write that number in your journals."

Once the students have recorded their estimates, she puts six craft sticks end to end, along a portion of the table's edge. Some of the children express surprise at how much of the table's length these sticks cover. They squirm waiting to adjust their written estimates. Others look pleased, as if the placement of the sticks affirms their thinking. "Now," says the teacher, "I want you to look at these sticks and think about your estimate again. How many craft sticks do you think it will take to measure this whole length? Write your answer below your first estimate. Think, do you want to change your number or keep the same estimate?" Once the estimates are recorded, the teacher places craft sticks end to end until the entire length is measured. The children count together to find that the table is almost fifteen craft sticks long.

Next, the teacher asks the children to draw a line that they think is one inch long in their journals. After noting the different lengths the students have drawn, the teacher represents a length of one inch by holding up her thumb and pointer finger about an inch apart. "This is about an inch and now I want you to think about measuring the table in inches. How many inches long do you think this table is?" she queries. She asks them to record this answer in their journal as well. Once again a variety of answers are provided. (See Figure 1–1.)

Abby makes a drawing to decide the relationship between the length of an inch and the length of the craft stick. (See Figure 1–2 on page 8.) She traces a stick, estimates the distance of one inch from the bottom of the stick, and places a mark there. Based on this visual model, she decides that three inches is the same length

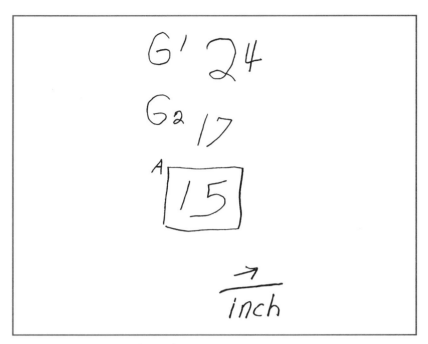

Figure 1–1   *Terrance's initial journal response.*

as one craft stick and begins to make a list of numbers, counting by threes. She makes a couple of false starts, becomes frustrated, erases her work and begins again. This time, she makes a list of the numbers one through fifteen. Her teacher overhears her say, "I know I need fifteen sticks." Next she draws a line to the left of her list and proceeds to count by twos to thirty. Finally, she makes a third column to the right by adding the two numbers to the left, for example, in the first line she adds two and one to get a sum of three. When the teacher asks about her thinking, Abby replies, "I don't know how to count by threes, so I counted by ones, and counted by twos, and put them together. So I got forty-five inches." The teacher is impressed with Abby's strategy for listing multiples of three. She also recognizes Abby's ability to use her understanding of the number of inches in each stick to estimate the length of the table in inches. Though the craft stick is closer to four inches long, three is a reasonable choice, particularly given that Abby overestimated the length of an inch in her drawing.

This activity quickly engages children in the measurement process and it gives the teacher some important information. Based on observations and student recordings, she can determine students' abilities to make initial estimates and whether their second estimates become more accurate. She has an indication of their abilities to estimate an inch. She can gain preliminary ideas

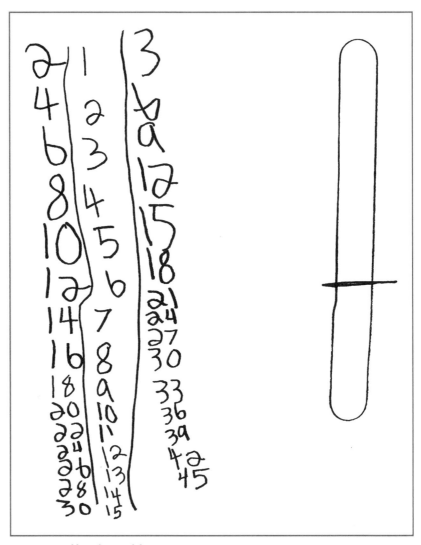

Figure 1–2 *Abby's chart and drawing.*

about which students recognize the significance of comparing the length of an inch to the length of the craft stick, whether they recognize that an inch is shorter than the length of the craft stick, and if they use the relationship between a craft stick and an inch to estimate the table's length in inches. While keeping the mathematical standards in mind, this cursory data can help her make initial decisions about adapting the *content* for different students. The lengths of items to be measured can vary. Some students can measure straight lengths while others could measure "crooked paths." She can have some students measure more lengths in order to better conceptualize the relative length of an inch while others work with different traditional units. Comparisons of *unit lengths* and *number of units needed* can involve informal or traditional units of measure.

Once content variations are determined, *process* is considered. The teacher has some students make "inch and foot strips" so that they can have a single model of each unit with them when they make their estimates. She posts some length measures around the room so that students can choose to use these visual images of length. She also makes inch and foot strips of Velcro® and puts them on the wall near the door. She has some of the students close their eyes and run their fingers along these strips whenever they enter or leave the classroom. She encourages these same students to pass their fingers over the lengths of the objects they are estimating before they make their estimates. Initially, she lets students choose the lengths they want to estimate, so that they can begin with items that are of interest. She provides some students with measuring strips cut to one-inch lengths and they are encouraged to use as many as needed, while others have only one strip and must reuse it to measure. She thinks about pairs of children that will work well together during this unit and subsets of students that she wants to bring together for some focused instruction.

Then the teacher must think about *product*—how her students can demonstrate their ability to estimate lengths at the end of the unit. For example, students might write an explanation of the estimation process, pretend they are interviewing for an estimation job and explain how their skills and experiences will help them to be an effective estimator, teach a kindergarten student something about estimation, estimate ribbon lengths needed for an art project, or participate in an estimation Olympics.

It's not necessary, or even possible, to always differentiate these three aspects of curriculum, but thinking about differentiating content, process, and products prompts teachers to:

- identify the mathematical skills and abilities that students should gain and connect them to big ideas;
- pre-assess readiness levels to determine specific mathematical strengths and weaknesses;
- develop mathematical ideas through a variety of learning modalities and preferences;
- provide choices for students to make during mathematical instruction;
- make connections among mathematics, other subject areas, and students' interests; and

- provide a variety of ways in which students can demonstrate their understanding of mathematical concepts and acquisition of mathematical skills.

It is also not likely that all attempts to differentiate will be successful, but keeping differentiation in mind as we plan and reflect on our mathematics instruction is important and can transform teaching in important ways. It reminds us of the constant need to fine-tune, adjust, redirect, and evaluate learning in our classrooms.

Differentiation Within a Lesson

A kindergarten teacher is thinking about a mathematics lesson she often leads during a particular week of the school year. The lesson focuses on one-to-two or two-to-one correspondence. The teacher is aware that one-to-one correspondence is an essential understanding on which most of the mathematics instruction for her young students is based. But she also knows that many-to-one or one-to-many correspondence is an important concept on which to build future understanding, especially in relation to place value, and tries to present opportunities during the second half of the school year for children to encounter this new idea. Building on the knowledge that children know they each have two legs and two feet, she finds it challenging and enjoyable to apply this idea within the context of the Lunar New Year.

This teacher often chooses to connect learning mathematics with other aspects of the curriculum. As a way to learn about similarities and differences among groups of people, students are learning about how various cultures celebrate important events. As it is the week of Lunar New Year, she launches this lesson by reading *Dragon Feet* by Marjorie Jackson (1999). The story focuses on two children and their family's celebration of the New Year, culminating with them all going to the parade and watching the dancing dragon. The dragon is an important symbol for many people with Asian ethnic backgrounds. It is a symbol of strength, goodness, and good luck. Lunar New Year parades often feature dragons dancing down the street.

The story ends with, "The dragon twists and turns and rolls its eyes. It dances on a hundred feet . . . ." There is a pause as the teacher turns the page and reads the final phrase, "and they all wear sneakers." There is much giggling as the students realize that it is children under a dragon costume who make the dragon dance.

Sharing this story as a class brings to life a special holiday several classmates celebrate at home, connects with the current theme in social studies, and contextualizes the mathematical questions that are the focus of the lesson: How many people? How many legs or feet?

The teacher turns to a picture of the two children in the story and asks, "If only these children were holding up the dragon costume, how many people would be making the dragon dance?" The children respond, "Two," in loud voices, the way children often do when they are positive about the answer. The teacher then asks Abdul and Ashley to come up and model the dragon. She hands Ashley a dragon mask made from a paper plate. Ashley holds the mask with the tongue depressor that has been attached to it and Abdul stands behind her. The teacher asks, "And how many feet would there be?" This time there is a pause and you can see several children moving their heads so that they can see each of the feet. Many children then raise their hands and the teacher calls on Megan who proudly announces, "There's four." Heads nod in agreement. "And how many legs?" asks the teacher. There is a momentary pause and then a confident response of "Four!"

The teacher is an experienced kindergarten teacher and knows that her students' quick identification of the four feet or four legs does not mean that this task is simple. She knows that her students will feel challenged as the number of people increases. Counting the actual feet or legs is one step in the process. Over time it is the one-to-two relationship of people to feet or people to legs that the teacher wants to focus on. Her students have worked hard at identifying one-to-one relationships, a correspondence that is more intuitive to young learners, but that still requires intensive investigations. For this reason, the teacher likes to connect the idea that there are four legs as well as four feet, when the visual representation of two people is prominent. She also likes to introduce legs into the situation as she knows that children find it easy to draw legs and that they sometimes forget to draw feet. When it comes time to make representations of the problem, she wants them to focus on the mathematics and not to struggle with their recording.

Breaking the one-to-one expectation is an important developmental stepping stone that helps students prepare for later work with grouping by tens. The teacher recognizes that even though the one-to-two ratio is the simplest of the one-to-many relationships, one that is helped immensely by the fact that all of her students have set recognition of two objects, it is far from an automatic association.

Next the teacher calls up three children and hands one of them the mask. After establishing that three people are making the dragon dance, the teacher again asks about the number of feet. First she calls on Lowell. Lowell comes up to the children and points to each foot with his index finger as he counts from one to six. He then turns to the class and says, "Six."

The teacher thanks Lowell and asks what others are thinking. Rachel says, "It's six, because that's what I counted." The teacher then asks if anyone has a different way to find the answer. Olivia responds, "It's six because we had four and two more than four is six." Aaron offers, "It's six because three and three is six."

Jessica comes up and again says the number names while trying to touch the feet one by one. One of the children steps back as she touches his foot and says, "Ouch!" It is important to give students opportunities to touch real objects, but in this case, some preparation is needed. Creating an environment where students feel safe with the idea that they can touch another child's foot or that someone could touch their feet is one of the many issues teachers need to anticipate with this lesson. Appropriate behavior needs to be modeled and children need to be ready for this occurrence.

Another group of three children come up to act as the dragon and this time the teacher asks about the number of legs. Their response is quick and the teacher believes they are ready for greater numbers. As the children have been sitting for awhile, the teacher has them all get into groups of four and more dragon masks are provided.

Time is given for these groups to move together in a dragon dance. The energy level in the classroom increases, as does the volume, but this teacher knows how important it is to shift the pace of a lesson and accommodate for little bodies that can't sit still for too long. Getting up and moving allows all of the children to refocus and consider the number of legs on each dragon they have created.

Once there is agreement that there are eight legs, the children are asked to reorganize themselves into groups of five. Though the teacher is aware that it is a relatively simple shift from five groups of four to four groups of five, she is curious to see how her students will work this out. Initially there is some confusion as there is now one too many masks. In time, the children essentially start from scratch to form four new dragons and one mask is dropped to the side. Ten legs becomes a resounding chorus as the children dance the dragon dance once more.

As the number of people in the dragon increases, so does the number of children who count directly to find the number of feet or legs. The teacher notes that Olivia holds on to her idea of two more each time and that Brad begins to use this strategy as well. There is much commotion and conversation. Mathematical disagreements arise naturally in this investigative environment and the teacher skillfully helps the children reach resolutions without taking over the discussions. The children are engaged throughout this process and enjoy taking turns at holding the dragon masks and walking in ways that "make the dragon dance."

In time the teacher brings them back to sit in their circle and they discuss what they discovered. She then poses one last question, "If there were four legs in the dragon, how many people would there be?" This question puzzles them at first; the inverse relationship is not nearly as obvious. It is much easier to visualize people and count their legs, than it is to think of legs and pair them to identify people. After a pause the teacher offers a hint. "How many people would there be if there were two legs?" Faces relax and "one" is identified by all. Stan then says, "So it has to be two people because we need two of the two-legs!"

"Do you agree with Stan?" the teacher asks. Children nod and then the teacher asks how they could *show* that Stan was correct. The idea of having two children stand up and then counting their legs is suggested and carried out. The teacher notes that the children have returned to counting people first and then legs, rather than counting legs by twos. She is not surprised. In the many years she has explored this activity or others involving one-to-many relationships, only one child has initially used skip counting as a way to investigate the relationship. The teacher believes this is another indication of how challenging this task is for young children.

Up to this point, the lesson has proceeded the same way as it has in previous years, but now it is about to change. Having just taken a workshop on differentiated instruction, she has thought about the lesson in new ways. She wants to provide more choice, more variations based on readiness, and more ways for her students to demonstrate their understanding of the concept. She feels that she is a novice in this area and unsure of where this will lead her and her students.

In the past, the exploration would continue with the teacher asking, "What if you were all part of the dragon, how many legs would there be?" The children would all stick out their legs and take turns counting around the circle. They would count as a group with one child saying "one, two" and the next saying "three, four." Along the way there would occasionally be a child who would say "wait, wait!" Such a child usually was confused and needed to go back to the first child and count from one, rather than from the last number said. The task provided a good counting activity, reinforced the one-to-two relationship, and provided a challenge to the students who had become comfortable with the smaller numbers in the dragon dramatizations. (See Dacey and Eston 1999, 103 for a description of this approach to the topic.)

Though she feels that offering choices to students has always been part of her kindergarten program, with the teacher's new focus on differentiation, she now realizes that the choices were not always connected to the learning goal. For this investigation she began to think about her planning and preparation with more focus on differentiation of the content, process, and product. At the same time, she did not want to take on too many new things or to overwhelm her students. She thought about other math activities that were currently being explored in the classroom and set out some familiar ones for the children so that she could focus her time and energy on more specific work around the dragon problem. Establishing an environment that supports choice is ever evolving in this classroom as the teacher needs to think about how independently children work, their interests, and the duration for which they can sustain a work session. After all, they are five and six years old, and learning how to work with others while engaged in learning about a focused idea is very new. The importance of and ways to plan and facilitate choices in math workshop are discussed throughout this book. They are an essential element of the differentiated classroom.

So with this in mind the teacher announces, "For the rest of our math workshop time, you must come see me as one of your choices. I will be at the bean table and we will explore some more dragon problems together. You can also choose to work with our number puzzles, our pattern blocks, our big blocks, or one of this week's two math games." As the teacher announces these activities, she points to the four icons for these choices that are shown on the bulletin board. "But remember," she continues, "you must see me as one of your choices." The children are used to a math workshop format that allows them to pursue different ideas or materials that have already been introduced. The teacher spends much of the fall helping her students to understand this format. This early work pays off; the children move easily to the different choices.

The teacher has a variety of materials available at the bean table including two word problem worksheets. The first asks "How many legs does the dragon have?" and allows the teacher to write a number—based on her familiarity with students' comfort levels with different-sized numbers—in the blank before the word *people*.

> *On Chinese New Year,*
> *also known as Lunar New Year,*
> *people celebrate with a dragon dance.*
>
> *_____ people are dancing a dragon dance.*
> *How many legs does the dragon have?*

The second, alternative handout identifies the number of legs, again with the teacher writing an appropriate number, and asks "How many people are dancing a dragon dance?"

> *On Chinese New Year,*
> *also known as Lunar New Year,*
> *people celebrate with a dragon dance.*
>
> *The dragon has _____ legs.*
> *How many people are dancing a dragon dance?*

It is important to have this alternative form available to ensure that all of the students will be challenged at some level. When children explore inverse numerical relationships, they are developing their algebraic reasoning.

When the children receive their sheets, they work in a variety of ways. Many make drawings (see Figure 1–3) or use chips to represent the people and then say two number names per chip. Carl combines kinesthetic, visual, and auditory modalities to find his answer. (See Figure 1–4.) His task is to identify the number of legs for seven people. First he makes seven single tally marks spread out across his page. Then he taps his leg twice, counts, "one, two," and writes *2* under the first mark. He taps again, says, "Three, four," and writes *4* under the next mark. He continues until he identifies the fourteen legs.

Other activities also are available in an attempt to provide different levels of difficulty and a variety of ways in which students can demonstrate their understanding of this idea. For example, the teacher has prepared strips of paper about ten inches long with a

_6_ people are dancing a dragon dance.
How many legs does the dragon have?

Figure 1–3   *One child's understanding of the relationship between the number of people and the number of legs.*

_7_ people are dancing a dragon dance.
How many legs does the dragon have?

Figure 1–4   *Carl recorded numbers to keep track of the number of legs.*

dragon head pasted onto the left side of the strip. The children are directed to fill in some of the space on the strip with Unifix cubes and encouraged to think of the cubes as the people making the dragon dance. Then they are asked, "If each cube is one person, how many legs would there be?" At the bottom of the strip the children fill in the blanks to indicate the number of people and the number of legs.

The teacher designed this task hoping that the children would choose an appropriate number of people. She thought that

Figure 1–5 *Students created take-home drawings of dragons using bingo markers.*

some students would pick a small number, such as three or four, if that fit within their comfort level. This is not, however, what happened. Instead, all of the children who explored this task placed Unifix cubes until they reached the end of the paper strip. After the fact, the teacher realized that she might have predicted this behavior. The space was there and so the children filled it. In retrospect, strips of different lengths would have provided the differentiation she had intended.

Some of the children ask to make a dragon picture that they can take home. Their teacher did not anticipate this request but wants to honor it. She begins to formulate ideas for an additional choice during math time tomorrow. She thinks about providing strips of paper with a line drawing of a dragon's head at one end. As the children love using bingo markers, she considers providing these for their use as well. She knows a prompt will be included on the paper to help the students focus on the number of people and the number of legs. (See Figure 1–5.)

Aaron is ready to be given the number of legs and asked to predict the number of people dancing a dragon dance. The teacher starts him with twelve legs as she knows Aaron might get frustrated with a greater number. He rubs his chin and sighs, gripping his pencil tightly. Then he smiles brightly and begins to draw twelve lines on his paper. "I just need to connect the legs," he announces proudly as he draws horizontal lines connecting each pair of "legs." He then counts his "people" and records 6. (See Figure 1–6.)

Another approach to the problem is to build dragons with modeling clay and toothpicks. The teacher envisions that the children would roll balls to indicate the people and then stick two toothpicks into each ball. Another surprise, this is not what

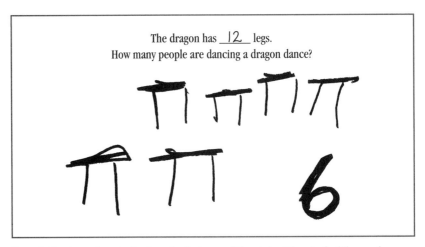

The dragon has __12__ legs.
How many people are dancing a dragon dance?

6

Figure 1–6   *Aaron drew twelve lines for the legs and then paired them to find the number of people.*

happened at all. Instead, many of the dragons looked more like porcupines with toothpicks sticking out all over one big ball of modeling clay! While building, the children talk about adding another person and two more legs, but the material is not structured enough for them to keep track of the relationship between the two variables. On the other hand, this lack of structure leads to an important mathematical insight for one of the students. After making her "dragon," Kim makes a chart. (See Figure 1–7). When she records *12* as the last number under the people heading, she returns to counting the toothpicks. After counting twenty-three toothpicks she proclaims, "This dragon needs another leg!" Her teacher asks how she knows that and she replies, "Twenty-three isn't even. It has to be even." She then adds one more toothpick and writes *24* on her chart.

Until this activity, the teacher was unaware that Kim knew that the number of legs would always be an even number or recognized twenty-three as an odd number. She was also intrigued with the chart Kim made. When asked about it, Kim replied, "It helps me keep track. I didn't have to make each one."

These tasks provided several types of differentiation. Even though the children were allowed to choose which of the tasks they want to complete, the activities still provided for different readiness levels, including a challenge for all students. A variety of materials were used in order to complete the problems and different products were produced to demonstrate understanding.

Following this work, the teacher leaves the masks in the meeting area. During exploration time, several children wander over and

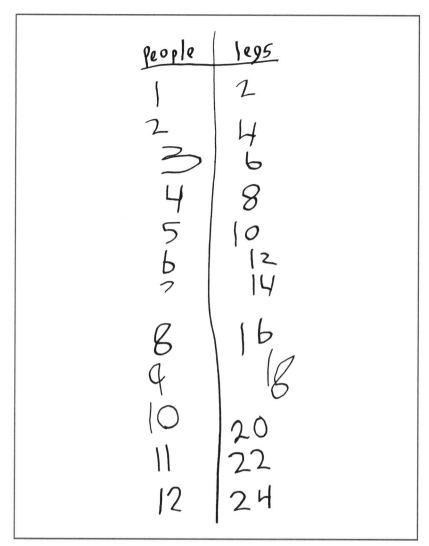

Figure 1–7 *Kim made a chart to show the relationship between the number of people and the number of legs.*

"make a dragon." Then they announce the number of people and the number of legs making their dragon dance. Next, the teacher introduces two new math games. The first is a game in which the children roll one or two dice for the number of people and then determine the number of legs. In the second, a concentration-type game, children match the number of people written on a yellow card with a blue card that shows the corresponding number of legs, along with a picture of those legs. The teacher notices that a few of the children are beginning to be able to start with either color card and still find the correct match.

Lucas begins to form a strategy for his play. He says, "I just double the number of people and that gives me the legs." His teacher prods his thinking by saying, "Tell me more." He replies, "It's like two and two is four and four and four is eight. You just double. It works every time!" The teacher smiles as she thinks about how much knowledge Lucas has gained and about how much he has taught her in the process. His "doubling" strategy helps her realize that it is a more concrete way of thinking about the one-to-two correspondence that has been the focus of this investigation. She also hears a level of confidence in his voice as he seems to recognize that it will work every time. She thinks about how Lucas has discovered a generalization or a way to think algebraically. He sees that this relationship is constant; it does not change over time.

After the activity, the teacher reflects on what she has learned.

Teacher Reflection

I don't think I would use the modeling clay again, although the children enjoyed working with it. It was just too open-ended. Some structure is needed in order to preserve the mathematical intention. I also think that I could have put out materials that would have been more helpful than the Unifix cubes. I have Teddy Bear Counters and Lakeshore People in my classroom and both clearly show the two-to-one relationship between feet or legs and people. I know some of my students would have found these helpful. It would have been interesting to see which children still chose the cubes, rather than a more concrete representation of the problem.

I was excited to see what emerged from the different problem setups. Before I began thinking about this problem, I didn't realize how many different ways children could represent their understanding. I was also surprised by how tired I was after the activity. This is the first time my students experienced multiple choices within one choice area. I needed to mediate a lot of different ideas at once! In fact one of my students was somewhat distraught at the end of workshop time. "But I didn't do all of them," he said in a frustrated tone. I wonder if this is because we usually complete the activity at a choice area or whether he didn't really recognize that each activity was just another way of solving a dragon problem. Maybe next time I should offer fewer choices, but it was really exciting to see the different ways my students were exploring this problem.

This teacher is not as much of a differentiation novice as she may have thought. This is true of most teachers. Every day teachers are trying to meet students' needs without necessarily thinking about it as differentiated instruction. Similar to this teacher, however, seeing teaching and learning through the lens of differentiation helps us to better meet students' needs and to do so more consciously. Over time, teachers can develop the habits of mind associated with differentiated instruction. Remember and think about the following questions as you continue reading and planning your lessons.

1. What is the mathematics that I want my students to learn?
2. What do my students already know? What is my evidence of this? How can I build on their thinking?
3. How can I expand access to this task or idea? Have I thought about interests, learning styles, uses of language, cultures, and readiness?
4. How can I ensure that each student experiences challenge?
5. How can I scaffold learning to increase the likelihood of success?
6. In what different ways can my students demonstrate their new understanding?
7. Are there choices students can make?
8. How prepared am I to take on these challenges?

Chapter 2
Changing Expectations

Some people describe mathematics as a subject that requires you to learn how to follow a series of prescribed steps in order to find the one correct answer. Such a description reflects the way mathematics is sometimes taught, but not the subject itself. Instruction that emphasizes a rule-based approach to mathematics focuses on factual and procedural knowledge. It is the way most of today's teachers were taught. Procedures for addition, subtraction, multiplication, and division, along with the associated basic facts, were almost the entire focus of the early and intermediate elementary school curriculum. Factual knowledge, such as vocabulary and basic facts, were stressed as well as specific algorithms for finding sums, differences, products, and quotients with whole numbers, fractions, and decimals. Students were expected to learn facts through memorization and to perform the same algorithmic procedures regardless of the specific numerical examples.

A common outcome of such rule-based instruction is that to find the sum of 499 + 11, many students (and adults) mindlessly proceed with the algorithm that they were taught. They add the ones, get 10, and record *0* in the ones column and *1* in the tens column. When explaining their work, they don't necessarily mention the distinct place values in the regrouping process. Often the rule "You can't write ten here," said while pointing to the ones column, is considered sufficient. They then add 1 + 9 + 1, find a sum of 11, and record again. Though they are now working in the tens column, the language associated with this step is often the same as with the ones column. Few of these students have any idea that there are eleven tens and that they are recording one ten, while regrouping the remaining ten tens to one hundred, allowing them to write a *1* in the hundreds column:

1	1 1	1 1
499	499	499
+ 11	+ 11	+ 11
---------	----------	----------
0	10	510

Add the ones.   *Add the next column.*   *Add the next column.*
9 + 1 = 10   *1 + 9 + 1 = 11*   *1 + 4 = 5*
You can't write 10.   *You can't write 11.*
Write the 0 and   *Write the 1 and*
regroup 1.   *regroup 1.*

While these place-value relationships may have been taught originally, they are often lost in rote practice. In fact, the traditional addition algorithm is often summarized as "add each column just like they were ones." This may be an efficient generalization for those that can follow it, but it doesn't develop conceptual understanding of addition or of relationships among numbers. Most problematic, it doesn't lead to flexible thinking grounded in conceptual understanding.

More flexible thinkers use a conceptual approach; they consider the numbers and values first and then determine the most sensible way to find the sum. In this case, a simple mental computation is all they need. Thinking of 499 as one less than 500 and recognizing that 10 + 1 = 11, the student combines the 1 with the 499 to get 500 and then simply increases this number by one 10 to find the sum, 510:

                      Think: 499 is one less than 500.
     10 + 1 = 11   *Split 11 into 10 and 1.*
    1 + 499 = 500   *Add the 1 to 499.*
   500 + 10 = 510   *Add the remaining 10.*

There are several mathematical concepts embedded in this method:

- Numbers can be split into parts without changing the sum.
- Numbers can be added in any order without changing the sum.
- Numbers ending in zeroes are easier to work with, so it makes sense to combine numbers to reach such landmarks.
- Ten ones are equal to one ten. So increasing the tens digit by one is the same as adding ten ones.

Such rich mathematical thinking is cultivated by teachers who focus on mathematical reasoning and facilitate the development of children's ideas. As we differentiate learning activities, these priorities must remain in place for all of our students.

Along with the lack of flexible thinking, other difficulties arise when facts and procedures are taught just as rules, without conceptual frameworks. Some students begin to believe that mathematics is only a set of isolated rules that have no meaning, some lose interest in learning mathematics, and all students become underexposed to mathematical reasoning. Further, when rules and procedures are learned in isolation of concepts, misconceptions can emerge in higher grades. For example, sometimes teachers provide simple rules in hopes of simplifying a procedure for students who require more support. In the early elementary grades, you might hear a teacher say, "You can't take a bigger number from a smaller one, so you need to borrow." When their students are working with the traditional algorithm for subtraction, this direction is sometimes given to students as a reason to regroup. Later when negative numbers are introduced, however, the generalization no longer holds true and may confuse students. Further, there are always students who only remember the first portion of this phrase and make the common error shown below:

$$\begin{array}{r} 382 \\ -\,139 \\ \hline 257 \end{array}$$

Such work does not demonstrate an understanding or a connection with the purpose of the procedure, that is, finding the difference between the two numbers.

When examples such as $31 + 234 + 6$ are given to students, teachers sometimes offer the procedural rule to "line up the numbers on the right." The intent is to help students with traditional approaches to addition that require the example to be rewritten in vertical form. Young children are more familiar with the way that a list of words is lined up on the left. As this arithmetic procedure conflicts with the more well-known language procedure, the rule to line up numbers on the right is given much attention. Yet later, when decimals are introduced, lining up the numbers on the right to find $3.04 + 2.1 + 5.7$ will lead to an incorrect sum:

$$\begin{array}{r} \overset{1}{3.04} \\ 2.1 \\ \underline{5.7} \\ 38.2 \end{array}$$

With both whole and decimal numbers, the concept that is mathematically important is that we add like values to like values: ones with ones, and tenths with tenths. It is this concept that we need to emphasize, not a procedural rule that could later lead to a misconception. As teachers, we should get into the habit of asking ourselves: Is there a mathematical concept that will help children understand what to do, regardless of the type of numbers? Am I limiting my less-advanced students' conceptual development by providing them with an oversimplified rule? Am I depriving these students opportunities to develop more complex mathematical concepts?

Understanding Models and Representations

It's not that facts and procedures aren't important, they are, but we don't want to teach them in ways that keep students from developing the conceptual understanding that underpins their procedures and connects the facts that they know. Ideally, all three types of knowledge—*factual, procedural,* and *conceptual*—work together to build mathematical power. Traditionally, a basic fact such as $7 \times 5 = 35$ was taught before students engaged in the various uses of multiplication or in the discussion of fact strategies. Today, more emphasis is placed on conceptual development and students are likely to first be introduced to a simple story problem associated with this fact. Let's consider the following problem explored in a second-grade classroom after the students had visited tide pools.

> *Marietta saw 7 sea stars in the tide pool.*
> *Each sea star has 5 arms.*
> *How many arms did Marietta see in the tide pool?*

The children have been working independently for a few minutes when a teacher joins a group of three children sitting together and asks them to explain their work. Lei shows her drawing of seven sea stars and points to her recorded answer, *35.* (See Figure 2–1.) The teacher asks her how she knows that there are thirty-five and Lei responds, "Oh, I counted them, one, two, three,

Figure 2–1 *Lei's drawing of sea stars helped her determine the number of arms.*

four . . . ." Lei proceeds to count the arms by ones until she has validated her answer.

Matt says, "I counted by fives." He then counts by fives, putting out a finger each time he says a number. When he sees that he has seven fingers out, he stops and says, "That's it. It's thirty-five."

Jodi shows her seven Unifix towers, each with five cubes, and says, "I got thirty-five, too." When the teacher asks if she can tell more about her thinking, Jodi separates five of the towers and says, "I know five fives are twenty-five, so five more is thirty, then thirty-five."

After giving the children the opportunity to describe their own strategies, the teacher wants to shift their thinking and ask them to consider what they can generalize about the approaches used to solve the problem. Now that she has honored their individual solution strategies, she wants to help them see that the essential mathematical features of their models are the same. The teacher says, "I see that you each found the number of arms in a different way. Is there anything the same about what you did to find thirty-five?"

"Hmm," Lei says, "I don't think so, because I'm the only one who made a picture."

"And," Matt adds, "I didn't use any materials at all."

"You used your fingers," Lei reminds Matt.

"Is there any way that Lei's drawing is like Jodi's cube towers?" the teacher asks.

Jodi scratches her head the way she does when she is thinking and then she says, "Oh, I see. Lei made seven sea stars and I made seven towers."

"We put five in each one," adds Lei.

The teacher begins to verbalize the following generalization, "So you each have seven groups of . . . ."

"Five," pipes in Mark putting his seven fingers back out, and extending the connection, says, "Just like I counted seven fives."

Over time, students will learn the fact $7 \times 5 = 35$ (along with the corresponding fact, 5×7), and it will be connected to procedures and concepts they have developed for multiplication. Through more examples, these children will develop the concept that repeated addition is one model for multiplication and that multiplication can be used when there are equal-sized groups. As you will learn from the teacher's reflection, she wants to honor each child's way of thinking, but now, she also pays more attention to helping her students consider what is the same about their different representations.

Teacher Reflection

I was pleased that these three children were able to see the basic aspects of the story problem in each of their models. When I first began encouraging students to create their own representations of mathematical situations, I was so impressed with their different thinking. I just wanted them to share their work. I wanted my students to be exposed to the different ways we can think about mathematics. Now I want more than sharing. I want them to see the similarities as well as the differences in their work. I think this helps them identify critical mathematical concepts. This is a new idea for me and I am still working on it, but it feels like the next step in my voyage as a teacher.

This teacher's words help us to think about teaching as a journey. For many, it is a continuous growing process where new ideas and teaching strategies are developed to address current concerns. Over time, these strategies lead to the discovery of new questions and the further adaptation of our practices. Such has been the case with changes in the way we teach mathematics.

Investigating Mathematical Ideas

Recent reforms in mathematics education emphasize that learning mathematics is an active process, one that involves students in exploring ideas, making and investigating conjectures, discovering relationships, representing ideas, and justifying thinking. Such activity often results when students pursue real mathematical problems or explore open-ended tasks, that is, problems for which they don't already recognize a procedure that will lead them to a solution or tasks that may be completed in a variety of ways. When exploring these types of problems, students wrestle with ideas and are less likely to follow the same solution paths. Allowing for different approaches to mathematical tasks can lead to rich discussions that help students establish and agree on facts, construct and utilize procedures, and develop and solidify concepts. This way of teaching has two advantages: It supports deeper mathematical thinking and it supports alternative learning preferences.

Teaching with this mind-set is part of our changing expectations of mathematics instruction. Teachers facilitate mathematical discourse, rather than delineate specific steps and demonstrate how to follow these prescribed procedures. Teachers focus on questions such as: Why do you think so? What are you thinking? How do you know? When teachers engage in this approach, they often are surprised at the range of what their students are thinking. The teachers come to recognize differences in readiness levels, in approaches to tasks, in the ways children describe their work, in the connections children make among ideas, and in the ways they model, represent, and describe their thinking.

Needing to address the differences we discover

In fact, many teachers who begin to teach in ways that allow these differences to surface are truly amazed at what they see and hear. Teachers recognize that they have uncovered information about their students that they had never known before. Focusing on the development of mathematical ideas and on making links among factual, procedural, and conceptual knowledge is a significant transformation in the teaching of mathematics, and it has raised two essential questions:

1. Once we reveal the wonderfully different ways our students think about mathematics, what do we do with what we learn?
2. How do we support differentiated thinking about mathematics while still focusing on unified mathematical ideas?

Let's consider a vignette from a first-grade classroom. It is late November and the students are working on ideas related to number sense. They are extending their set-recognition skills and connecting visual images of numbers to symbolic notations. Students are also working on moving beyond needing to count all of the items in a set. This task helps them consider ideas of counting all or grouping items in a meaningful way so that they can arrive at a total. Simultaneously they are exploring part-part-whole relationships by looking at ways numbers can be separated into parts (decomposed) and then joined (composed). The teacher knows her students have familiarity with common arrangements of sets found on dice and dominoes since they have been using them during math workshop since school began. The teacher believes they are ready to examine less familiar arrangements. She wants to use visual images to expand the children's ideas about *number* and to extend students' repertoire of visual models. For example, she wants her students to recognize a set of five in a configuration other than the standard arrangement and to realize that a set of nine can be decomposed into parts other than the traditional five and four. Studies have indicated the importance of the visual cortex in mathematical thinking (Sousa 2001), and so activities that explicitly help students to develop visual perceptions of number are important.

The children are gathered in a circle and the teacher has prepared visual image cards to support these ideas. (See Figure 2–2.) Initially, the teacher will hold up a card briefly and then ask the children to identify the number of squares that they see. Over time, she believes this repeated activity will support them learning to break the whole into recognizable and manageable parts and then to combine those parts to tell how many in all. This activity also offers children an opportunity to use numbers and number sentences to describe what they see.

The teacher begins with simple examples to make sure all of the children are successful. After a few examples of sets less than six, she holds up a card of eight red squares. (See Figure 2–3.) There are a variety of responses to this more difficult example. A couple of the children raise their hands immediately. Nicolita looks like she will burst if she can't share her answer soon. Nat taps his finger on his forehead as if he is trying to recapture the image as he counts. Macy immediately drops her head, avoiding the teacher's eyes. The teacher looks around and says, "Before you tell me how many you saw, I want you to tell me what you think about this card."

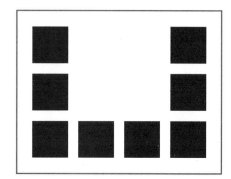

Figure 2–2 *Example of a visual image card.*

Figure 2–3 *A visual card of eight.*

"This one was harder," replies Jim.

"What made it harder?" the teacher asks.

"There are so many," offers Macy.

"I couldn't count each one," explains Paul.

"I did. There are eight," claims Nicolita.

"I got eight, too," confirms Joey.

The teacher asks if anyone else got eight and some hands rise in response. She then queries, "How did you know there are eight?" and shows the card again. She purposely does not confirm the answer as she wants the children to decide for themselves.

While pointing to the bottom row Nicolita explains, "See there's four here," and then pointing to the top two groups of two explains, "and here's four up here. So four and four, that's eight."

"Do you see the groups of four that Nicolita is showing?" asks the teacher. Heads nod and she asks, "Did anyone see eight a different way?"

Joey responds, "I saw two groups of three and two in the middle."

"Oh," responds the teacher. "Can someone come up and show me where you think Joey sees two groups of three and two in the middle?"

After Carla shows the groups and Joey confirms her identification, the teacher says, "So Nicolita saw two groups of four and Joey saw two groups of three and two in the middle. How did this help them know there were eight squares in such a short amount of time?"

"I didn't have to count each one," responds Nicolita.

"What does Nicolita mean by that?" asks the teacher.

"Oh, I know," Mimi says. "She just saw four. She didn't count them."

Then Leo's eyes light up and he says, "So if you can see a lot at once you can get it faster."

The teacher then suggests that they try some more cards. This time she returns to some easier examples, but in a purposeful way. First she shows a card with a row of two squares, followed by a card with a row of four squares. In both cases, the children recognize the number of squares immediately. The next figure she shows is a row of two squares on top of a row of four squares. Students raise their hands quickly and the teacher can see how excited the children are about their instantaneous recognition. After the children agree that there are six squares, she asks, "How did you see them?"

The children talk a bit about seeing the group of four and two and the teacher decides that they have done enough for today. The idea that decomposing numbers can help you find the total number has been introduced and the children have recognized that numbers can be decomposed in different ways. It's time to let these ideas incubate.

The next day she shows a new card with an arrangement the children have not seen before and asks, "Who can tell me what we did yesterday with cards like this?" Once students have connected with their previous learning, a few more of the visual image cards are considered. Today, more of the children are able to decompose the numbers in order to find the number in all. After the final example, the teacher says, "Cam sees four and six squares and Mike sees two and eight squares, and they both saw ten in all. How could we write this?" The teacher writes the corresponding number sentences on chart paper and introduces the next activity.

"I want you each to make your own arrangement of squares. When you go to your tables you will see some glue sticks, white paper, and some cut-out squares. Pick a number four through ten. Take that number of squares and make a design. Then I want you to write what you see." After the students repeat the directions and the teacher is confident of their understanding, students move to the tables where the materials are ready for use.

Paul makes a design with the squares, and then writes the number of squares in each of the three components of his configuration. (See Figure 2–4.) Note that he doesn't record the total number. Mimi and Gina record numbers for parts of the whole and the

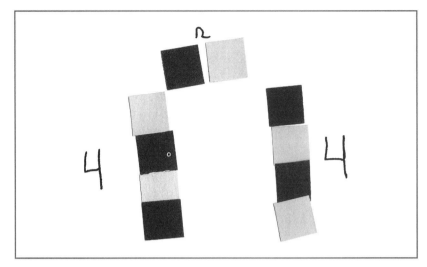

Figure 2–4 *Paul wrote numbers for each part of his design, but did not record the total.*

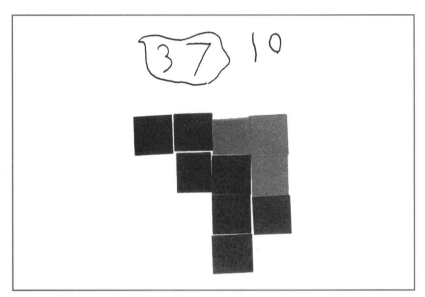

Figure 2–5 *Mimi recorded subtotals as well as the total number of squares in her design.*

total numbers. Mimi records *3* and *7* for the two groups she sees and then *10* for the total number of squares. She doesn't use the standard notation of addition, but circles the *3* and *7* to indicate that together, they make *10*. (See Figure 2–5.) Gina records numbers for three parts and *maks* 7 to indicate the total. (See Figure 2–6.) As is often the case with first graders, she has recently lost a tooth and is excited when she decides that her design looks like a toothbrush. It is important to her to communicate this as well.

Figure 2–6 *Gina recorded three subsets, the total, and identified her design as a toothbrush.*

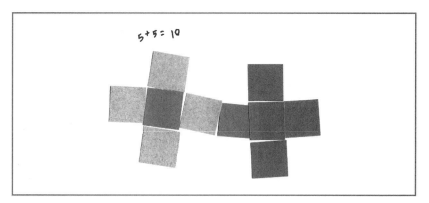

Figure 2–7 *Macy used an equation to describe her design.*

Macy and Julio both write number sentences for their designs. Macy first counts ten squares and arranges them in two sets of five. Then she arranges them in a design and records the corresponding number sentence. (See Figure 2–7.) The teacher notices that Macy didn't make a design and then decompose it to count, but rather, made a design to fit a decomposition of ten that she already knew, that is, $5 + 5$. Julio wrote a number sentence with three addends and the teacher is fairly certain that he did so because of what he saw in his design. (See Figure 2–8.)

Leo makes a design using eight squares and writes $4 + 4 = 8$. The teacher asks him where he sees the two groups of four and he replies, "I just know that." When asked what he can see, he adds the second number sentence $5 + 3 = 8$. (See Figure 2–9.) The teacher is pleased that Leo is able to connect with the visual image

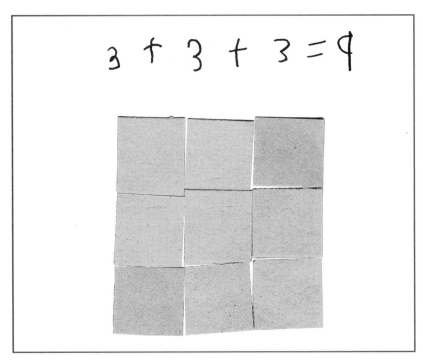

Figure 2–8 *Julio wrote an equation with three addends.*

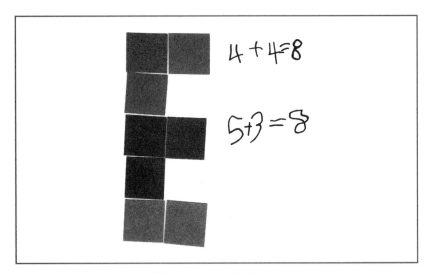

Figure 2–9 *Leo identified two different equations for the same design.*

and asks if there is another way he can see his design. He turns his paper around and says, "I can also see three plus five." Paul, who is sitting next to Leo, has watched this response and says, "You can turn the paper and the numbers."

With prompting, Joey is also able to identify another number sentence. Joey takes ten squares and makes a design based on a pattern. When he finishes, he asks the teacher if he can use another square so that he can finish his pattern. He records *10 + 1* first, perhaps because he knows he has just added one square to his group of ten. The teacher queries, "Is there another number sentence you can write for your picture?" Joey responds, "It would make no sense that nine plus one equals ten, so it's nine plus two equals eleven." Though the teacher appreciates Joey's thinking, she wants him to focus more on the visual image. She prods Joey by saying, "I want you to look at your picture and tell me what you see." Joey then says, "Oh, OK," and writes *7 + 4 = 11*. (See Figure 2–10.)

A small group of students is able to identify more than one decomposition of their designs, and write corresponding number sentences. Nicolita's work is the most complex. She sees and writes six different number sentences without teacher assistance. (See Figure 2–11.) When she shows her work to her teacher, she is able to re-create the connections between the equations she has recorded and her design. She uses her hand to show each way she decomposed the figure. When she gets to her last sentence, $1 + 1 + 1 + 1 + 1 + 1 + 1 + 1 + 1 + 1 = 10$, she just chuckles and says, "Well, I just put that because I knew it and wanted to write a long sentence. You can always do that, right?"

Figure 2–10   *Joey was able to write three equations for his design.*

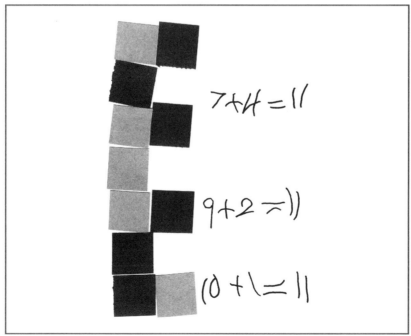

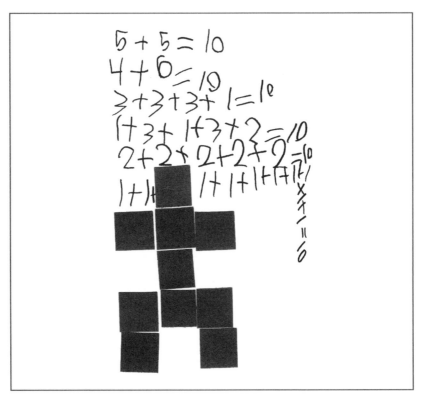

$$5 + 5 = 10$$
$$4 + 6 = 10$$
$$3 + 3 + 3 + 1 = 10$$
$$1 + 3 + 1 + 3 + 2 = 10$$
$$2 + 2 + 2 + 2 + 2 = 10$$
$$1 + 1 + 1 + 1 + 1 + 1 + 1 = 10$$
$$x + 1 = 10$$

Figure 2–11   *Nicolita described her design with numerous equations.*

So, what have the students learned from this activity? What decisions does their teacher need to make now? The teacher began reflecting on her students' work by making a list of the mathematical behaviors she observed:

- visualizing subsets within a larger set and assigning numbers to those subsets;
- identifying the total squares by decomposing the visual image into parts and then combining the parts;
- writing an addition sentence that matches the total number of squares (two addends, more than two addends);
- recording with conventional notation;
- using a known number fact and creating a visual arrangement of the squares to match; and
- being able to decompose the figure in more than one way and to write more than one corresponding number sentence (with teacher questions, independent of teacher intervention).

After writing the list she began to think about her students in terms of these behaviors. Thus far the teacher had met her students' diverse needs by providing an activity with multiple entry points. That is, students could function on different levels of readiness and still complete the same task, as evidenced by the differences in the student products. Now, she felt it was time to further differentiate. She identified three different kinds of needs based on the mathematical understandings and comfort level she saw her students utilize:

1. Students who are only connecting to number sentences that they already knew or who are not using standard notation.
2. Students who are able to relate number sentences to the visual images and are able to now work on identifying more than one way to decompose a set along with the corresponding equations.
3. Students who appear to have mastered these concepts and are ready for a more challenging activity.

Teacher Reflection

I have been challenging myself to focus on what students can do in order to determine what next steps to take to help them meet the learning outcome we are aiming for. My ultimate goal is to have all my students working in an area "just right" for them. I looked over their work and thought about whom I had interacted with during class time and what types of interactions were needed now. I wanted to use this information to tailor the next set of activities to better match their needs. I was pleased that everyone had independently met some level of success, and thankful that their needs seemed to group in a meaningful and manageable way.

I started by thinking about the group of students for whom the task seemed just right. In many ways what they need is time to work with these ideas; more time to practice if you will. I considered next steps to be giving them more opportunities to create more images to describe and in time challenging them to generate at least three different number sentences for any given arrangement they might make.

Next I considered the group who seemed the least flexible or comfortable with this task. My gut told me they needed more instructional time with me, where I could model ways to utilize standard notations in this task and to stretch their ideas of multiple solutions. When I get to this point in my planning I always wish I had another adult in the room so that I could really set aside some uninterrupted time to work with these students. These are the kids who do not pick up easily on all the ideas shared during our class discussions or

(Continued)

minilessons. I think they work best in a small group. They are also the least comfortable with math concepts and often solve all problems by counting all the objects. My hope is to use the visual images to help them chunk numbers they know so that they can think about counting on as a strategy for finding a total. Even though they can give a basic fact such as 4 + 4, I don't know that this knowledge goes very deep for them. The visual images are designed to help them consider multiple solutions.

In planning for this group I need to consider next steps with the task as well as ways to carve out some instructional time with them. It's only three or four children, which leaves at least twenty children on their own. I know we have established work norms so that children are prepared to work independently when I am working with a small group, but just as in reading, I need to make sure the work they are engaged in is significant. Perhaps if we have a brief class meeting where I show an arrangement of squares that I have made, offer the challenge of finding at least three ways to figure out how many squares, and share some notations for this, the majority of the class will have something more to work on while I meet separately with the children needing more instructional time.

Then I thought about the group who found the task relatively easy. I know I can always increase the size of the number to add a challenge for them. I also wondered about giving them snap cubes and demonstrating ways to build three-dimensional models. If this is the case, might they generate equations with more than three addends? This is something new to consider. I also know I could offer them a challenging word problem that asks them to consider multiple ways to compose and decompose a number. With a problem such as, *I bought a dozen eggs. I used some for cooking breakfast. How many eggs could I have left?*, students are utilizing some of the same mathematical concepts as they are with the visual images but in a different context. I know this will provide a challenge for these students at this time.

When the class begins math workshop the following day, the teacher launches her plan. After the initial group meeting in which more ideas about figuring out how many squares are contained in a specific arrangement along with ways to notate these solutions are shared, most children move right into making more arrangements with squares. Before they leave the meeting area, the teacher asks four children to work specifically with her.

In order to give these students an opportunity to learn together in a more focused way, she shows them an arrangement of four squares. Everyone is quick to identify how many. When asked how they determined the number, "I just know" is the unanimous response. She continues with some other small numbers to build their confidence. She does not want to add the notation piece at this point, as the children "just know" the total. Finally she shows them a more complex arrangement of nine squares and the group works on ways to consider how many squares and on ways to record their solutions. The small-group work seems to motivate the students and they agree to create more arrangements and try recording multiple solutions or use standard notation. The teacher seems pleased as she regroups and asks five other children to come to work with her at the meeting area where she has snap cubes waiting for them to consider.

Like the second graders working with the number of arms on a sea star, these first graders were all working in their own way, at their own level. They were operating using factual, procedural, and conceptual knowledge. Their teacher also recognized that the visual image activity helped them develop and solidify more complex mathematical concepts while they were building some facility with basic facts. She observed her students using counting strategies, identifying basic facts, conserving number, and applying the communicative property of addition. She was delighted when one of the students, Nora, shared her thinking.

Nora was one of the children who the teacher thought needed more practice. After working for two more sessions Nora creates an arrangement of squares and associated number sentences. (See Figure 2–12.) "I noticed that you have written four number sentences to go along with this arrangement of squares," the teacher comments. "Tell me more about your work."

Figure 2–12 *After practice, Nora was able to see different equations represented in her design.*

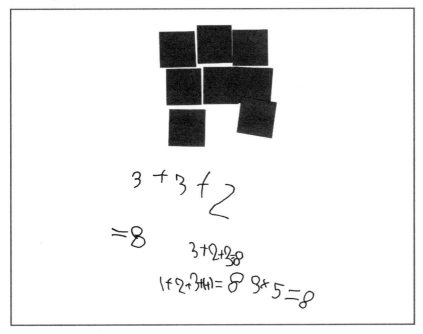

"It'll still be the same answer but one [said while pointing to 3 + 2 + 3 = 8] is three, [she pauses briefly] four, five [another brief pause], six, seven, eight. The other [said while pointing to 3 + 3 + 2 = 8] is three, [brief pause] four, five, six, [brief pause] seven, eight. See it's the same, but it's not. Any way you do the numbers it's the same. It's always eight," Nora spoke with conviction.

"Why does it keep coming out to eight?" the teacher questions.

"Because any way it would be the same [with this Nora motions to the equations as well as turns the paper as though it were a steering wheel on a car]. But it would be nine [pointing to the empty spot] if you put one more here."

"I see you also wrote two other number sentences," the teacher adds.

Nora places her finger to separate the top row of three from the rest of the squares and says, "Yeah, I tried to think about each group of squares. See three and five more make eight. This one [1 + 2 + 3 + 1 + 1 = 8] looks like this." Nora tips her paper slightly to the right. "See the one on the top, then two, then three, and then one and one more makes eight."

Identifying attributes of a worthwhile task

Nora and her classmates responded well to this series of tasks. Their teacher was pleased that the visual image activities led to a lively exploration of mathematical concepts. Relationships were discovered, affirmed or reaffirmed, a variety of ideas emerged, symbolic notation was connected to visual patterns, and students were eager to explain their thinking. What type of task yields such results? While it is easier to recognize a specific task as being one that will be worthwhile when explored with a specific group of students, some general attributes of a worthwhile task can be identified.

It focuses on significant mathematical ideas.

The task should be connected to big ideas in mathematics and be problematic, that is, the solution should not be apparent immediately or a variety of outcomes should be possible. In this case, number sense and connecting standard notation to visual images are the big ideas. When instruction emphasizes significant ideas, students are more likely to make connections across mathematical strands. For example, a couple of weeks after the students worked with visual images in this way, the class was involved in data collection. Paul has used arrows to indicate that he could "turn around the numbers" in his summary statement about his data. (See Figure 2–13.)

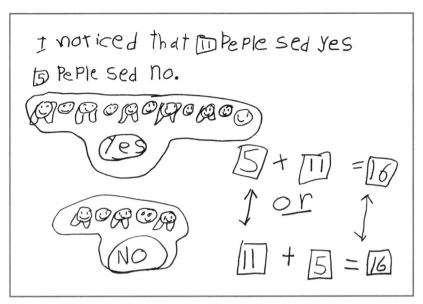

Figure 2–13 *Paul summarized his data and then made a connection to the order property of addition.*

It is developmentally appropriate.

At the primary level, this means that ideas are within reach both from a cognitive level and an experiential one. Students should be encouraged to construct their own strategies or ideas and be prodded to connect their intuition and natural language to their mathematical experiences. Concrete manipulatives and drawing materials should be available for use at all times to support their work. As was demonstrated in the exchange between Nora and the teacher, asking students to explain their ideas often extends students' thinking.

It is contextualized.

Presenting mathematical ideas in connection to literature or art activities (such as making their own designs) can help young children enter mathematical activities. Situating mathematical tasks within everyday contexts also helps capture young children's interests and gives them insights on how to begin open-ended tasks.

It offers an appropriate level of challenge.

To be worthwhile, a task must offer a cognitive challenge that requires decisions to be made and new ideas to be explored, and yet not be so challenging as to feel overwhelming. When a task has multiple entry points, it is possible to engage students with a broad range of readiness.

It encourages multiple perspectives.

An interesting task stimulates a variety of strategies, representations, and mathematical ideas and thus encourages students to engage in mathematical discourse in which they explain and justify their thinking. When students shared the different ways they *saw* a figure, other students were able to extend their visualizations of the set as well.

Note that these characteristics of a worthwhile task serve two purposes. They provide attributes of a task that build broader and deeper mathematical ideas and that support differentiated instruction. That is, a task that is contextualized is developmentally appropriate, offers an appropriate level of challenge, encourages multiple perspectives, makes room for a variety of learners, and supports a variety of learning needs. While a variety of tasks are available in published materials, teachers often find that they are more successful with tasks they adapt or create themselves. Whether using tasks as written, adapting them, or creating them from scratch, teachers first need to assess where their students are in comparison to the goals of the curriculum.

Chapter 3

Getting to Know Our Students
Places to Start

$\mathcal{B}$ack when we were in school, teachers assessed our mathematical work in the same way that our spelling tests were scored. We wrote our answers in a list and they were marked as either right or wrong. The number of incorrect responses was written at the top of the page, followed by an x. Teachers considered this number of incorrect or correct answers evidence of our learning and then they kept these scores in a record book for future reference. Feedback was limited to these scores. Little or no attention was given to analysis of our work and process was seldom valued.

Thankfully, this is no longer the status quo in most of today's elementary classrooms. As our expectations for teaching mathematics have changed, so have the ways in which we gather evidence of learning. In recent years, teachers have begun to examine their students' mathematical thinking more closely. They observe students as they work individually or in groups, use manipulatives, and tackle more complex tasks. They keep anecdotal records of these observations. Daily work, in which children are often expected to write or draw to communicate and represent their mathematical ideas, is looked at intently and provides assessment data that inform instructional decisions. As well as correctness, teachers look at the work in relation to curriculum standards, developmental readiness, strategy choices, misconceptions, and conceptual thinking.

More focused assessment tasks may be given at both the beginning and the end of units. Mathematical portfolios may be kept that include samples of work completed during different times of the year and across curriculum strands. Interviews may be conducted with individual students. Together, these assessment techniques allow teachers to get to know their students as individual mathematical thinkers and thus teachers can more effectively match instructional practices to their students' various needs. As described by this teacher in the following reflection about the analysis of student work, these assessment practices require more time. But when teachers make the commitment to value their students' work, the results are informative and rewarding.

Teacher Reflection

Sometimes I'm overwhelmed by my students' work. It can take a long time to analyze their recordings. I think about what the work is or isn't telling me about my students' understandings, their misconceptions, or their connections. When I think back to when it took very little time and effort to mark answers as correct or incorrect, I know I used to have a nagging feeling about this. On some level I realized that anyone could have corrected their work and that it didn't really tell me much about my students and their progress.

When I am not feeling overwhelmed, I do feel great joy while reflecting and commenting on their work. I see such possibility and get a sense of deep satisfaction about my role as a teacher. I look for patterns of thinking and use pieces of the work to help frame our next minilesson(s). I try to give authentic, purposeful feedback, too. I want the students to feel that I care about their thinking because I do! Each piece of work is evidence of learning.

This feeling is similar to how I feel when I listen to my students in class. I marvel at how children can communicate their ideas and how clever their thinking can be. I want them to feel the satisfaction that I feel, to take pride in their work and ideas.

I can remember getting worksheets handed back when I was a child. I never looked at the work again, only the red mark on the top of the page. It was the grade, not the learning, that I came to value. In contrast, I think carefully about the comments I write on my students' papers. When my students read them, or share them with a parent or family member at home, I want the children to use my comments as a way to reconnect with their thinking and to see the work as evidence of their own learning.

Though it certainly matters if an answer is incorrect, I try to see if I can figure out where any of the students got off track. For me, that's most important. When this happens I can plan instruction to help redirect the learning. If I can't make sense of their work, then I know that I need to spend more time with those students so they can help me understand what they were doing or thinking at that moment. When work is handed in that is incorrect or incomplete, I want to take the time to have students think about it again. I don't want children to feel as though their work is never finished, but at the same time, I don't want them to view each piece as a separate task that they can easily discard when they hand it in saying, "Done!"

The students' work is interesting and informative. It has great value to me; it shows me what and how my students are learning. Isn't that the heart of the matter? I know that is not how I felt about my work in math class as a child, but it is how I want my students to feel now.

This teacher has captured many of the differences between assessment practices when she was a student and those she incorporates into her classroom. While other changes in assessment and evaluation of student learning have occurred during this time as well, such as the significant attention paid to high-stakes, mandated testing, the focus here is on those assessment practices and habits of mind that support differentiated instruction on a daily basis. Such practices include formal and informal techniques for collecting data, and most likely, many are already incorporated into your classroom. Through the lens of differentiation, however, the purposes of these data-gathering strategies become more focused and refined as do the assessment tasks we want to use with our students. Like this teacher, our sights should always be set on getting to know our students better and to understanding their ways of making sense of the mathematics they are learning. Our goals are to gather evidence of learning and to gain insights into best next steps.

Pre-Assessment

To differentiate according to readiness, we need to determine what our students already know. Note that some of the earlier classroom scenarios began with an activity that allowed teachers to pre-assess their students' knowledge and level of familiarity or proficiency with the concept at hand. Many activities can serve this purpose if they include opportunities for discussion, group work, or recorded responses and explanations. It is the teachers' clarity of purpose and attention to students' work that allow such activities to become sources of pre-assessment data. Let's consider another teacher's words as she reflects on pre-assessment.

Teacher Reflection

When I am thinking about pre-assessment, I know I am trying to identify children's zones of comfort and proficiency. I am looking for data that will help me answer questions such as: How familiar are my students with this new concept? What working knowledge, skills, and strategies do they have in place to support them in this, supposedly, new area of learning? What misconceptions might they have? How comfortable are they with the mathematical language associated with this topic?

(Continued)

I try hard not to make assumptions about my students anymore. Some of them come to school with a wealth of mathematical knowledge and experience. Many students do not, and the range among them seems to be increasing each year. I want to meet each child where he or she is. It's hard to find that zone for each child, that place between where things are too hard and out of reach, and too easy and potentially uninteresting or not challenging. Though I know in reading it can be fun and good practice to read a book that is too easy, I also know that if that is all you are asked to read, you have considerably less opportunity to improve and become a more proficient, independent reader. When a book is too hard, it can also be frustrating and lead to reluctance and lack of productivity. The same is true in math. I want to identify the tasks and investigations that will be just right for my students, that will challenge their thinking without overwhelming them. And, I want to do this quickly, so that we all feel good about what we are doing.

Many aspects of the importance of pre-assessment have been identified by this teacher. So, just how soon in the year should we begin this pre-assessment process? It is common for teachers to begin assessing students' reading abilities immediately. Teacher-developed, system-created, or standardized assessment tools may be used. The results of these initiatives allow teachers to get a broad sense of their students as a group and to begin to capture the range of their readiness levels. These data allow teachers to identify initial ways to differentiate their reading instruction. It is less common for teachers to attend to their students' mathematical readiness with the same intensity. While we recognize that the development of language and literacy skills remains the top priority of early childhood education, we believe that early assessment of mathematical readiness must also occur.

Anecdotal Records and Screening Devices

From the first day of school, teachers have a myriad of ways to get acquainted with their new students. They are eager to learn about what their students know and their comfort levels with the various academic subjects, social interactions, and rules and routines of school. For example, in kindergarten teachers might begin to collect anecdotal data about their students' mathematical understandings during the first week by observing them explore mathematics-related manipulatives for the first time and become familiar with the possible uses of these materials. As children dive in, so do their teachers, who listen, watch, and often record what they see and hear:

- Page counted to twelve as he stacked blocks to make a tower.
- Kim didn't seem to want to explore the materials. She kept gravitating back to the baskets of books.
- April connected Unifix cubes in a train. She used only two colors. "I made a pattern." Though not consistent the whole length of the train, her first six cubes were an AB pattern.
- Jane and Dave were using Cuisenaire rods. They made "stairs." "This is the tallest," Jane said.
- Bruce and Kayla stopped at each bin but moved on quickly. "Now what?" Bruce kept asking.
- Counting buttons; Evan got to nineteen but said, "thirteen, thirteen, sixteen, seventeen, eighteen, nineteen."

Anecdotal notes like these help the teacher get a feel for students' comfort level, engagement, and working knowledge. Over time, patterns of thinking or behavior might emerge for an individual as well as for the whole class that can help the teacher make more informed decisions for instruction. New information abounds during these first few days and weeks and teachers can sometimes feel overwhelmed. Recording these simple observations can help us to focus and to remember what we have witnessed.

Even before some children come to school, kindergarten screening tools are administered. Most, if not all, tools ask the child to count a group of objects. Though these screening devises are cursory and are designed primarily to determine if a child has a special need for which the system must be prepared to provide accommodations, rather than for determining school readiness levels, tasks related to mathematical understandings are part of the overall picture. Early on, we can recognize the importance of providing our students with tasks that help us to find out more about their mathematical ideas and that further inform the first glimpses of our new students.

Interviews

For many teachers anecdotal records based on interactions in the classroom and screening scores are enough to get started; for others, they do not yield enough information. Interviews are sometimes conducted in which each child is asked to respond to a series of tasks or questions. In kindergarten, as well as the other primary grades, interviews are important components in initial assessments for literacy. Just as we want to get a baseline on what letters and sounds, if any, a kindergartner knows at the beginning of the school year, so too, do we want to get an initial appraisal of selected skills associated with mathematics.

Kindergarten assessment interviews are usually designed to help the teacher learn relatively quickly what each student knows about counting by rote, counting groups of objects, recognizing and writing numerals, and making connections among sets, number names, and notations. Often teachers construct their own interviews and use their state standards as a way to decide what kinds of questions to ask. One kindergarten teacher uses the following questions in her interviews:

- How high can you count? (Child makes prediction and then proceeds to count rotely.)
- Can you count another way? (backwards, by tens, by twos, by fives, in another language)
- What numbers do you see? (Child is handed a sheet with the numerals 0–30 written in random order. Teacher has a similar sheet and checks each one read correctly or notes incorrect responses.)
- What numbers can you write? (Child is given a piece of paper with designated space to write up to ten numerals.)
- How many counters are there? (Child is given a set of fifteen to twenty-five objects to count. Teacher notes one-to-one correspondence, correctness of counting sequence, and ability to keep track of what has already been counted.)
- Can you show me a set of five (then ten, and then twenty) objects? (Teacher looks for accuracy and for strategies that involve duplication of or adding on to known sets.)

The assessment interview can be repeated a couple of times throughout the year to track skill progression and development. (For a more complete discussion of this interview see Dacey and Eston 1999, 180–91.)

Many math educators, researchers, and research groups have designed more comprehensive assessment interviews. For example, the *Early Numeracy Interview Booklet* (Communications Division for the Office of School Education, Department of Education, Employment and Training 2001) is one part of a more comprehensive program that can easily give teachers in kindergarten through grade 5 a guide for some key assessment tasks. According to this program, an interview is "a powerful tool for assessing students' numeracy development during the first five years of schooling. . . . Time spent conducting the one-to-one interview is invaluable in enhancing teachers' understandings of students' mathematical understandings and the strategies they use. For this reason it is recommended that the classroom teacher administer the interview" (7–8).

Andrea Guillaume has written extensive interview protocols in *Classroom Mathematics Inventory for Grades K–6: An Informal Assessment* (2005). Referred to as CMI, this assessment program is similar to a reading inventory and is designed to be used by the classroom teacher. Protocols span across the elementary grades and include each of the content strands. Many of the assessments utilize common classroom manipulatives and there is also a section teachers can use to assess attitudes toward mathematics.

Leading mathematics educator/consultant Kathy Richardson has developed a series of assessment tasks designed for use as individual interviews. To date there are nine different assessment tasks in Richardson's *Assessing Math Concepts,* each focusing on an essential concept of mathematical understanding (Richardson 2003). Designed for use across the primary and intermediate grades, each of these tasks is tailor-made to help a teacher find the place at which a student transitions from a comfortable, grounded understanding of mathematics to a place where more practice, application, or instruction is required.

Similar to Vygotsky's zone of proximal development, our job is to challenge students' comfort level and then to help them find their next boundaries. Through assessment, we try to identify evidence for what the child knows or has mastered, areas where initial ideas are formed but additional experience with them is needed, and those concepts and skills that require further scaffolding or additional readiness development. Richardson (2003) also suggests how the teacher can make strategic decisions for future instruction based on data gained through interviews and provides ways to continue to assess students' work.

Sometimes a classroom teacher becomes concerned because a student's performance is considerably different from what was expected. Using a norm-referenced screening device, teachers can better home in on the strengths and weaknesses of a child in question and compare the student's performance to a standardized expectation. The *Test of Early Mathematics Ability* (TEMA3) is an example of such an instrument (Ginsburg and Baroody 2003). In its third edition, TEMA3 is designed for use with children four years zero months through eight years eleven months and is administered individually by a math specialist or other staff member responsible for testing of this type. When requesting special services, this type of data can be quite helpful, and it also assists teachers in identifying important gaps in learning.

It is becoming more commonplace for schools or school districts to require some initial assessment in mathematics. We are all being asked to be more accountable. In turn, each teacher needs to determine his or her own best way to use data gathered from an assessment, be it formal or informal. There was a time when such initial data were used to determine ability groups in mathematics. Often referred to as *tracking,* these groups were thought to be homogenous in nature and tended to be a long-term assignment. That is not the goal assumed here. While we do recommend that students' instruction be differentiated based on readiness, we do not assume, nor do we recommend, that groups will always be formed, or that when groups are appropriate, that they will always be homogeneous or that their membership will remain unchanged for too long.

Open-Ended Tasks

Along with individual interviews and anecdotal records as ways to collect information about what their students know and how they represent their ideas, some teachers find it useful to give every student an open-ended task or problem. One second-grade teacher offers her students the following task during the first week of school.

> *What do you know about 12?*
> *Show 12 in as many different ways as you can.*

Haley's response contains a range of ideas. The inclusion of standard notation, along with the creation of a word problem, shows that she is aware of the kinds of problems we explore during math time and some of the symbols we use to communicate mathematical ideas. She tells her teacher that her first drawing shows, "ten ones together to make one large one with two small ones left." This lets Haley's teacher know that she has some understanding of working with tens and ones and some familiarity with a model of our base ten system. Haley then draws twelve "ones" as an additional representation and indicates her awareness of another mathematics manipulative when she says, "These are twelve tiles."

What do you know about 12?
Show 12 in as many different ways as you can.

12   12 + 0 =
     0 + 12

11 + 1   1 + 11

I had 11 pese of gum.
My frand gave me
1 pese   of gum. I had 12
Pesise of gume.

Figure 3–1 *Haley's response to an open-ended task showed connections to equations, physical models, and a story problem.*

She seems to have some ideas about the communicative property for addition as she has written *12 + 0 = 0 + 12* as well as *11 + 1* next to *1 + 11*. (See Figure 3–1.)

The teacher was particularly pleased to see the equation with two addends on each side as it shows an initial understanding of the equal sign as indicating equality or balance, rather than the traditional misconception many children have that it's the sign to tell you where you write the answer. In the following reflection we gain insight about how the teacher thinks about this task as a way to gather early data about her students.

Teacher Reflection

I like using this task as one of the very first problems I give my second graders. The range of responses is pretty amazing. I have found that twelve is a number that most, if not all, of my incoming students feel comfortable with and yet it

(Continued)

still provides mathematical interest. Some children try to dazzle me by writing a long list of equations, others try adding "clever" responses, such as "I know twelve is a dozen," or "Twelve on the clock is for noon and midnight." I think by second grade, many students know we use problems like this one to get a feel for what they know and can do. Sometimes they even write a multiplication sentence. One child recently wrote, "*6* tims *1* + *6* tims *1*."

Though the range of responses is great, I don't want to read too much into them. After all, it's only one task and students sometimes need a week or two back in school before they really get going. But it is a place to begin and does help me develop some ideas about what my new students know. I don't have a specific number of responses I am looking for, though I do look for accuracy, flexible thinking, and engagement. I also check to see if there is any evidence of a child looking uncomfortable during this work. It's just a start. But it really helps.

This teacher reminds us of the balanced way we need to think about assessment tasks. No one task can be given too much attention and yet each appropriate task does provide us with some relevant data. It is particularly important to take a similarly balanced perspective on information that is passed from grade to grade. In many schools data are shared from one grade to another by way of lists of test scores and portfolios that contain end-of-year assessment interviews or packets. Many teachers receiving this information find it to be very helpful, while others prefer to begin to make their own judgments before reviewing any of the previous data. In either case it is important to remember the significance of gathering evidence from multiple sources.

Looking Beyond Readiness

So far we have concentrated on early assessment tasks that address readiness, often the sole focus of mathematics teachers. But we also want to differentiate instructional activities according to interests, preferred learning styles, intelligences, and mathematical dispositions. We can collect this data through parent questionnaires, student input, teacher observations, and conversations with previous teachers. Collection and use of these data are ways to acknowledge that we expect our students to be different from one another and to show the children (and their parents) that we care about getting to know them as individual learners. The following reflection shows us how one teacher has used letter writing or special conferences as a way to gather information from parents.

I like to offer parents and guardians an opportunity to write a letter to me or to make an appointment to come in and talk for a few minutes at the start of the school year to help me get to know their child. I got this idea from a book Lucy McCormick Calkins wrote called *Living Between the Lines* (Calkins 1991). Over the years I have found that not all parents respond or pick up on this offer, but those who do give me insights I don't think I could have gained without their input. I realize that many people are not comfortable talking or writing to someone they don't know, particularly a teacher who is seen as having the status of authority over their children. But those who respond to this invitation have shared some pretty extraordinary pieces of information with me.

When it comes to talking about math, parents frequently let me know that they themselves were not successful or didn't like math. They would like this experience to be different for their children. Other parents let me know how much they excelled at math and how they have similar expectations for their children. They tell stories of how their child has impressed them at an early age and identify family traits and interests they share. "We love to look at the baseball stats in the newspaper." "I love to sew and my child already knows a lot about measuring because I ask him to help me mark patterns." These comments give me a perspective on how the families view mathematics and how mathematics is embedded in their daily lives.

One family wrote of their deep concern that their second child seemed to have a significant math disability. They wrote, "It's like numbers don't exist for him. He avoids all situations where we might be talking about numbers. I'm not even sure he can tell you his birth date or age." I know this can be gut wrenching for a parent. As I read the letter, I was struck by their apparent feeling of helplessness and of their crying out for assistance. It is at times like these that I want to reach out to families to help them see that we are all in this together, that we have similar goals, and that we will work hard to figure out the nuances of their child's difficulties and sources of their confusion.

Questionnaires

Some teachers ask parents to complete questionnaires. While they are not always returned, when they are the information gleaned can be important. Some kindergarten and first-grade teachers send a questionnaire home to gather information about their students. (See Figure 3–2; see also Blackline Masters.) Questions about hobbies, collections, and activity choices in and out of school provide insight into interests children have that may connect to mathematics. Collecting coins, playing cards or logic games, doing puzzles, having an interest in sports-generated statistics, and constructing intricate block designs often relate to skills that support and utilize mathematical thinking. Children's general interests are also relevant to mathematics as they allow us to position tasks in contexts

Dear Parent or Guardian:

I am always so excited about the start of the school year and a roomful of eager children. I look forward to getting to know each and every one of them, as well as their families. As no one knows your child as well as you do, I am hoping that you will have the time to answer these few questions. There are no right or wrong answers, just responses that will help me to better meet your child's needs when learning math. I am very interested to help children realize that math is an important part of the world, and therefore exciting to learn. I believe by connecting the learning of math to other important aspects of your child's life, I can make it more relevant and exciting. Please feel free to call me if you have any questions. Thank you.

1. What are your child's favorite hobbies, interests, pastimes, books?

2. In what ways is mathematics part of your child's life at home?

3. What, if any, concerns do you have about your child's knowledge of mathematics?

4. What is a mathematical strength that you see in your child?

Figure 3–2 *Parent or guardian questionnaire.*

that can help to capture students' curiosity and to illustrate the usefulness of what they are learning. Some teachers, however, prefer to use forms that do not require narrative responses. (See Figure 3–3; see also Blackline Masters.)

Questionnaires can also be used to gather helpful data from students, such as a general interest survey given to first-grade students early in the fall. (See Figure 3–4; see also Blackline Masters.) Students can also tell us about how they learn best, for example, whether they like to work in groups or alone, the levels of challenge they prefer, the noise level they find comfortable, and where they like to work in the classroom. Asking children about these

Dear Parent or Guardian:

This first day has been a wonderful start to the school year. I am excited about getting to know each of my new students. I am hoping that you will help me by completing this questionnaire about mathematics. There are no right or wrong answers! Please feel free to call me if you have any questions. Thank you.

1 = agree
2 = somewhat agree
3 = somewhat disagree
4 = disagree

My child will stick with a math problem, even when it is difficult.   1   2   3   4

My child lacks confidence in mathematics.   1   2   3   4

My child has strong computational skills.   1   2   3   4

My child's favorite subject is mathematics.   1   2   3   4

My child becomes frustrated solving math problems.   1   2   3   4

My child does math homework independently.   1   2   3   4

As a parent, it is my job to help my child with math homework.   1   2   3   4

Math is talked about at home and is part of our everyday life.   1   2   3   4

I do not always understand the way my child thinks about
math problems.   1   2   3   4

Math is taught better today than when I was in school.   1   2   3   4

Comments:

Figure 3–3   *Alternative parent or guardian survey.*

preferences helps them realize that we care about how they learn best. It also allows even young children to reflect on their learning preferences. (See Figure 3–5; see also Blackline Masters.) As the following teacher's words suggest, knowing our students' interests and preferences can help us relate to them more deeply and to better prepare to meet their needs.

What Interests You?

1. What activities do you like to do after school?

2. What are your favorite sports or games?

3. What do you like to do at indoor recess?

4. If you could plan a school field trip, where would the class go?

5. Who is your favorite character from a book or a video?

6. Which of these things do you like most? Put a 1 there.
   Which of these things do you like second best? Put a 2 there.

   ____ music   ____ reading

   ____ sports   ____ being outside

   ____ acting   ____ drawing

   ____ playing with friends   ____ using blocks

Figure 3–4   *General interest survey for first graders at the beginning of the school year.*

Teacher Reflection

I have found it fun and informative to give this interest survey early in the year. I think my second graders can and should be encouraged to tap into their feelings about learning. I mean, isn't this meta-cognitive skill a big part of helping children know who they are and that they are valued for their individuality? Though I feel I was treated with respect by most of my teachers, I can't say that I felt they really knew me, knew what mattered to me most. Our connection was always around how I responded to the work they were expecting me to complete. Maybe they knew my siblings by name or my mom, but I don't think they knew I liked to cook with my grandmother, knew how to ride a horse, or found it useful to see pictures in order to help me think more clearly. I find it very helpful to know bits of information like this about each of my students. They can provide a bridge for our communication. I see the teacher-learner relationship as more of a two-way street than I felt it was when I was a child. This matters to me and I think it does to my students and their families, too.

Who Are You as a Learner?

1. If you could learn about anything at school, what would you choose?

2. What do you know a lot about?

3. How do you work best in school?

_____ alone _____ partner _____ small group _____ large group

4. Where do you like to work at school?

_____ desk _____ table _____ rug _____ library area _____ other

5. Do you learn best when your classroom is

_____ quiet _____ somewhat quiet _____ somewhat noisy _____ noisy

6. Do you like schoolwork to be

_____ easy _____ somewhat easy _____ somewhat hard _____ hard

7. What else helps you to learn?

8. What makes it hard for you to learn?

Figure 3–5   *A learning survey for second graders at the beginning of the school year.*

It is also worthwhile to gain insight into students' mathematical dispositions, or their attitudes toward mathematics. As all teachers know, positive attitudes contribute greatly to successful learning. Ideally, students enjoy mathematics, have had positive mathematical learning experiences, think of themselves as successful learners and users of mathematics, and view mathematics as a useful tool in their lives. Simple observations, such as noting how a child sits or looks during mathematical activities can often provide quite a bit of information. Does her body language suggest that she is tense? Do his eyes indicate that he is disinterested? Is the position of her shoulders a sign that she is confident? Is the angle of his upper body an implication of eager anticipation? These behaviors can often be

What Do You Think About Mathematics?

1. Math is important to learn because . . .

2. When I am learning math I feel . . .

3. One thing I am good at in math is . . .

4. One thing I am not good at yet in math is . . .

5. This year in math I want to learn about . . .

Figure 3–6 *Student math interest inventory.*

observed during the first week of school and can alert the teacher to those students who might need closer attention.

Again, questionnaires can be used, such as a form used to collect data from first- and second-grade students about their mathematical dispositions. (See Figure 3–6; see also Blackline Masters.) Kindergarten children, or those less-able readers and writers, can be interviewed using these questions. Student responses suggested a variety of beliefs about mathematics. For example, when asked, *Why is math important to learn?* some students indicated its relevance to their daily lives with comments such as "it helps you in life," or "in life you need to know how many or how much." Other responses were school-based; they contained expressions of concern about their future education with comments such as "in third grade the teacher will ask you," or "you have to know your numbers if you want to go to college."

Responses also revealed how students felt about math. Many students gave short positive answers such as "happy," "smart," "great!," "cool," or "excited." Unfortunately, even at this early age, difficulties and ill feelings were also suggested with responses such as "nervous," "like my brain is about to pour out of my ears," "confused," "sad, because I don't like math," or "like I want to go home."

Interestingly, naming an arithmetic operation was the most common response to what a student was good at, was not good at, or wanted to learn more about. All of the children were able to identify something they were good at with "adding," or "pluses," being the most common response among those who identified negative feelings when learning mathematics. Teachers who collected the data were pleased that some of the students identified "doing problems" or "learning different ways to do problems," as either their strength or as something they wanted to learn. They also recognized that their students' responses alerted them to feelings that could potentially impact learning, both positively and negatively.

Getting to know our students does not happen overnight, nor is it accomplished in the first few weeks of school. Most important, this information is not static; attitudes, interests, and readiness change throughout the year. Thus it is daily routines and lessons that provide teachers with the greatest source for assessment data for the greatest number of students. Teachers are always gathering data within their normal classroom activities and adjusting lessons accordingly. Probing questions (How do you know? Can you tell me more? Can you restate what she just said?) allow teachers to gain a better understanding of what their students know and how they think about mathematical ideas. Asking students to record their thinking with words, numbers, or drawings also provides mathematical artifacts that teachers can compare over time. Conversations overheard at recess or lunch can update teachers on their students' current interests or concerns.

Post-Assessment

Open-ended problems or tasks can also be given as post-assessment tasks. Two colleagues, a first-grade teacher and a second-grade teacher, have each chosen to assign such a task at the end of their units on time. The teachers designed the question so that a broad range of responses could be captured:

> *Your younger sister wants to learn how to tell time. Make a list of the most important things she needs to know. Or, describe how you would teach her to tell time using pictures, numbers, and words.*

Due to the open-ended nature of the task, students can control some of the difficulty level themselves, for example, by limiting their illustrations to times on the hour or half hour. Similarly, students may choose to use drawings, charts, or diagrams to communicate their ideas or they may rely more on prose. This task also gives teachers an opportunity to discover what their students choose to include, perhaps because it is what they know best, or what they believe it is most important, or what they find most interesting.

As expected, the children are intrigued by the task. At this age, even children without a younger sibling are aware of and proud of the fact that they now know more than younger children. They are often solicitous to kindergarteners who get upset on the playground and are proud to use their newly acquired literacy skills to read to younger children. The teachers view this task as a way to modestly celebrate their students' mathematical knowledge. The first-grade teacher chuckles as she hears Jason announce, "There's a lot I can teach my sister about time. She hardly knows anything and I know bunches of stuff."

Madison is in first grade and Hannah is in second grade. Both girls rely mostly on clock faces to explain their thinking. Note that both recognize the importance of labeling the hands on the clock, but that the older student refers to their purpose, rather than to their size. Hannah's work is also more sophisticated in that it includes three examples, distributes the numbers more evenly about the clock face, and indicates that there are twenty-four hours in a day. (See Figure 3–7.) But, Madison has drawn a recognizable clock and has written the corresponding time correctly. (See Figure 3–8.)

Jessica is a first-grade student with a somewhat unique response. (See Figure 3–9 on page 62.) She is the only child in either grade who represents the people involved and one of only three students who connect analog and digital representations of the same time. The teacher is not surprised by her drawing as she knows that relationships are important to Jessica. She is surprised by Jessica's inclusion of the fact that there are sixty minutes in an hour, a detail that many students do not retain for some time. Jessica does not, however, focus on how to tell time and the teacher plans to have a follow-up conversation with her, and a couple of other students, to gain more insight into their thinking.

Derek, also a first-grade student, uses a list format to communicate what he would teach his sister. (See Figure 3–10 on page 62.) Through other samples of work in the unit, the teacher knows that Derek can draw a reasonable facsimile of a clock face and notes his preference for using words, rather than drawings, in this response.

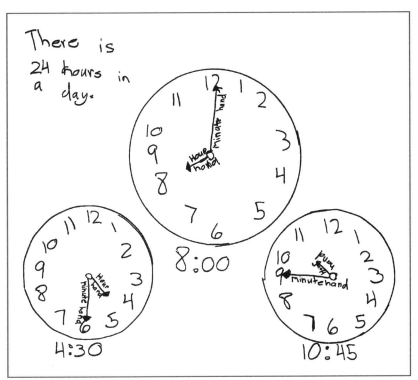

Figure 3–7   *Hannah's response included three different times and identified the hour and minute hands.*

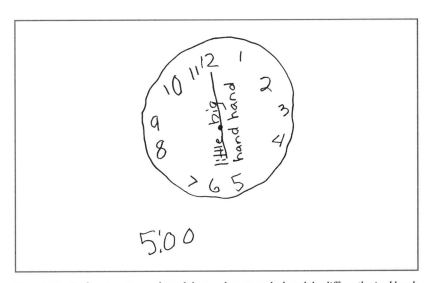

Figure 3–8   *Madison's response showed the numbers on a clock and the differently sized hands.*

Joey and Abigail are both second-grade students and their responses are quite detailed. Joey's clock shows the marks for minutes and he includes a drawing of a second hand as well as minute and hour hands. (See Figure 3–11 on page 63.) He has a chart and

Figure 3–9   *In response to this task, Jessica showed herself teaching her little sister how to tell time.*

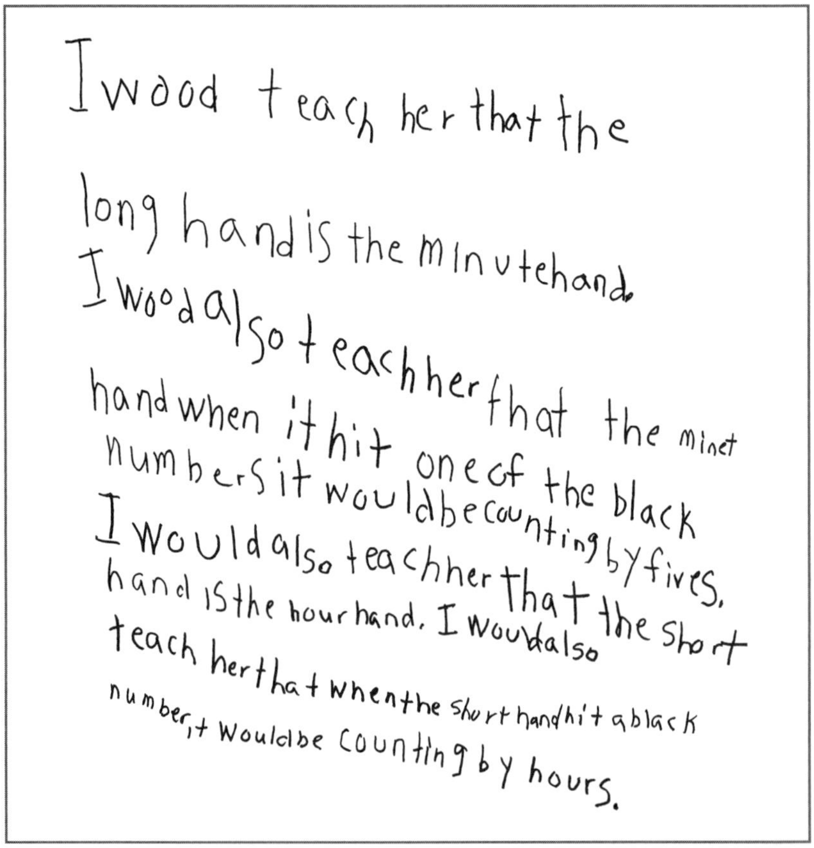

I wood teach her that the long hand is the minute hand. I wood also teach her that the minet hand when it hit one of the black numbers it would be counting by fives. I would also teach her that the short hand is the hour hand. I would also teach her that when the short hand hit a black number, it would be counting by hours.

Figure 3–10   *Derek provided a narrative response to this task.*

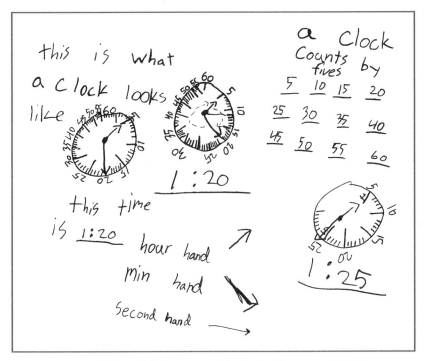

this is what
a clock looks
like

1:20

this time
is 1:20

hour hand

min hand

second hand

a Clock
Counts by
fives

5	10	15	20
25	30	35	40
45	50	55	60

1:25

Figure 3–11 *Joey's clocks included minutes and the relationship to counting by fives.*

a drawing to show how counting by fives is used to tell time. Abigail also has a chart for counting by fives and has connected the multiples of five to the numbers on the clock. (See Figure 3–12 on page 64.) Though two of her clock faces show somewhat simple times to the hour, her comment regarding how to interpret the hour hand when it is between two numbers is quite sophisticated.

The two teachers share their students' work and enjoy looking at the similarities and differences across the grade levels. They notice that three of the children describe the second hand as the "red hand." Too often, they realize, some students need additional examples to help them distinguish the information that is mathematically relevant from that which is not. They both commit to finding a clock with a second hand that it not red. They decide to include this work in the students' portfolios. Next year, they want the students' teachers to have these artifacts to help them determine readiness for future work in this area. They believe this task could be used as both a pre- and a post-assessment. They also talk about how they could further differentiate the task. Though they think the open-ended nature of the task allows for a variety of levels and ways of responding, they wonder about other ways students could respond. For example, perhaps some students could have demonstrated more knowledge if the task had not

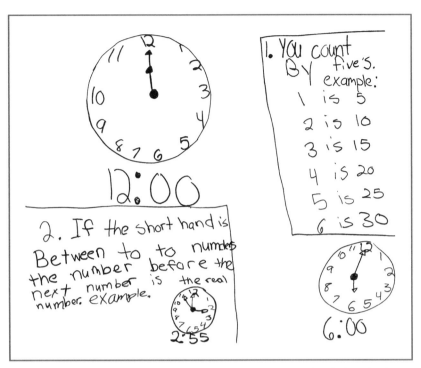

Figure 3–12 *Abigail's response included a description of what to do when the hour hand is between two numbers.*

required writing. Maybe students should have the choice of creating a dramatization of this scenario.

Pre-assessments, post-assessments, interviews, questionnaires, and observations—so what do we do with all these data? Many teachers comment that they get overwhelmed by the amount of information they collect. In a professional development course, one teacher bemoaned, "Sometimes I feel like I am drowning in paperwork. Every piece is important; I don't want to give it back to the student in case I need to refer to it in some way. It's all so interesting, but I'm beginning to want to find a way to figure out what I need to know versus just what is nice to know."

One recommended practice is to take a few minutes a day to write two to three items about what you know about five students. The idea is to focus on each student by the end of the week. Over time, teachers begin to see patterns among their students that can be useful to understanding developmental sequences. Furthermore, these notes can serve as summative statements of what teachers feel confident that their students understand. Or, the notes can provoke the next questions to guide instruction, such as "Can you read me your pattern?" or "What can you tell me about your pattern?" Throughout this process, teachers are frequently asking: What more do I need to know about my students to offer them an effective and engaging math program? Creating thoughtful rubrics and checklists can also help teachers to assess student work in a more expedient manner.

Teacher collaborations

Sometimes teachers experience uncertainty or confusion in regards to particular students. No matter how much data they collect, they feel that they still have not gathered information that allows them to figure out how to best reach these students. Some teachers who face this situation have learned the benefit of turning to each other for assistance. Ellen and Margie are an example of such a partnership. Both experienced second-grade teachers, they have been teaching for over twenty years and have been introduced to many math curriculums during that time. They are now in the third year of implementing another new series. Although they both embrace the curriculum, they also feel that the professional development provided by the school system was not enough for them to feel completely confident while teaching the units. They would both like additional support in their classrooms, but their system has no more funding for mathematics education this year and has plans to focus next year's professional development on science.

Both Margie and Ellen feel confident in their own mathematics abilities, but the lack of this program's formal assessment procedures leaves them unsure as to what each student is learning. After many conversations in the teachers' room, they decide to provide for their own professional development. With the support of their principal, they develop a plan that they hope will work for them. They agree to meet once at the beginning of each unit to reconsider it together. Also, they will visit each other's classroom during each unit and look for *evidence of learning,* a term their professional development presenter used when they were looking at student work. They also will meet before the visit to review the mathematics in the lesson and any particular concern they might have. Finally, they will meet to debrief the lesson.

Today's lesson is in Ellen's classroom. Ellen has twenty-three second-grade students with many different levels of mathematical understanding. The focus of the lesson is solving story problems involving addition and subtraction. Ellen has introduced her students to a hundreds chart throughout the year and encourages them to use this tool to help solve problems. On each table there are story problems in envelopes labeled *A, B,* and *C.*

In their preconference, Ellen shared that she would like Margie to listen to how her students are solving the problems and to see if their representations on paper match their mathematical thinking. With a class of twenty-three students, Ellen feels she is unable to do this in a single lesson. There are times where she wishes she could teach the old way when everyone had the same problem at the same time. Her life certainly was easier then. Ellen is also concerned that some of the students are not effectively using the hundreds chart. Over the course of the year, they have had many opportunities to use the chart and she was hoping to see more growth. She wanted all of her students to count forward or backward by tens and ones, not always just by ones. Students have shown confidence in decomposing numbers into tens and ones in class, but Ellen was concerned that some of her students did not apply this skill when using the hundreds chart. She expressed particular concern about Josh, who rarely explained his thinking.

When the lesson begins the students are assigned, based on their readiness, to solve three problems in one of the envelopes. As the students work, Margie and Ellen interact with various students and make notes about their conversations and observations. To a third observer, they would appear to be team teaching. Following the lesson they meet to share what they saw and heard.

Once Ellen is assured that Margie thought the lesson was successful, they begin to review their notes. Margie was anxious to tell Ellen of her interactions with Josh when he was working on a problem from set B:

> *Lucinda had 28 pennies in her pocket.*
> *She spent 17 of them.*
> *How many pennies does Lucinda have now?*

Margie describes how Josh took the hundreds chart, started on 28, and counted back seventeen ones. As she had heard Ellen's concern about this strategy being relied on too heavily, Margie asked him if there were another way to solve the problem. Josh said, "I could go up ten and then back seven. Is that what you mean?" Margie told Ellen that she was confused by his use of *up* and *back,* so she asked him to show her on the hundred chart. Josh put his finger on 28 and said, "See I am going to go up ten," as he placed his finger on the 28 and moved it up one row to land on 18. "Then," he continued, "I count back one to seventeen." To her, *up* meant forward and she would have expected a greater number to result. She was glad she had asked him to show her what he was doing.

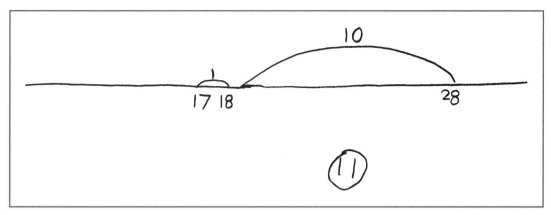

Figure 3–13 *Josh used an open number line to solve a problem.*

Margie then explained that when it was time to record his thinking on paper, Josh groaned and clearly didn't want to write what he had just verbalized. When she looked at his folder, she found that he had explained his work on the first problem by simply writing "I went backwards." Margie then told Ellen that she wondered if Josh counted by ones as it was an easy strategy to record. She thought a different visual model might be helpful to him and so she showed him an open number line. She demonstrated how he could use this model to indicate his moves on the hundreds chart. Josh decided to try out this method of recording. (See Figure 3–13.)

As we learn from Ellen's reflection on this experience, she was quite pleased with their exchange.

Teacher Reflection

When we first started these class visits, I was nervous about having Margie in my classroom. I wasn't sure what she would think about my teaching and I was used to being alone with my students. I tried to calm my nerves by remembering that I asked for her support as a means of getting to know my students better, to gather evidence of what they were learning. Now I really look forward to these opportunities to work together and to share our thinking. I was delighted with Margie's interaction with Josh. I remembered learning about the open number line as a model in one of our training sessions this fall, but I never would have thought to use it in this situation. Maybe I was too stuck on the hundreds chart for this idea to enter my mind. It really took another person's perspective for me to realize what I had missed. I mean Josh knew how to work with tens and ones, but somehow the hundreds chart didn't encourage him to do so. Or, the requirement to record an explanation limited his thinking. With an open number line, he would not have to write all of the numbers and so larger groupings would be appealing. I wonder if that model would be better for some of the other students in my classroom as well. I hope I can be as helpful when I visit Margie's class next week.

This example helps us to remember that it is important not to assume that students do not know something just because they have not provided evidence of that knowledge within a particular task. It speaks to the importance of differentiating mathematical models within assessment tasks, as well as instruction. It also reminds us to constantly adjust our lenses as we look for evidence of student understanding.

We believe that getting to know each child is at the heart of differentiation. By using a wider variety of assessment practices and specially designed data-gathering techniques, teachers can have a greater understanding of each student as a unique learner and, as a result, have a deeper and broader view of the learning trajectory for each student. Making decisions about for whom, why, and when to differentiate becomes clearer when it is based on what we know about our students and our curriculum. Information about students' readiness, learning preferences, and interests enables teachers to offer different ways for students to develop and to demonstrate their mathematical knowledge. Ways to match, adapt, or create curriculum in order to meet a variety of learner needs is the focus of the next two chapters.

Chapter 4

Casting a Wider Net for Readiness

Transforming lessons for
Individual
Exploration, according to
Readiness

*T*hrough assessment we uncover many of the similarities and differences among our students' thinking. It offers us an opportunity to look for patterns in our students' learning, both as individuals and as a group. Inevitably, assessment data for any classroom reveal a range in students' experiences, interests, and readiness. In response to these differences, teachers work diligently to delineate standards for all learners, to build inclusive classroom environments, and to vary their teaching styles in order to address these differences. Yet, no matter how carefully learning outcomes are identified, habits are developed to encourage community, or diverse instructional strategies are employed, teachers remain most concerned about the range, great or narrow, of student readiness. Consider the following words of this first-grade teacher.

Teacher Reflection

I often struggle with finding what is "appropriate" for all my students. Even now, just days into the new school year, I am already feeling that I am not prepared to meet the different levels of math readiness in my students. Yesterday, Hazel spoke up at morning meeting and quickly, without knowing it, revealed to me some of the ways she thinks mathematically. It's only the second day of first grade and as we were talking about the number of children in our class, twenty-three, I hear her say, "I can make twenty-three with two tens and three more. I can also make it with eleven and twelve if I split up the tens and ones." I've been teaching for a few years and this is the first student who has demonstrated such thinking so early in the year. Just last night I was reviewing the first

(Continued)

few lessons in our math curriculum and they are all about working with numbers under ten. How is that going to challenge Hazel?

Later I asked her to talk with me about math. Hazel beamed and exclaimed, "I love math! I love to count and figure out the numbers. My mom says I think in numbers." I took a moment to ask her a few informal questions. I know I will take the time in the coming weeks to more formally assess her mathematical understanding, but her eagerness and confidence called out to me. I don't want to wait too long to get a clearer picture of her abilities and to tap into her obvious interest and potential in math. I just wish it were easier. I asked her to solve a few word problems that I remembered from the end of the school year. It was clear that she has fluency with adding and subtracting numbers to at least one hundred. She spoke in terms of values; ones, tens, hundreds, and thousands. She clearly is clever and accurate when calculating. Later I also noticed her making complex patterns with Unifix cubes as the children explored materials during our first math lesson. When I spoke with her about her work she was very articulate, and again accurate. Already I have the sense she meets or exceeds our first-grade curriculum goals.

While this child seems particularly advanced in her understanding of numbers, I feel there are always children in my class who have already met some of the goals of the given curriculum. I'm just not sure how best to extend the lessons for them, especially when the curriculum seems right for the majority of students. I don't feel stuck like this when thinking about readiness in literacy. I know I have a host of books at varying levels to meet the challenges of my emerging, early, or independent readers. If I don't have enough titles for them at a given level, I feel comfortable asking the teachers at the grade level above mine if I can borrow some books. I wish it were that easy in math. Do I ask to borrow a copy of their math curriculum? If I do, won't they feel like I'm stepping on their toes? I have a close friend who might be willing to share her curriculum, but then what will the children do next year?

Hazel may very well be the student who represents the more advanced students in her first-grade class this year. Perhaps she is not alone. More than likely there are classmates whose profiles are dramatically different. A second-grade teacher provides us her thoughts on students who are less ready for math challenges.

Teacher Reflection

I am worried about two of my students, Bryce and Michelle. Today we were doing some money problems where the children had to figure out the value of a collection of coins in a piggy bank. It was as if Bryce and Michelle had never seen or used coins before. I did not hear them use the correct names of the coins and though they assigned values of one cent, five cents, and ten cents, they mixed up the values of the nickels and the dimes. I did not see any attempt to count by fives or tens when they were trying to determine the total value. In the end their answer was off by a lot and they didn't seem to have any way of judging whether their response was reasonable or not. I think what is most concerning to me is that we have been working with coin problems off and on for several months. But, it's as though Bryce and Michelle were seeing it all for the first time today. I wish I had a better way to help cement money-related skills and ideas for these children.

While these two children struggle the most as we work with coins, other students experience similar difficulty with other areas of our curriculum. I just never have enough time to sit with them and give them the support that they need. We have more help with reading. My school system has a specialist who comes to my room three mornings a week to work with my students who are having the most difficulty. And, I have more resources for these students. My classroom library has many picture books and early readers. There are so many books to choose from; I know I will have new materials for them. But, I can't just redo the same math problems our curriculum offered them last year.

Considering ways to manage and meet the range of readiness in our mathematics classes is no easy task. Most early childhood and elementary teachers feel much as these teachers do. What we take on as a rudimentary challenge in literacy becomes seemingly impossible to many, when it comes to mathematics. We're often not sure how to challenge those students who are beyond grade level, and sometimes it feels as if the students who are less ready can slip easily through our grasps. At times, nothing feels just right or appropriate.

But how do we define *appropriate*? It is a word used frequently in the educational arena. Too often, we aim for the middle or average group and just hope the others will manage. Returning to Vygotsky's zone of proximal development helps us think more clearly about what is appropriate for each student. It is that area that provides challenge, without going beyond the student's comfort zone or edges, that is, without being too easy or too hard. We can't possibly provide a separate curriculum for each of our students, nor would that be advisable. The social interaction and exchange of ideas among students is too important a component of learning. So how do we expand our curriculum so that it is appropriate for students whose grasp of mathematics differs greatly from that of the majority of students?

Transforming Tasks

Choosing mathematical tasks is one of the most important decisions that we can make. While it is difficult for one task to be appropriate for all learners, most tasks can be transformed to be more inclusive, to allow a greater number of students access, and to provide additional students with possibilities for more expansive thinking.

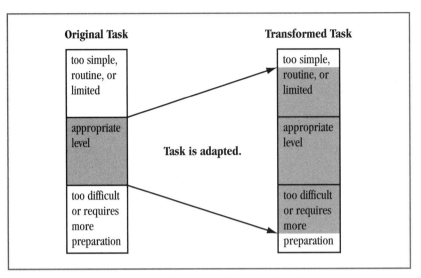

Figure 4–1 *Tasks can be transformed to meet a wider range of readiness.*

When we do this, we are casting a wider net that can "catch" a broader range of students. Our goal then is to transform or modify tasks, to meet a wider range of readiness. (See Figure 4–1.) Note that the range of learners does not change, nor the field that is deemed *appropriate*; rather the tasks themselves are stretched to be better aligned with our students' needs. To do this, we begin with the tasks in our curriculum and consider how they can be modified.

Teachers have discovered a variety of ways in which tasks can accommodate different levels of readiness. One adaptation a teacher can make is to allow students to have some control over the difficulty level. This, for example, can be done with story problems. Instead of the standard format where all the numbers are provided, a story may be written without numbers and the student asked to provide them. For example, students may be asked to write numbers in the following story so that it makes sense:

> *Lucas has _____ stamps.*
> *His mother gave him _____ more stamps.*
> *Then Lucas used _____ stamps to mail some letters.*
> *Now Lucas has _____ stamps.*

Students can choose numbers according to their comfort levels, but *must* recognize the mathematical relationships among their chosen numbers. This is an important point. Whenever we expand tasks in order to allow more access, we never want to do so in ways that undermine the integrity of the mathematical challenge. All students must have access to tasks that require mathematical thinking, not just rote learning or less complicated thinking.

Students can also make choices within simple practice assignments. Imagine a standard list of ten addition examples. By changing the directions, *Complete exercises 1–10*, students can make choices according to their readiness. Consider the following alternatives:

Pick five of these examples to complete.

Pick five examples that have a sum that is less than five hundred and tell how you know that will be so.

Pick one example and find the sum. Next, create four different addition examples that will have the same sum.

Pick one example and find the sum. Then write four subtraction examples with a difference equal to that sum.

Another approach is to open up a problem so that there is more than one answer. Problems with more than one answer allow room for expansion. Some students will be quite satisfied with finding one answer and it may take them some time to do so. Other students may find one solution quickly, but be able and interested to find more possibilities. By removing information or by creating a greater number of choices, many problems can be adapted to allow for multiple answers. Examples of such problems include:

How might you color half of this figure?

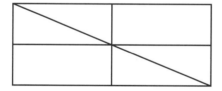

Jocelyn has fifteen pencils.
Some are sharpened and some are not.
How many of each type of pencil could Jocelyn have?

Danny has some pennies and nickels.
He has five coins.
How much money could Danny have?

Standard story problems can also be transformed by providing students with a "number story" and with "answers." Students are asked to create questions within the given context that will yield the answers provided. Students can make choices about which questions they provide; they may also identify more than one question for some of the answers. (See Figure 4–2 for an example of such a problem, along with possible questions.)

Here are the answers, but some may need the cents sign (¢): 4, 22, 2, 48, 26*

Number Story:
Colin has three nickels and seven pennies.
Lisa has nine nickels and three pennies.

What could be the questions?

Possible responses: (Students may provide one or more questions for one or more answers.)

4: How many more pennies than nickels does Colin have?
   How many fewer nickels than pennies does Colin have?
   How many more pennies does Colin have than Lisa?
   How many fewer pennies does Lisa have than Colin?

22: What is the value of Colin's coins?
    How many coins do Colin and Lisa have together?

2: How many more coins does Lisa have than Colin?
   How many fewer coins does Colin have than Lisa?

48: What is the value of Lisa's coins?

26: How much more money does Lisa have than Colin?
    How much less money does Colin have than Lisa?

Other choices for answers are possible, but it is usually best to limit the list to four or five possibilities.

Figure 4–2   *Example of students' answers to* What's the question?

Some tasks have multiple solutions in that there are a variety of ways to respond to them. The problem in Chapter 3, which required students to describe what they would teach their younger sister about telling time, is an example of such a task. Teachers usually create these tasks by thinking about the topic and identifying a broad question that taps into what children know, see, or recognize. Examples of open-ended problems include:

Write and draw to tell about money.

How could you use dollars, dimes, and pennies to find 48¢ + 59¢?

Dana added 26 and 47 and got a sum of 63. What could you show and tell Dana to help him find the correct sum?

Use mathematics to talk about this picture of a picnic.

How would you describe a square to someone who has never seen one?

What are some patterns you see on the hundreds chart?

The answer is 87. What could the question be?

How is measurement used in your home?

Materials

Teachers have long recognized that children operate on a variety of levels in terms of their needs for concrete models. Therefore, the types of materials available may make the difference as to whether a problem is accessible. Consider the problem that follows:

There are some strawberries on the table.
Maria and Tom each eat two of them.
Now there are nine strawberries left.
How many strawberries were on the table in the beginning?

Teachers can make a variety of materials available to children when solving this problem, including real strawberries; strawberries made from felt; individual pictures, stickers, or stamps of strawberries; red Unifix cubes, tiles, or counters; or arbitrary counters that aren't red. This is not to say that all students would choose to use these materials. Many students prefer to draw, while others feel they do not need any visual or concrete models to solve a problem. These students may have developed a deeper or more abstract sense of numbers or may more easily visualize numerical situations in their heads. As we learn from the following teacher's reflection, however, having a range of materials available can provide students with access to this type of thinking.

---

*T*eacher *Reflection*

When I first began teaching kindergarten I thought that as long as there were physical materials available, my students would be fine. "Hands-on" had been the buzzword in my teacher training and I knew that I would make sure my classroom was filled with math manipulatives. Over the years I've come to recognize that using materials is more complex than I realized. I began to think about "concreteness" along a continuum that included real items, manipulatives that closely related to the real object, random manipulatives or counters, and

---

(Continued)

pictures. I tried to always have a variety of materials available that represented different levels of abstraction. I would assign my students to use different materials based on what I perceived as their need for concrete representations. As I did so, I came to realize that what children found helpful went beyond or differed from the continuum I had constructed in my mind. For example, orange Cuisenaire rods are more abstract than pictures of real carrots for some children. For others, touching the rods is more important than the realistic images of carrots in pictures. Now, I think it's best to make many different kinds of materials available and let my students choose what works best for them. If I find a student struggling, I will suggest a different model and this is often successful. But I would rather intervene once it is necessary than to impose my thinking right from the beginning. I now realize that my students make fairly good choices and this helps them to become more independent learners.

Tiered Activities

Sometimes even open-ended tasks need to be differentiated in order to be successful with a wide range of student readiness. In this case, tiered activities can be used or created. Such activities allow students to focus on the same general concept or skill, but to do so according to their levels of readiness. Consider the following example from a second-grade classroom.

The students are gathered in the meeting area where the teacher shows them four number cards: 4, 5, 11, and 17. He also has drawn a picture of these number cards on chart paper. He pulls out a black top hat from behind his chair. The students watch closely as he places the cards in the hat and then shakes it. He then looks quizzically at the hat and says, "If we pull out two of these numbers, I wonder what their *sum* would be? Can you help me find out?" Heads nod and Jasmine and Andrew are invited to come to the front of the meeting area. The teacher holds the hat high enough so that the children have to reach to choose a card. Jasmine announces that her card is 5 and Andrew shows the class his card, 17. The teacher asks the children to talk briefly with their neighbors about the sum of these numbers. The class agrees that the sum is 22.

After another example, the teacher shows the students' names listed in three groups on a piece of chart paper. Within each group the students are recorded in pairs so that partnerships can be formed quickly. Each group is also color-coded to correspond to the folder in which students will find copies of tailor-made direction sheets for their group. Red is associated with the first level of the task, blue with the second, and green with the third. (See Figure 4–3; see also Blackline Masters for individual

Red Group

Getting Started
- Write the numbers *3, 6, 8,* and *10* on the blank cards clipped to this sheet. Write one number on each ca
- Put your number cards in the bag and shake it.

To Play
- Pull out two cards. Record the numbers and their sum.
- Return the cards to the bag and take another turn.
- Do this at least fifteen times.

Stop and Think
- List all the sums you get.

What Did You Learn?
- Do you think you have all the different sums that can be made by adding two of your numbers at a time?
- Talk together about why you think you have all the possibilities.

Blue Group

Getting Started
- Write the numbers *4, 5, 11,* and *17* on the blank cards clipped to this sheet. Write one number on each card.
- Put your number cards in the bag and shake it.

To Play
- Pull out two cards. Record the numbers and their sum.
- Return the cards to the bag and take another turn.
- Do this several more times.

Stop and Think
- Make a list of all the sums you could get when using these four number cards.
- Continue to play.

What Did You Learn?
- Make a list showing all the sums you made.
- Do you think you have them all?
- Talk together about why you think you have all the possibilities.

Green Group

Getting Started
- Write the numbers *12, 15, 19,* and *24* on the blank cards clipped to this sheet.
- Put your number cards in the bag and shake it.

To Play
- Pull out two cards. Record the numbers and their sum.
- Return the cards to the bag and take another turn.
- Do this a few times.

Stop and Think
- How many different sums do you get when you pull two of these number cards from the bag?
- How do you know you have all the possibilities?

What Did You Learn?
- Write about your thinking.

Figure 4–3 *Task descriptions for tiered second-grade sums investigations.*

tasks identified by color.) Before releasing the students the teacher explains, "Since we do not have enough top hats, we will be using paper bags. I can't wait to see what you discover. Let's get started!"

The teacher is thrilled by how seriously each group takes up its challenge. He is happy that the children are so engaged and delighted that they are getting a lot of practice with addition. The task also provides them an opportunity to consider conservation of number. He wonders what his students will do when they come across the same two numbers to be added. Will they find these sums each time as though it were the first encounter or might some notice the repetition? The teacher is also curious to see how students will determine the sums. As with any math lesson, counters are within reach for children who prefer to make the problems more concrete. Students know that hundreds charts are available to them as well. The teacher expects to observe a wide range of strategies from counting all, to counting on, to utilizing some basic facts knowledge. He believes he will see some of these behaviors across the three groups. That is, some students who are ready to work with greater numbers may sometimes rely on less complex strategies, while students not ready to work with greater numbers may occasionally feel enough comfort and familiarity with the particular numbers chosen to use more advanced strategies.

As the teacher checks in with the students working in pairs, he hears initial predictions: "I think we'll have a ton [referring to the sums] because we have the highest numbers," Eliza says. Eliza and her partner are working with 12, 15, 19, and 24. As the teacher moves on to Harry and Melissa he hears Harry chime, "Same, same, same!" He thinks that Harry has recognized the fact that the number of sums is limited but as he gets closer, he realizes that Harry is referring to having pulled the same two addends from the bag three times in a row. But over time, "Same!" becomes a common chant. One child even bemoans, "So boring. Same!" as he pulls out the 4 and the 11 for the fourth time. He is hoping that this emotion will cause the students to look more closely at their growing list of combinations and sums and begin to make a general statement about why the repetition might be happening. The wheels of ideas are churning and he notices that one group is debating if $4 + 11$ is the same as or different than $11 + 4$. These students are more focused on the order of the addends and not on the sums they yield.

The next pair he sees is trying to accomplish the task with a more abstract approach. The students decide to abandon the random pulling of cards from the bag and place all four cards face up on the table. They then try to write all the possible combinations of numbers by making a list of equations. The teacher is pleased to see this change of strategy, but then realizes that their list also includes $11 - 5 = 6$ and $11 - 4 = 13$. The teacher acknowledges the pair's decision to write equations and then asks them to reread the directions. "But, I thought we were supposed to find all the ways," Craig protests. Cassandra points out her recognition of the error when she says, "Oops, it does say make a list of all the sums." Reluctantly, they erase their equations involving subtraction.

Teacher Reflection

Once the work in pairs began, I realized that I had underestimated the time this task would require. It took a lot of time for students to collect their data. I recognized that we would not be ready to debrief our work today. I gave them a warning about this, telling them that we would return to the task on a second day. Telling the children this helped to relax them, to understand that this was a big investigation.

Students need to feel comfortable sharing their ideas with the whole class. More time with this work will help them to prepare for our discussion. It's not just one group of students that need this time. Seeing Cassandra and Craig's inclusion of the subtraction equations reminded me that all of my students need considerable time to process a task when it is at the right level of challenge. They are both quite comfortable creating different equations during our morning number of the day routine. Here, they were falling into a familiar pattern of response. Now that they know this task is somewhat different, they will look more thoughtfully at their data.

I can't wait to have a chance to talk as a class about this investigation. We did have to stop midstream, which was hard for some children, but I hope it will also break the momentum of pulling random cards and help them to refocus on what they have recorded. Carrying the work over to a second day will also give them additional practice time. Sometimes I feel for some of my students; there just isn't enough time to really practice. Additional practice within an investigation feels great!

On the second day, procedures are reviewed and the children quickly get back to work. As the teacher circles the room, he hears a new kind of sentiment. "Wow, we got five plus eleven or eleven plus five a lot." "Let's make a list to see if we missed any." It is exciting to see how the children now refer to the information they gathered on the first day. Today, the students are looking more closely at their data, instead of just writing the random numbers they pull, along with their sums, on their lists. The teacher soon recognizes that the focus of the second day is more on the

"Stop and Think and *What Did You Learn?"* stage of the investigative process. The teacher has used this phrase throughout the year as a way to remind students to reflect on their work during the problem-solving process.

"We already have this one" became a familiar mantra. "We keep getting the same number!" Ezra declared, "I mean the same sum." Energy is beginning to shift and the individual groups, regardless of the addends they are using, are starting to think in more generalized ways. "Let's make a list," Lucinda suggests in her small group. "I know, let's look at what we have and then match them up," Iris suggests. Though this pair of students did not identify each of the six sums, their "matching" led to their affirmation of the order property of addition and their recognition that each pair of numbers has one unique sum. (See Figure 4–4.)

After a bit more time for investigation the teacher suggests that the groups begin to wrap up their work and get ready to share. When the students gather they are excited to tell what they have discovered and want to know what others have done. The teacher begins by recounting the directions of the tasks; he wants to make sure that everyone remembers that each group only used four number cards. He hopes that the students will use their individual experiences with their different numbers as a way to connect with the bigger picture, or underlying mathematics in the problem. Two pairs, working with different sets of numbers, present their data when Sabrina suggests, "Everyone has four numbers, so everyone is going to get the same number of sums. We got six different sums, too. I bet everyone did."

Though many students could not make this dramatic leap, others were considering Sabrina's idea. As a beginning, every group agrees that they each got six sums. The teacher is not convinced that all the students believe that's all they will ever get with their four numbers, no matter how long they kept trying, but it is a start and a validation of their hard work. Some students are clearly ready to examine this idea further and begin to offer conjectures as to why there were six different sums.

"See I think it's six. I mean you can't add twelve and twelve because there is only one of them," Jasper explains. He continues, "I can add the first number to the other three, but then the next one doesn't." Jasper is very eager to share this idea. He comes up to the board and writes his group's four numbers. Next he draws a line from the twelve to each of the other numbers. He continues, connecting each number to each of the other numbers, and then announces, "See, it has to be six."

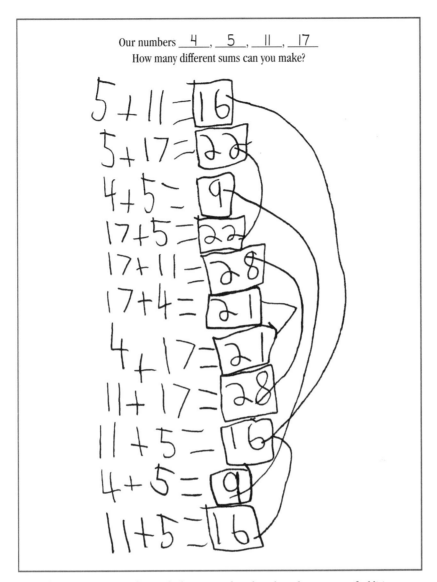

Our numbers __4__ , __5__ , __11__ , __17__
How many different sums can you make?

$$5 + 11 = 16$$
$$5 + 17 = 22$$
$$4 + 5 = 9$$
$$17 + 5 = 22$$
$$17 + 11 = 28$$
$$17 + 4 = 21$$
$$4 + 17 = 21$$
$$11 + 17 = 28$$
$$11 + 5 = 16$$
$$4 + 5 = 9$$
$$11 + 5 = 16$$

Figure 4–4   *Iris and Lucinda matched equations based on the order property of addition.*

The teacher thinks this is a good place to stop. Some of the students were nodding eagerly while Jasper presented his reasoning, but other classmates were beginning to fidget or tire. The teacher recognizes that further consideration of this idea will need to be differentiated once again. But, all of his students experienced a meaningful investigation and found a preliminary way to convince themselves that they had found all the sums. Later the teacher would think about the next challenge for the students who agreed with Jasper. Perhaps he might give them a set of five numbers or maybe another set of four numbers in which two of the number pairs have the same sum, such as 8, 9, 21, and 22. He could also save this task and reconsider it in the context of the money unit they would do next. It would be simple to translate this task to four coins in a hat. But right now, it was time to shift the focus to another subject.

This teacher had created a common task for each group, but tiered the assignment based on readiness. The greatest number of students was in the middle or blue group, but the teacher thought it was important to develop tasks for students who are on different places on the learning continuum. In his reflection, we learn about why the teacher made the changes he did and what he thought about as he designed modifications for this task.

Teacher Reflection

The second graders in my class enjoy working together to learn math. They are an eager group and have already had a lot of experience talking about how they solve problems. They like to share their strategies, but I'm not always sure how much they learn from each other when we share. Some of the children seem to get overwhelmed if the numbers we are using are too big, while others find the work tedious if the numbers are too small. I find a great need to differentiate work on number concepts and operations, but have not always been successful when trying to keep the work relevant for all the children. I've played around with changing numbers in problems, or giving practice packs that are designed to hit the target for a particular group of students. This works, but inevitably when kids are working on different assignments there isn't any real need to come together and share. I feel this can fragment the class and I don't want to do that.

I noticed a colleague working on a type of problem I had not seen before. The goal was to have children investigate what happens when you have a set of possible addends and ask them to only add two of them together at a time. The overarching goal of the problem is to have students generate a list of all the possible sums and then to consider what this means. I quickly recognized how this problem offered students a way to think algebraically, while they had a context for practicing the operation of addition. I wanted to give it a try.

In an attempt to make the problem accessible to all of my students, I tiered the directions and carefully selected the number sets with which each group would be working. It dawned on me that this type of problem lends itself to exactly the type of investigation we could focus on as a class, while differentiating the actual level of addition work. I believed that all of my students could take on the algebraic challenge that the problem suggested, so long as the numbers they were using were within their operational range. I was thrilled to see how this played out.

From the onset, my class loved the playful way I picked two of the four number cards from the hat. "It's like a magic trick!" one student exclaimed.

Though I want to dispel the idea of math being "magic," it was a fun place to start. I was momentarily stopped in my own tracks, however, when one student asked what *sum* meant. I guess I take it for granted that this word is part of the math vocabulary of second graders. In particular the word added an interesting spin, as one child offered, "Not *some,* like you are only going to use some of these cards, but *sum,* as in the total." Another student offered, "Think of it as finding how many."

Once the students let me know they were comfortable with the task and the parameters I had set, they headed off to work in their assigned groups. I did feel a need to explain that some groups would be working with different sets of numbers. I did not tell them that I had also differentiated some of the outcomes listed on their "Getting Started" sheets. I felt I needed to differentiate this part in order to give more challenge for my stronger students, while also giving more direction for those who are easily overwhelmed by the process.

The story from this second-grade classroom demonstrates the effectiveness of tiered assignments. This is usually the case when the teacher has a clear rationale for creating the assignment and makes sure that the activities include mathematical ideas at varying complexities so all students can be challenged appropriately. Simultaneously, the teacher made sure that the task could be approached from a variety of entry points and was thus accessible to all students. Finding the right combination of accessibility and challenge is the goal of a tiered approach.

Creating tiered assignments

So how do we create tiered assignments? As always the first step is to identify the important mathematical ideas. Consider second graders studying geometric shapes, focusing on quadrilaterals (as a general name for all four-sided figures) as well as on identifying rectangles, squares, trapezoids, and parallelograms as particular types of quadrilaterals. Teachers can use "shape critter" tasks to reinforce this particular content goal while also providing students with opportunities for deductive reasoning and problem posing. The shape critter tasks ask students to identify similarities and differences among critters made of shapes. It often helps to begin with the middle level, focusing on what you would expect most of your students to be able to do. (We will call this level, or tier, blue.) A shape critter card can then be developed for that audience. (See Figure 4–5; see also Blackline Masters.)

The blue card begins with "whirly do figures," quadrilaterals with a curlicue. Four-sided figures without the curlicue do not fit the rule, nor do figures with more or fewer than four sides even if

Each of these is a whirly do.

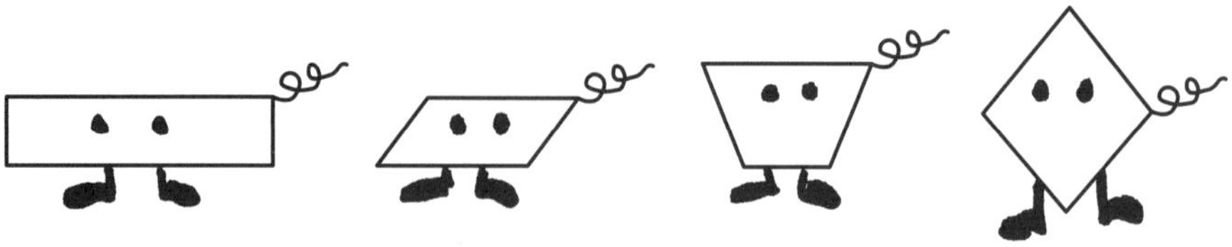

None of these is a whirly do.

Which one of these is a whirly do?

Make up a name for these critters and write it in the blank.

1. Each of these is a _____.

Draw one more critter above. Be sure it fits the rule.

2. None of these is a _____.

Draw one more critter above. Make sure it does not fit the rule.

Figure 4–5   *Blue tier shape critter card for grade 2.*

they have a curlicue. Students then are asked to complete a critter series by naming the critter and adding a figure to each section.

Two other tiers can then be developed by adjusting the middle (blue) tier. For example, in a simplified version (red), the whirly do figures in the top half of the card have curlicues, so the student does not have to consider this characteristic; they need to focus only on figures with more or fewer than four sides. The second half of the card is the same as the blue tier. (See Figure 4–6; see also Blackline Masters.)

In a more challenging version (green), the whirly do figures on the top half of the card are the same as the blue tier, requiring students to attend to both characteristics. In the second half of the card, however, students completely create the critters and accompanying drawings. (See Figure 4–7; see also Blackline Masters.)

A tiered task for first-grade students provides a mathematical focus on pattern finding and algebraic reasoning. (See Figure 4–8 on page 88; see also Blackline Masters.) Though most of the students would probably work at the middle (blue) tier, this example shows how the tiers can reach a wide range of readiness. All tiers involve the same growing pattern of trains for which the first three models are shown: a one-car train, a two-car train, and a three-car train. In the simplified (red) tier, students begin by physically building the four-car train and drawing the five-car train. They answer specific questions about six- and seven-car trains and then identify the number of each piece that would be needed to build a ten-car train.

In the more challenging (blue) tier, students move to generalizations right away. While physical materials and drawings are options that they could choose to use, students are not directed to do so. The task begins with the question about the six-car train. Then students are asked about a ten-car train and expected to draw and write to explain their thinking. In the most challenging (green) tier, students begin with the question about the ten-car train. The next question asks them to reverse their thinking; that is, they are told the number of pieces needed and are asked to identify the number of cars in the train.

In kindergarten, teachers find a need to target practice with initial concepts in number focusing on recognizing the numerals 0–10, making a set of objects to match these numerals, and ordering numbers 0–10. (See Figure 4–9 on page 89; see also Blackline Masters.) How to direct students to the appropriate task, when they are not yet able to read directions independently, always needs to be considered. In the primary grades where the number

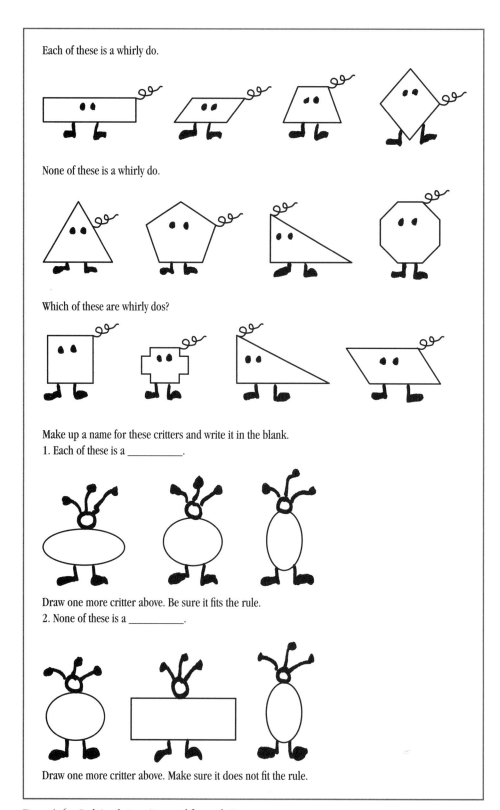

Each of these is a whirly do.

None of these is a whirly do.

Which of these are whirly dos?

Make up a name for these critters and write it in the blank.

1. Each of these is a _____.

Draw one more critter above. Be sure it fits the rule.

2. None of these is a _____.

Draw one more critter above. Make sure it does not fit the rule.

Figure 4–6   *Red tier shape critter card for grade 2.*

Each of these is a whirly do.

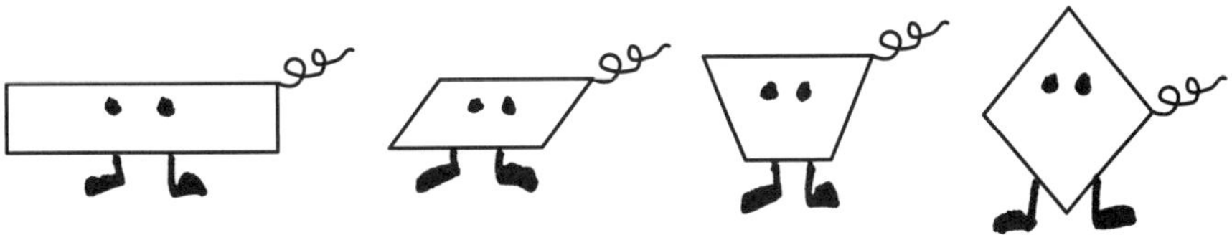

None of these is a whirly do.

Which one of these is a whirly do?

Make up your own critters.
Write their name in each blank.
Draw the pictures.
Write your rule on the back.
Trade cards with a friend and find the rules.

1. Each of these is a _____.

2. None of these is a _____.

3. Which of these are _____?

Figure 4–7   *Green tier shape critter card for grade 2.*

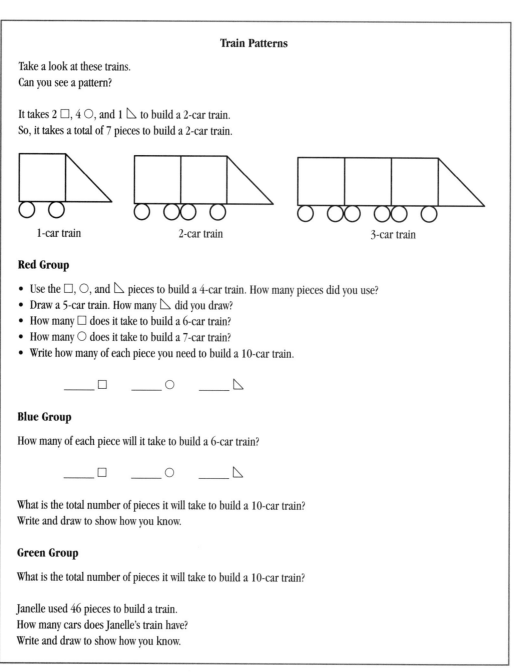

Train Patterns

Take a look at these trains.
Can you see a pattern?

It takes 2 □, 4 ○, and 1 △ to build a 2-car train.
So, it takes a total of 7 pieces to build a 2-car train.

1-car train   2-car train   3-car train

Red Group

• Use the □, ○, and △ pieces to build a 4-car train. How many pieces did you use?
• Draw a 5-car train. How many △ did you draw?
• How many □ does it take to build a 6-car train?
• How many ○ does it take to build a 7-car train?
• Write how many of each piece you need to build a 10-car train.

_____ □   _____ ○   _____ △

Blue Group

How many of each piece will it take to build a 6-car train?

_____ □   _____ ○   _____ △

What is the total number of pieces it will take to build a 10-car train?
Write and draw to show how you know.

Green Group

What is the total number of pieces it will take to build a 10-car train?

Janelle used 46 pieces to build a train.
How many cars does Janelle's train have?
Write and draw to show how you know.

Figure 4–8   *Tiered task for grade 1.*

of emergent readers is likely to be greater, this question requires additional thought. With this particular task, one teacher found it worthwhile to model for all children the instructions for the more challenging (blue) task. Once direction was established, the majority of children were sent on their way to begin working while

---

Ordering Numbers

Red Group

    Materials: 3 paper plates, counters, and number cards 0–6

    Task: Create a specific set of objects based on quantity.

- Turn over a number card and make a set of objects to show how many.
- Keep going until you have made 3 different sets.
- Which set has the most?

Blue Group

    Materials: 6 paper plates, counters, and number cards 0–6

    Task: Create a specific set of objects based on quantity.

- Turn over a number card and make a set of objects to show how many.
- Keep going until you have made 6 different sets.
- Put the sets in order.
- Which set has the most?
- Which set has the least?

Green Group

    Materials: 6 paper plates, counters, and number cards 0–10

    Task: Create a specific set of objects based on quantity.

- Turn over a number card and make a set of objects to show how many.
- Keep going until you have made 6 different sets.
- Put the sets in order.
- Which set has the most?
- Which set has the least?
- Which sets are missing?

Figure 4–9 *Tiered task for kindergarten.*

the teacher met with the handful of students for whom she designed the simplified (red) task. Once she got them under way, she checked in with the few students who were ready for a more challenging (green) task. She added additional number cards and expectations to their task. Being flexible and trying to strike the right balance of challenge is always a goal, though hard to achieve with all that teachers do every day.

Compacting

Along with tiered tasks, some teachers consider *compacting* content for more ready learners. This strategy recognizes that some content can be accelerated or eliminated for these learners. What remains is a more *compact* version of the standard curriculum.

The process is similar to all models of differentiation: Key curricular ideas are identified, students are pre-assessed, and appropriate learning decisions are made based on that data.

Though compacting is often associated with gifted learners, it is important to remember that a variety of factors impact students' readiness. A student may have come from another school district or another country where the material was already considered. Students' interests or family culture may have already provided significant learning opportunities within a particular content area. For example, Grace is a first-grade student whose father's favorite hobby is woodworking. Grace loves spending time with him in his "shop." Together, they often make gifts for her cousins. Last winter they even worked on a doll house for Grace's room. Her special job was to measure the rooms for the wallpaper. She then had to cut the wallpaper so that it would fit on the walls. As a result, Grace's exposure to standard measurement and measuring tools is well beyond her grade level. Though other mathematical units are well suited to Grace, measurement is one that can be compacted.

Though compacting can serve a variety of students, teachers are sometimes reluctant to actually eliminate content from the curriculum. As we learn from this teacher, outside support for compacting can be helpful.

Teacher Reflection

Jamie seemed to walk in the door already knowing everything covered in our curriculum. Fortunately, my school system has been holding workshops on differentiated instruction. The presenter introduced me to the idea of compacting. I never thought about just eliminating some of the lessons. I was always trying to find a way for Jamie to be more involved, even if it was just to help others. I was disinclined to try compacting, but didn't know what else to do. I made an appointment with my principal and asked for her advice. She was supportive and encouraged me to try this approach.

Now Jamie and I hold a miniconference at the beginning of each unit. After pre-assessment, we look at the list of the unit's lessons together. He sees me check the ones that he is still responsible for and cross some of the others out. Jamie is an independent learner and together we identify projects that he can do in lieu of participating in the other lessons. The plan is also shared with his family. Jamie is so much happier now that we have begun to compact his learning. He now offers to help his classmates more readily and looks more engaged during our class discussions. It's as if a burden has been removed from both of us. We no longer have to just make the curriculum work; we can change it more than I realized.

Additional Resources

Though this teacher has been successful with the compacting strategy, it does require teachers to monitor independent work and to have additional resources available. Teachers also need more resources for those students who need additional support. This need is felt particularly by some teachers who use nontraditional textbooks that have fewer practice exercises or problems. Exchanges with other teachers and Web sources can be helpful. The goal is to provide mathematical materials equivalent to our multilevel classroom libraries for reading.

Multilevel problem decks can provide for the broad spectrum of readiness within grades 1 and 2. Grade-level decks can be purchased and then teachers can redistribute the decks among themselves so that each class set contains cards for additional grade levels. If purchasing is not an option, problems can be found in old textbooks or in sample textbooks for each grade level. Cut out problems from lessons and paste them onto file cards of the same color. Then cut out examples of more challenging problems often included in special boxes within texts and highlighted as brainteasers or some similar title. Paste these problems onto file cards of a different color. You may want to search for problems across two, three, or four grade levels. Label the cards from each grade level with a different letter or use some other identification scheme. Then sort the problems by strand. So, for a particular strand such as geometry, you would have:

basic problems below grade level (color 1–A)

advanced problems below grade level (color 2–A)

basic problems at grade level (color 1–B)

advanced problems at grade level (color 2–B)

basic problems above grade level (color 1–C)

advanced problems above grade level (color 2–C)

This organizational approach allows students at all readiness levels to have access to more advanced problems as well as basic ones at their grade level. Though the initial creation of the deck is time consuming, teachers find that it serves their students well and can be used over many years.

Card decks can also be available to kindergarten students, but the limited number of readers makes this resource less useful. Some tasks cards, such as those involving patterns, are accessible to these young students. Some kindergarten teachers have found it helpful to combine pattern materials designed for preschool, kindergarten, and first-grade students.

Technology also offers teachers many resources. If one or more computers are available in your classroom, Webquests, applets, and practice games can help meet a variety of readiness levels. Webquests are interactive activities that involve resources on the Internet. They are generally organized around a central question or task such as designing a park or planning a family vacation. A worthwhile site for learning more about Webquests is: http://school.discovery.com/schrockguide/webquest/webquest.html.

When children are learning new mathematical skills, they need to practice those skills. As you know, exactly when practice is needed, the focus of the practice, and the amount of time that practice is appropriate varies greatly among students. Computer games often provide different levels of challenge and more and more practice games are available for free on the Internet. A game in which the focus is merely to practice should not be played for too long; once a skill is mastered, there is no reason to play the game. But for the brief time when a practice activity is needed, the computer game can make it readily available within a motivating format.

Each of these curriculum adaptations is a response to variation in readiness. In order to provide for a wider range of students, teachers can cast a wider net by:

1. allowing students some control over the difficulty level by having them
   - provide the numbers in the problem
   - choose exercises to complete
2. transforming problems so that they allow for
   - one or more solutions
   - a wider range of responses and understandings
3. providing multiple models such as
   - real objects or pictures of real objects
   - closely related manipulative models such as teddy bear counters for people
   - random counters or chips
4. varying the challenge offered students through
   - tiered tasks
   - curriculum compacting
5. extending resources by
   - sharing materials with teachers at other grade levels
   - using Internet resources

Decisions to make these kinds of adaptations or to provide differentiated learning opportunities are grounded in knowledge of our curriculum and our students. As we choose among modifications we must remember that all students deserve challenging, thought-provoking problems and tasks. Too often, in the spirit of "helping," some students are provided with simplistic tasks or rules to follow that are not connected to conceptual understanding. For example, oversimplistic statements such as "take-away means subtract" do not allow students to understand the variety of language or uses associated with subtraction.

Knowing our students and our curriculum are essential first steps, but making decisions about what content and teaching strategies are appropriate is where we begin the hard work of providing all of our students with improved access to the curriculum. It is in the conscious act of matching our students' needs with what our curriculum and pedagogy have to offer that differentiation helps us meet our instructional goals most effectively. Many times readiness is only one piece of the puzzle. This matching of tasks to learners also has to consider language, learning styles, and preferences. There is a need to develop ways to adapt tasks according to these factors as well.

Chapter 5
Breaking Down the Barriers

*T*he term *universal design* originated in the field of architecture. This philosophy of design is committed to providing inclusive environments that work better for everyone: door levers rather than knobs, curbless showers, and doors that open automatically are examples. Door levers are easier for older, arthritic hands and for anyone else carrying packages with only an elbow free for use. The idea is to build this way right from the beginning, rather than to retrofit spaces when special circumstances arise. So with this philosophy, all bathrooms would be built with wider doorways, not renovated when a family member needs to be in a wheelchair. In this type of environment, barriers to independent living are removed at the design stage. Access for people with physical disabilities is considered from the inception and everyone benefits from these decisions.

Many of our students face learning barriers in our classrooms. Students' readiness levels are not always apparent, even when conscientious teachers observe their students closely and provide tasks designed to pre-assess learning. Sometimes there are barriers that keep students from accessing prior knowledge or from demonstrating what they have learned. When not attended to adequately and respectfully, language, learning styles, sensory preferences, and anxiety can keep children from reaching their full potential as successful mathematical doers and thinkers.

Recently, educators have begun to think about a teaching philosophy that embraces universal design. What would our curriculum plans look like if we designed activities that worked for everyone right from the beginning rather than remediating or reteaching or in architectural terms, retrofitting, once original plans prove unsuccessful or inadequate?

Language

We begin with language and its impact on learning mathematics by thinking about a class of second graders. The students are working with laminated hundreds charts and transparent chips to explore patterns and skip-counting. The students choose a number and place chips on their charts as they skip-count by that number. Then they choose another number and investigate that outcome as well. After a few numbers are explored, each child chooses a result to record by coloring in the numbers they land on on a copy of the hundreds chart and by writing about the patterns they observe. After working for about thirty minutes, the children gather in the meeting area to discuss their findings. The teacher notices that Janella appears confused throughout the discussion. The teacher is somewhat surprised. Though Janella is often unclear on directions and has a more limited grasp of English than many of the other students, she usually does well when concrete materials are used. Today she seemed to be working successfully during the investigation, but once on the rug, she was silent and fidgety.

Later in the day, the teacher finds time to sit with Janella. The teacher asks her to use the materials and skip-count by twos. Janella sighs, looks concerned, and bows her head. With further prodding and her teacher's insistence that she just wants to listen to her thinking, Janella begins. She counts quietly, "one, two," and places a transparent chip on 3. Then she counts, "four, five," and places another transparent chip on 6. She follows this pattern several more times, placing chips on 9, 12, and 15. Before long, the teacher realizes that Janella thinks that skip-counting by twos means to "skip two and land on the next one." The teacher wishes she had said, "What numbers do you say when you count by twos?" The teacher comments on what a good job Janella did with keeping the pattern and acknowledges the sense Janella made of this task. "I can see how you followed your pattern of skipping two numbers. I should have been clearer," says the teacher and they work together to clarify the expectations of skip-counting by twos.

Fortunately, Janella's misconception was discovered because she cued the teacher to her confusion and the teacher followed up with her individually. It would have been easy for the teacher to have missed Janella's visual cues or to have been unable to find the time to follow up on her instinct that something was amiss.

Janella might have submitted her work without identifying it as a "two pattern," and when viewing the work, the teacher might have assumed that Janella had submitted a three pattern.

Misconceptions involving language are sometimes hidden. Children may pretend to understand or be able to submit work that can be deemed correct in spite of their literal interpretations, misperceptions, and confusions. Children who are learning English or who have language difficulties may be reluctant to communicate their thinking. Note that the teacher first made sure to make sense of Janella's work and to compliment her for following her pattern consistently. She also took some responsibility for the confusion. This stance helped Janella feel more comfortable and to be open to clarification.

Students who are confident in their thinking are often more willing to expose their misconceptions as they are less concerned about having a different perspective. Consider Sabrina, a first-grade student, solving the following story problem:

> *There are 9 children jumping rope.*
> *3 more children join them.*
> *How many children are jumping rope now?*

Sabrina uses Unifix cubes. She counts nine yellow cubes and connects them. Then she counts three red cubes and adds them to her "train." She demonstrates her ability to count on, rather than counting all, as she places her finger on the last yellow cube and says, "Nine." Then she counts, "ten, eleven, twelve," as she touches each of the red cubes exactly once.

Satisfied with her work, she begins her written representation. It is only the first week of school, but she knows already that her teacher expects her to show her thinking. She draws a picture of the cubes and records the number *9* on the left and *3* on the right. Below the train she writes *12* and draws a circle around it. Finally, she writes the number sentence *9 + 3 = 12.* Her teacher stops by to look at her work and says, "You found the sum, twelve." Sabrina looks up at her teacher and says, "Some? I thought I'm supposed to count all of them!"

Sabrina enjoys mathematics and has a positive attitude about her ability to add. Just yesterday she had informed her parents, "I'm awesome at adding!" Yet even children such as Sabrina can miss the nuances of our mathematical language. This can be particularly difficult when we use several terms to refer to similar ideas such as *in all, all together, total,* and *sum* or when a word such as *sum* sounds exactly like another word with a different meaning.

Sometimes it is difficult to separate language difficulties from mathematical ones. Ross is being interviewed by his kindergarten teacher late in the spring. "What is one less than six?" the teacher asks. "One," he replies. His teacher then asks, "What is one less than three?" Again, Ross replies, "One." Next the teacher asks, "If you have three raisins and eat one of them, how many do you have left?" As she says this she points to imaginary raisins on the table and pretends to eat one of them. Immediately Ross responds, "Two." When asked about six in the same problem format, Ross correctly identifies five as the answer. The teacher is not sure if the real-world model or the gestures were essential for Ross to understand what to do, or if he just didn't understand the phrase *one less*. She wonders if he thought he was supposed to name the number that was less, one or six. She was pleased that he was able to answer the question about the raisins and that she could work with Ross to connect real-world ideas with abstract mathematical language.

These classroom examples emphasize the important role of language in the teaching and learning of mathematics. For some students, talking about mathematical ideas can help to solidify concepts and further develop confidence. Occasionally, students such as Sabrina have a minor difficulty or misunderstanding that can be addressed easily. For others, language can be a significant barrier, one that keeps them from grasping new ideas or from demonstrating what they know.

While language has always been important, today the relationship between language and mathematics is even more prominent. Now that the significance of problem solving is recognized, mathematical tasks are often presented within language-rich contexts. Rather than a story problem beginning with the simple phrase *eight birds,* students are often asked to listen to or to read, *After the rain there were eight birds playing in the puddle.* The once familiar phrase *show your work* is now often replaced with *explain your thinking.* These approaches to mathematics necessitate careful attention to mathematical vocabulary and to the language of mathematical reasoning so that these barriers to learning can be ameliorated.

The language of mathematics is both complex and subtle. It takes considerable experience for children to become comfortable with it. Even a simple mathematical statement can be more challenging than teachers realize. A kindergarten teacher told us how surprised she was by how one of her more advanced students responded to the task, "Place your number cards in order, one through nine." The student searched carefully through his number set to find the card with the number 1 on it and the card with the number 9 on it. Then he placed the card for 1 to the left of the card for 9 and proudly announced, "Got it!"

We need to be sensitive to language issues. According to the 2000 census data, nearly one in five Americans speaks a language other than English at home (U.S. Census Bureau 2003). Before students are asked to complete mathematical tasks, we need to make sure that the language of the task is understood. To do this, teachers can:

- have students read the task repeatedly, as in a choral reading format;
- encourage students to dramatize story problems;
- ask students to summarize the task in their own words;
- preview specialized vocabulary;
- have vocabulary lists available when students write about their ideas;
- use pictures, models, and gestures to clarify ideas whenever possible;
- have students try out their thinking in pairs or small groups, before speaking in front of the whole class;
- make sure that symbolic notation is mapped carefully onto everyday situations and concrete models;
- speak slowly and avoid idioms and contractions; and
- pose problems in familiar contexts that students will recognize.

We also need to pay attention to particular terms that may be problematic. For example, many mathematical terms have a different meaning in everyday usage. One classroom teacher helps children note these different meanings through dramatizations. She begins by reading *Amelia Bedelia Helps Out* by Peggy Parish (1979). The teacher pantomimes Amelia as she dusts the crops and sows the seeds. The children giggle as Amelia misinterprets directions left by her aunt. After the story, as an example of what could happen in the classroom, the teacher dramatizes telling Amelia to make a table to show her data. Then acting as Amelia, she pulls out a hammer and nails and says she needs to find some wood. The children laugh and talk about how Amelia Bedelia makes sense of the directions. Throughout the year the teacher refers to Amelia whenever she wants to make a distinction between a mathematical and every-day meaning of a particular term. Examples of words found in the primary curriculum that have different everyday and mathematical meanings include:

count	range
face	ruler
fair	set
left	side
mass	table
odd	turn
one	volume
plot	yard

Homophones, or words that sound the same but have different spellings and meanings, can be similarly problematic. Sabrina's confusion between *sum* and *some* is an example of this difficulty. Again, special attention should be given to these terms and humorous examples can be helpful. One teacher tells her students about the following conversation and asks them to figure out what happened.

> *Two people leave a doctor's office when one says, "What was your weight?" The other replies, "Five minutes." "Oh," says the first. "Mine was one-hundred thirty pounds."*

Examples of mathematical words with everyday homophones include:

cents/scents	sum/some
eight/ate	symbol/cymbal
fair/fare	week/weak
hour/our	weight/wait
one/won	whole/hole

Some everyday words sound very similar to mathematical terms, including *cents/sense, half/have, quart/court, sphere/spear*, and *tenths/tents*. Teachers should enunciate these words carefully, note them in print when they are first introduced, and listen carefully to students' pronunciation of them.

As with universal design, attention to language will benefit all of our students. When we listen carefully to our students and ourselves, and attend deliberately to the language used, children are better able to access their previous learning as well as to better understand the tasks they are asked to perform. Like all language skills, learning the language of mathematics is an important goal for all primary students and can remove barriers to learning mathematical ideas.

Multiple Intelligences

Along with language, students differ greatly in the ways they prefer to explore mathematical ideas. Howard Gardner emphasized the differences among students' thinking when he developed his theory of multiple intelligences. He has now identified eight intelligences: linguistic, logical-mathematical, spatial, bodily-kinesthetic, musical, interpersonal, intrapersonal, and naturalist (Gardner 2000). When lessons and activities do not tap into different ways of knowing, barriers result. As limited knowledge and facility with basic facts can also become a barrier to success with more complex computation, let's consider the goal of learning basic facts through the perspective of multiple intelligences.

Attitudes about how to best learn these basic facts has changed in recent years. Most experienced teachers first learned their basic facts through memorization accompanied by timed tests. One hundred facts were presented on a single sheet of paper and they and their fellow students were given three to four minutes to complete the items. Often this ritual was repeated on a weekly basis. In between, they might have identified different ways two numbers can sum to seven, for example, or practiced with flash cards. There was little or no instruction on conceptual models that could be linked to these facts or on ways to make connections between one fact and another.

Today's teaching tends to place more emphasis on conceptual understandings to support the learning of basic facts. Even kindergarten students begin to recognize that changing the order of the addends does not change the sum, that is, they can predict that $5 + 3$ will have the same total as $3 + 5$. Many young children intuitively realize that to find $9 - 5$, they can think, "What do I add to five to get nine?" Counting on strategies are developed as well as a variety of fact strategies. For example, doubles such as $7 + 7$ are emphasized and then used to find $7 + 8$.

So is this a better approach to learning basic facts? The answer is not simple. Placing an emphasis on conceptual development is definitely a better way to learn addition. In the previous approach, students often memorized the facts without ever developing an understanding of what addition was or how it could be used. Fact strategies may not be the best way, however, for all students to learn their facts. Such strategies often assume a mathematical-logical intelligence that may not match students' strengths. This is not to say that strategies should not be taught; rather, strategies should be part of a diverse approach designed to reach all intelligences. Possibilities for addressing students' multiple intelligences while they learn basic facts are summarized here:

Linguistic

- read a book and then make up addition and subtraction story problems related to the characters in the story
- talk about fact strategies

Logical-Mathematical

- create fact strategies
- practice with puzzles, such as magic squares or magic triangles

Spatial

- connect quantities to visual images by using dice, dominos, and other everyday objects, such as egg cartons
- decorate fact cards

Bodily-Kinesthetic

- dramatize story problems and fact strategies
- use counters to model problems

Musical

- clap beats to match numbers used in problems
- create songs about facts

Interpersonal

- practice with fact buddies
- discuss fact strategies in groups

Intrapersonal

- set personal fact goals
- keep a journal about fact strategies

Naturalist

- find examples of doubles in nature
- categorize facts that are best solved by particular strategies

Consider this first- and second-grade combination classroom where students are working with both addition and subtraction facts. Among the many small groups is a cluster playing *Cover Up*. In pairs, the children have some beans and a paper cup. Lisa and Ricky are working with the number nine. While Lisa closes her eyes, Ricky places five of the beans under the cup and four in front of the cup in clear view. Lisa looks at the four beans closely and then she moves her finger on the number line from four to nine as she counts aloud from one to five. She announces, "It's five!" with confidence and Ricky grins as he lifts up the cup and they count to check her response. Next Ricky closes his eyes and Lisa hides seven beans under the cup. Ricky looks at the two beans and then tilts his head up as if he were looking at something. He whispers, "Nine, eight," and then tells Lisa, "There's seven."

Melissa and Jackie are playing with six beans and Mark and Ann have twelve. Some of the children use fingers to model the situation and some refer to a number line. Counting is almost always involved, as today many of the children have started with a new total number of beans. Their teacher keeps careful records of their working numbers and changes them when the children are ready for a new challenge.

A cluster of three students is working on computers. They are each playing a game that provides basic practice with addition facts. Chips, hundreds charts, and drawing materials are available for use. The game allows the user to choose the level of difficulty for each round. The basic levels focus on facts to ten and provide more time between examples. Lucy has decided that she is ready for a more challenging level today and she is excited about it.

Mallory and Cole are writing a poem about addition. There is much conversation about whether or not *ten* rhymes with *again*. Cole claims that in order to rhyme, the words "need many of the same letters." Mallory tells him, "This will work. We say it like it was *agen*." They are quite proud of their work and ask the teacher if they can share it with the class. When the class is back together as a whole group, they get the microphone from a props trunk and read the poem that follows with a hip-hop rhythm and snapping fingers.

> *To add on nine, think of ten.*
> *Then just go back one again.*
> *For nine plus five do ten plus five.*
> *Back one to fourteen, and you jive.*

Not all of the younger children understand the strategy, but they enjoy the performance and many of both the first and second graders want to write their own addition poems. The teacher decides that the day's language arts time could be used this way for those that are interested. The less advanced students tend to write about facts to ten. For example:

> *Four plus four is eight.*
> *That's right. That's right.*
> *Now shut the gate!*

Sharlie, Meg, and Dani work on their poem several times during the next two days. They work together to create the first two lines when Sharlie says, "This is OK, but we need an example." The teacher chuckles to herself as she hears this. She is always asking the children to give examples or to provide further details of their thinking. During snack time the next day they complete the next two lines. The final lines are written during recess. The following day they present their poem to the class. The teacher asks if other students can make pictures to show how this strategy works. In this way, other students are able to connect to the poem and make sense of its ideas. The poem follows.

> *Use your doubles as a start.*
> *Then back and forth, it's an art.*
> *For seven plus six think seven plus seven.*
> *Back one from fourteen and you're in heaven.*
> *For eight plus nine think eight plus eight.*
> *Up one from sixteen and you're at the gate.*
> *For five plus four think four plus four.*
> *Add one to eight and you're out the door.*

Sam, Jess, Doug, and Matty enjoy playing board games. Today they are playing *Addition Threesome* to practice their facts. The game boards are blank partial addition tables. The sums are written on tiles and turned over. On each turn, a player picks up a tile and places it correctly on the board. The first player to place a tile that shares three complete sides with other tiles is the winner. Sam and Jess are working with the addends five through nine, while Doug and Matty focus on one through five. (See Figure 5–1.)

Billy and Mary Ellen are connecting their addition and subtraction facts. Together with their teacher, they have each identified ten facts that they want to practice. They then make their own fact cards for these examples. The teacher has shown them how to make triangle fact cards. (See Figure 5–2.) Triangle cards help students to connect the three numbers. The goal is for them to

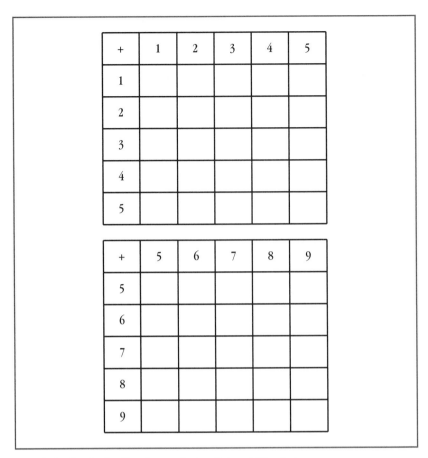

Figure 5–1 *Two levels of board games for practicing addition facts.*

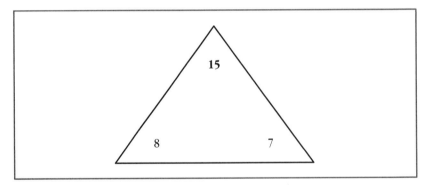

Figure 5–2 *Triangle fact card showing all three numbers in a fact family.*

identify the correct number, no matter which one is missing. The two children exchange fact cards and take turns covering up one of the corner numbers for their partner to recall. As the teacher checks on them she hears Billy give Mary Ellen a hint. "Think about five plus five," he suggests when Mary Ellen struggles with 5 + 6.

When the teacher believes that the students are working well at their separate activities, she calls a specific small group to meet with her at the back table. The students are aware that their goal is to become confident in their abilities with addition facts as an extension of the other practice work they have been doing. The teacher also wants these students to feel more comfortable and flexible with numbers. She believes that efficient retrieval of these facts will help achieve these goals. Fact cards have been created and the children have been asked to bring them to the table. During the past few weeks the students have sorted their fact cards into three labeled envelopes: *Facts I Know!*, *Making Progress*, and *Too Hard Right Now*. Initial conversations centered on the purpose of knowing math facts and ways to learn them. Time was also spent deciding how to label each envelope. Today the group is meeting to discuss and honor the progress these students have been making with moving more cards into the first two envelopes.

Their teacher has thought long and hard about how to approach basic facts in a way that supports differentiated learning, particularly for students who may not naturally link one fact to another.

Teacher Reflection

I've tried various approaches and activities over the years in order to encourage my students to learn their basic addition facts. For some of my students, I know that this is not something that will really be in place until third or fourth grade. I don't want to over manage development of this skill, but rather encourage children to begin to take ownership of their learning of basic facts. I've noticed over time that my strongest and most self-assured math students have basic facility with number facts. Sometimes facts have been learned through memorization, but mostly, it seems to me that these children just feel comfortable playing with numbers and building a repertoire of known facts or ways to know them. I wanted to let all of my students in on what seems to be their secrets. I want to give all children an opportunity to work with facts as individual pieces of knowledge or offer them an opportunity to analyze them by chunking or grouping them in some meaningful way.

Using the envelopes to sort the fact cards is one step in this process. I also ask my students to think together about the necessity of basic facts—we begin to help them see facts as a tool that can help them in the future. I recognize that many of my students are still developing the idea of what it means to add, and thus memorizing basic facts may feel too premature, while other students delight

(Continued)

in reciting facts they know. Even my kindergarten colleagues tell me that some of their students are eager to share that two and two is four and five and five is ten. It seems to me that using the facts that are "easy" to know or recall can be the stepping-stones to future success in this area. The challenge is to have all students be able to identify facts "they know" and take pride in this knowledge first. Then over time, we can help them increase the number of known facts.

Using the envelopes as benchmarks for learning is a tangible way this teacher helps her students take ownership of their learning and allows for variability in the manner in which students make strides in learning their addition facts. She moves slowly with the class establishing the idea that each individual student makes his or her own decisions about what is presently too hard, is something that is currently being worked on, or is established and can be called up with ease.

There are times when the students in the small group all agree that a fact is easy to recall, as in $1 + 1$ or $2 + 2$, or the opposite, that $7 + 6$ is one of the hardest. Then again, one child comments, "That one is easy for me, because six and six is twelve and one more is thirteen." Individual strategies are always acknowledged while trying not to make one idea more celebrated than the next. A strategy that works for one student or many, more than likely does not work for all. The goal is to increase student learning and facility with addition facts, not to cause children to feel inferior about their ideas.

Initially when the students looked at the fact cards and talked about what they noticed, they sorted the cards in a variety of ways. Some children grouped them by common addends, for example all facts with an addend of five. Other students put facts together that had the same sum. Other students put all of the double facts, such as $6 + 6$, together. The idea is to tap into what makes sense for each child and not to set an explicit way of organizing the cards. The teacher also makes preliminary decisions about how to group students for this work and how many of the basic fact cards to use at one time.

The notion of using the labeled envelopes is the next step and students talk as a whole class about how to sort the facts. They are asked to think about this in the same way that they might choose a book for reading. They are used to the idea that some things are easy, that some things feel ready to be worked on, and that some things feel too hard. Selecting reading texts in this way is familiar to this class and it is another example of where differentiation is tightly woven into the fabric of the classroom environment. These first and second graders assume that everyone is not working on the same ideas in the same way.

In the small group, students are asked to review the cards in their *Facts I Know!* envelope first. They begin by working with the cards on their own. When they feel comfortable, they ask a classmate if they want to review together. Some pairs compare cards and talk about how they know the fact, while others like to "test" each other. Next they look at the cards in the *Making Progress* envelope. Students are encouraged to think about the facts they know in order to help them with this next set. Russell shares, "Wow, I can move these cards. When we were using our cards the other day I tried to think about all the cards that use a four. I first added two, because I know all the ones with a two and then I added two more, since I already know this. So, it's really like eight plus four is eight plus two is ten and ten and two makes twelve. I'm not super fast, but I know I know them!"

Trying to keep the focus off of speed when learning basic facts is difficult. For many people "knowing" your basic facts depends on how fast you can retrieve the answer. Russell reminds us that one can still feel very secure in "knowing" a fact even if is not recited in a split second.

"This one used to be too hard for me," Miranda offers while looking at $3 + 8$. She continues, "I know I can count up, but counting on eight took too long and sometimes I missed one or counted too many. I might get ten or twelve as the answer. I made a challenge for myself to just remember that three and eight make eleven. I kept saying it over and over in my mind." The notion that once something was too hard and now it is not is a very powerful step in learning. Seeing the cards as fluid and that movement from one envelope to another is a form of progress is another tangible aspect of this activity.

Engaging Multiple Senses

Being strategic and mindful of the purpose of the activities in which we ask our students to engage helps teachers to make powerful instructional choices. Having some control over their learning helps children to be more powerful learners. As we learn from the following teacher reflection, when we are trying to remember something, it is helpful to have several senses engaged.

Last summer I read *Differentiation Through Learning Styles and Memory* by Marilee Sprenger [2003] for a course I was taking. It really made me think about memory. One part of the book that really struck me involved not being sure about whether we have turned off something. I can't remember if it was an iron or a stove in the example, but I remember the suggestion was to use all of the senses. Our eyes can see the dial move and our fingers are touching it, but we are not using our auditory memory. Just saying something like "I am turning the iron off now" can really make a difference! I began to think more about how I could improve my ability to remember things. I started looking at the key pad when I wanted to memorize a telephone number. Making a visual pattern of the numbers was much easier for me than just remembering what I heard the information operator say or what I saw in a phone book.

Next I began to think about my students and how challenging it is for some of them to learn their basic facts. I wondered if I were including enough alternative ways for them to practice their memory skills. This year I have made practice time more varied. The students have more of a choice in how they practice and I try to make sure that over time, visual, auditory, and sensory memory are involved. It seems to be helping. Just yesterday Billy asked me if we could add another practice time to our week!

Anxiety

Anxiety can also be a barrier both to learning and to demonstrating what has been learned. Mathematics anxiety has received much attention in recent years and though early studies focused on adults, it is now recognized that it may begin early and is difficult to change once it is established. This anxiety is a major contributor to limiting the number of mathematics courses taken later in life. As a result, many people take only required mathematics courses, which can greatly limit career options. It seems essential then that we begin to address this learning anxiety in the primary years.

While mathematics anxiety is not completely understood, experts recognize it as a specific anxiety, one that generalized anxiety alone cannot explain. Those afflicted experience a severe dread of the subject and tension that interferes greatly with their ability to work with numbers or to perform mathematical tasks in front of others. It can interfere with working memory to the point where new information cannot be stored or cannot be retrieved during a test. As one second-grade student explains, "I get all sweaty when we have a fact test."

Family attitudes, social factors, teacher judgments, and negative classroom experiences can all contribute to mathematics anxiety. Ideally, parents, teachers, and other school personnel work together to prevent its occurrence in the first place. For example, family math nights help many parents recognize that learning and doing mathematics can be enjoyable. The evenings can also be structured so that those parents who have their own mathematics anxiety are comfortable identifying themselves. Follow-up conversations can help them to understand the importance of not modeling or perpetuating negative attitudes for their children.

Schools should be sure to project a positive attitude about mathematics. Most schools have ample displays of children's writing and art work. Walls are often lined with posters related to books. We rarely are greeted with a colorful and dynamic display related to mathematics upon entering a school building. Even a colorful bulletin board for "Numbers in the News" can help connect mathematics to the real world and make it more meaningful.

So what about our classrooms? It is clear that difficulty learning mathematics and low achievement in mathematics contribute to anxiety. Teaching mathematics in a rote, context-free manner makes it more difficult to learn and may result in more students suffering from anxiety. Providing rich contexts allows more students to relate to the subject and often suggests entry points to problems being explored. Small-group work may be less threatening than whole-class discussions, and concept building, rather than rote rules that can be forgotten easily, helps empower students' faith in their ability to do mathematics.

There are some caveats, however, to this approach. Overemphasizing oral explanations and justifications can increase anxiety. Some children develop a great fear of doing mathematics in front of others, just as having the teacher walk near may cause some children to freeze. As one first-grade student put it, "I hate when it is my day to do the attendance chart. I get so scared I can't count right." Children who feel this way may benefit from writing (or taping) and rehearsing explanations first, and then repeating them to the class. Also some students may perform better when creating explanations with a peer who will report to the group.

The following are some other ways to prevent or reduce mathematics anxiety.

- Promote self-talk in which children verbalize what they are doing with statements such as "First I am going to . . . ," in order to focus their attention and help them believe that they do know what to do. This is sometimes called *anchoring*.

- Build confidence by helping students recognize what they *can* do. Use questions such as "What do you know about this?" Keep samples of their work so that they can see their improvement over time.

- Have available, or have students help you create, collections of manipulatives that are aesthetically appealing, visually interesting, and represent favorite activities or characters for students in your class.

- Keep number lines, hundreds charts, and calculators available so that students can use these devices to ensure accuracy.

- Use multiple sources of assessment and de-emphasize high-stakes testing. Understandably, teachers are under much pressure from all of the attention given to mandated tests. It is important not to share this pressure with the students. Test anxiety correlates highly to mathematics anxiety and vice versa.

- Have students keep a journal where they can record their feelings about mathematics. Journal prompts such as: *When we start a new topic in math I feel . . .* , *When I am asked to explain my thinking in math I feel . . .* , *When I am asked to come to the board in math class I feel. . . .* Teachers and students must be aware of these feelings in order to reduce them.

- Limit activities that are timed. Time is one more pressure that can greatly add to anxiety.

- Choose partners carefully. For some students, this may mean being in a group that works at a slower pace. For others, it may mean the need to work with the same partner throughout a unit.

- Let students set personal goals. When students set their own objectives, it gives them a greater sense of control, which in turn lessens anxiety.

- Integrate mathematics with other subject areas. Some students feel more comfortable performing mathematical tasks when they are related to an area of their interest or strength. A student who just received a new puppy may enjoy collecting data about class pets, while a student whose favorite subject is science may be interested in collecting and analyzing data related to an experiment. Students also tend to develop more positive attitudes toward mathematics when it is perceived as connected to their world.

It is easier to prevent mathematics anxiety than it is to reduce it. If you think one of your students suffers from this affliction or appears to be developing attitudes and behaviors rooted in being anxious while learning mathematics, you may want to talk with his or her parent(s) and your school's guidance counselor. Though difficult to imagine, even students in grades K–2 can exhibit anxious behaviors during math class. In most cases, classroom interventions are not sufficient. Anxiety management training usually also involves breathing exercises, visualization techniques, "I can do it" mantras, and desensitization. Working with parents and other professionals, teachers can work to prevent or lessen any future concern in this area.

Learning Challenges

The need for outside help is not limited to anxiety. Barriers, both visible and invisible, are very real for many students. The list of diagnosable learning disabilities seems to be growing by leaps and bounds as we learn more about how our brains function and what happens if an area is underdeveloped or functioning in a unique way. For many students the level of engagement and pace of learning in our primary classrooms is overwhelming. While this is not a book about specific learning disabilities, we would be remiss not to take to heart the physical, emotional, and intellectual challenges of many students as they try to navigate the precarious terrain of mathematics. As we strive to get to know all of our students we can also recognize that no one classroom teacher can fully differentiate the mathematics curriculum for each and every student, every day. We need to be able to use all of the resources available to craft programs and meaningful experiences for each student.

In *Teaching Inclusive Mathematics to Special Learners, K–6,* Julie Sliva (2004) offers many techniques and insights that can help us meet our goal. Being able to distinguish what barriers might be present for a student is the beginning and her book offers many evaluation forms to help us make these decisions. Strategizing with colleagues and working collaboratively with assistants, tutors, remedial staff, and special educators is essential.

As illustrated in the following reflection, in many ways, each educator can have a critical piece of the puzzle and together, the whole child can be seen more clearly.

Teacher Reflection

Watching Bess during math class was painful. Only a second grader and I could see that she was already overwhelmed by the math curriculum. As her classroom teacher I could pinpoint areas of strengths, but the gap between her working knowledge and that of her peers was ever widening. I wished I could slow down and reteach her concepts I know she was taught in kindergarten and first grade. But to slow the class to a pace that best suited Bess would not work for her classmates. I could see from her previous report cards and from speaking with her former teachers that Bess started off in a different place than her peers and that each year she made marked progress, but never enough for her to feel comfortable or confident. I don't like to have students pulled out from my class, but I was feeling stuck and thus went to our special education liaison for help. Testing in grade 1 revealed that Bess did not have a diagnosable learning disability and thus no IEP [Individual Education Plan] was developed for her. At the same time, everyone who has worked with her has recognized her struggle. I found myself pleading for extra help for her.

We have been talking as a staff about how we have remedial support in literacy but very little in this same vein for math. No matter how important we all agree that math is for our students, literacy is still the name of the game in the primary grades. I wished for Bess that this was not the case. I don't worry about her literacy development. She reads on grade level and her writing shows a carryover from our word work. She also has a great sense of humor that she is beginning to include in her written persona. She is a wonderful artist. But when it comes to working with numbers, it's as though she is in another world.

I feel she would benefit greatly from having one-on-one instruction in math in addition to our math time. I'd like to figure out a way to more thoroughly assess her strengths and to find the holes in her learning. Is this really only happening in math? How much of it is based on experience? Does Bess's attitude affect her learning? I have heard her say she hates math. I have never heard her speak this way about any other learning activity.

Student profiles vary considerably. In this situation Bess's teacher is working to find a way that will help Bess make gains in mathematics comparable to her level in literacy. Her teacher sees the inconsistencies across learning domains and is perplexed. While growth is noted, Bess's teacher is rightly concerned.

In many schools Child Study Teams (CST) are formed as a venue for teachers to voice concerns about the lack of progress a student is making. Teachers are encouraged to share trepidations, raise questions, review student work, and share anecdotes about what is happening in class. Bess's teacher was able to take advantage of this support and used the CST in her school as an opportunity to more fully focus on Bess's mathematical profile and to collaborate with fellow educators about her continued concerns. In preparation, she completed a form about the student's strengths or weaknesses and answered a few guiding questions for the pending conversation. In addition she made copies of some of Bess's current math work. Though Bess may not ever know that a meeting focused on brainstorming possible ways to help her make progress in mathematics will take place, her teacher wanted to be sure that she represented Bess in a fair and respectful manner. She also made sure to contact Bess's mother. Though she had been reporting to her readily about her concerns and her mom concurred, Bess's teacher wanted to make sure that she had permission to go ahead with this next step.

Teacher Reflection

I see the Child Study Team as a great opportunity to tap resources to better serve Bess. Though my school does not require parent permission for this meeting to take place, I wanted Bess's mom to know that I continue to have concerns and that I wanted to seek the support of my colleagues in order to better differentiate for Bess in class and to see if it was possible to have her receive additional support.

At the meeting I was able to place Bess's case in the center of a circle of professionals who were all willing to share their expertise in order to help her. I appreciated that our principal set the stage by reminding all of us that we needed to be respectful of each other's ideas and that teaching, like learning, can make one feel vulnerable. I didn't realize how personally I was taking Bess's struggle in math until my principal said this. I was worried that one of the other teachers might question my style of teaching and profess to know more than I did. Thankfully this did not happen. I shared my views about how I see Bess as a learner—her strengths and weaknesses, understandings and confusions—and how I felt she was feeling as a student. We reviewed progress reports from her previous teachers, and in fact, her first-grade teacher was able to be a member of the team. We concurred on so many levels as we both shared stories about Bess's learning profile.

One of the guiding questions that I raised was, "Why is Bess so successful in language arts and yet seems to be struggling in mathematics?" We agreed that we all felt this was true, but we were not able to answer why this was happening. Our math specialist agreed to come and observe Bess and to also take her out of the class for a few sessions to see if she could pinpoint any specific holes in Bess's understanding of mathematics. We reminded ourselves that last

(Continued)

year Bess went through a series of tests that yielded no finding of special needs, but also wondered what type of testing was done that specifically looked at mathematics. Our math specialist agreed to review the tests to check for this level of detail.

As the meeting proceeded, I could feel a sense of relief pass over me. It felt so good to share this responsibility with other professionals. Prior to the meeting, I wasn't sure I wanted to bring up my other guiding question but I felt secure enough at this moment to ask, "Is there anything in my style of teaching, expectations, or the curricular decisions I make that is creating these confusions for Bess?"

The special ed liaison for my grade level responded thoughtfully, "Do you have any specific thoughts about this yourself? This must have been hard for you to ask. I'm not sure I would feel comfortable opening myself up in this way. I would be happy to come and observe Bess if you feel I can help at all."

I really appreciated that no one made any quick judgments. I was afraid that they thought my class was not very structured or that I didn't follow the curriculum the way they interpreted it to be. At that moment I really did feel like a member of a team.

In the weeks that passed after the CST, Bess's teacher found the follow-through from the meeting added to her feeling of inclusiveness. The math specialist worked with Bess and pinpointed an instructional level at about the range first described by the teacher. Bess clearly had gaps and in fact, her instructional level was more of a kindergartner, as counting was the only way she made sense of joining groups. Even then her one-to-one correspondence was shaky. In conjunction with the in-class observations by the special education teacher, it was agreed that Bess would truly benefit from a tailor-made remedial program targeted at her current level of proficiency and that it would be too much of a stretch for Bess's teacher to take this on alone. Since the staff had been discussing the discrepancy in remedial reading and math services, it was agreed that a pilot program would be developed around Bess's needs. She would work with a tutor-teacher for twenty minutes, three times a week, on specific mathematical skills. It was also agreed that this opportunity would be offered to other second-grade teachers in the event that they had a student with a similar profile that had not been discussed at a CST. Working together, the math specialist, tutor, special education liaison, and classroom teacher developed and implemented a program of intervention for Bess. It's exciting to think what can happen when barriers are acknowledged and time, effort, and resources are utilized to put service in the best places to support learning.

More and more schools are looking at ways to increase instructional support in mathematics. System specialists now work more closely with teachers and students on assessment, curriculum design, implementation, and direct teaching. Some school systems are hiring assistants and tutors who focus on mathematics, and special education staff, who often have stronger backgrounds in literacy learning, are beginning to augment their skills. Many schools, however, still find that budget limitations keep all staff members from participating in professional development opportunities in mathematics or from receiving curriculum materials. To remove barriers as successfully as possible, schools *must* provide these opportunities and materials to *all* professional staff and be committed to success in mathematics for all. Teachers must nuture open channels of communication with parents, specialists, assistants, tutors, and their students. They need to be willing to take risks, ask questions, examine their beliefs and behaviors, and make accommodations so that everyone achieves success.

Chapter 6
Scaffolding Learning

S*caffolds*, a term related to architecture and construction, are temporary structures that remain in place as long as they are needed. Workers use scaffolds to get to parts of buildings that would otherwise be inaccessible; similarly, we use scaffolds to support students' learning. Training wheels are used when a child is first learning how to ride a two-wheel bike. These extra wheels allow children to ride safely and successfully, something that would be impossible without the added support for balance. These wheels are removed when the child establishes his or her own sense of balance and is ready to ride without them.

Too often in the past our mathematics instruction has focused exclusively on students working independently, without support. Most of the time was spent working silently on the completion of seat work. Little or no assistance was given. At the end of a week or unit, each child took a test to determine what was learned. Fortunately, learning mathematics is no longer viewed as something that is done in isolation. Whole-class discussions and small-group work provide opportunities to share ideas and talk about what has been learned. These groups in and of themselves are a form of scaffolding. Many learners can do more when the classroom environment is communal. Help from a peer or collaboration with others are viewed as an integral part of the learning process.

With isolation no longer the norm, we can ask, "What can students do with support that they are not currently able to do on their own?" Another way to ask this question is, "What scaffolds can be put in place to allow students to be successful learners of mathematics?" Teaching with an emphasis on scaffolding presents a more integrated vision of teaching and learning. Teaching and learning are no longer separate, static activities, but interwoven events. The teacher develops a coaching style aimed at helping all children reach their potential. Scaffolding allows children opportunities to accomplish tasks that they would be unable to complete alone. Teaching, the act of supporting learning, is then viewed in a way more synonymous to how Vygotsky (1978) described the zone of proximal development. In this chapter we consider scaffolds that involve asking questions, focusing on strategies, making connections, and using graphic organizers.

Question Strategies

One of the ways that teachers support learning in the classroom is by asking questions. It is important that our questions require students to go beyond their current comfort level and understanding. Frequently, simple questions are posed at a level of thinking that requires only recall of information, for example, "What do we call a figure that has three sides?" By analyzing the questions we ask, we can make sure that we are inviting students to engage in more complex and deeper levels of thinking.

Though Benjamin Bloom first published his taxonomies in the 1950s, they remain helpful today. His cognitive taxonomy describes six levels of cognition: knowing, comprehension, application, analysis, synthesis, and evaluation (Bloom 1984):

Knowledge: To know is to recall information that has been learned. Sample activities include telling, listing, naming, and reciting.

Comprehension: To comprehend is to understand. Sample activities include explaining, summarizing, paraphrasing, retelling, and showing.

Application: To apply is to use what has been learned. Sample activities include demonstrating, illustrating, solving, dramatizing, adapting, and incorporating.

Analysis: To analyze is to examine an idea critically. Sample activities include comparing, categorizing, and deducing.

Synthesis: To synthesize means to put together in a new or different way. Sample activities include creating, inventing, formulating, transforming, and producing.

Evaluation: To evaluate is to determine the worth or value based on a set of criteria. Sample activities include making judgments, predictions, decisions, and estimates.

Since its inception, some people have viewed Bloom's taxonomy as linear and assumed that one can only move to the next level after the first levels have been mastered. Other educators see this view as problematic and believe students have been held back from potential learning opportunities because it was believed they would not be able to handle more advanced work in mathematics until they achieved more basic skills. No doubt everyone can think of students for whom the opposite was true, students who by nature engaged in analytical thinking even though they found it difficult to recall basic factual knowledge and thus did not perform well on certain types of tests. Seeing Bloom's taxonomy as more fluid can help us better challenge and serve our students.

One way to use Bloom's taxonomy is to categorize the questions we ask or tasks we provide to make sure that students are exposed to all levels. For practice, try categorizing the level of each of the following questions or tasks. The generally agreed-on responses are identified beneath the list. Note that more than six examples are listed and thus some levels will be labeled the same. This repetition is to make sure that final choices involve more than a simple process of elimination.

1. How else could you explain what Chad was saying?
2. Which estimation of the dog's weight do you think is best? Why?
3. Invent a new way to add these numbers.
4. What is the name of this shape?
5. Which strategy do you think is best? Why?
6. How does Sally's method compare to Janet's?
7. How many of these numbers have a 6 in the tens place?
8. What color do you think will be next in the pattern?
9. What is a story you could dramatize for 6 + 6?
10. Tell how rectangles and squares are the same.

1. comp. 2. eval. 3. synth. 4. know. 5. eval. 6. anal.
7. know. 8. eval. 9. app. 10. anal.

Although six different categories are provided, they are not necessarily discrete. For example, evaluating a pattern to predict what comes next (evaluation) requires that you first analyze the elements in the pattern that have been provided. Similarly, to dramatize a story for 6 + 6 (application), one must first have knowledge and comprehension of 6 + 6. Because of this overlap, it is sometimes difficult to distinguish one level from another. An additional concern is that some educators believe that synthesis, which involves creative thinking, is a more complex level of thinking than evaluation. One way to avoid these concerns is to create three categories: knowledge and comprehension, application and analysis, and evaluation and synthesis. Regardless of their exact organization, the goal is for the students to be engaged in a more complex level of thinking.

Scaffolding is one way to help students reach more sophisticated levels of cognition. It does *not* require us to start with a simple query and build up to more complex questions, as illustrated in the following sequence of questions:

- What is the name of this shape? (square)
- How would you describe a square?
- What is the name of this shape? (rectangle)
- How would you describe a rectangle?
- How is the square similar to the rectangle?
- How is the square different from the rectangle?

A more challenging approach would be to simply ask, "How are squares and rectangles alike or different?" Beginning with this question requires students to do more of the work. They may want to draw the figures or to think about how they look. Sometimes we ask more demanding questions and then backpedal when students do not seem ready for the challenge. Too often, teachers backpedal after only two or three seconds, without giving time for students to collect their thoughts. Waiting longer can yield surprising results. There are other ways to scaffold this task than lowering its level, for example, having geometric materials readily available in the classroom or asking students to first discuss their ideas with a partner.

Scaffolds are appropriate for our more ready students as well. If a task is really a challenge for them, then they too should initially need some form of support. As we see in the following reflection, until we push our more advanced students, we may not recognize their need for assistance.

I used to think my top students could just work independently no matter the task at hand. When I started to differentiate more and give them more difficult assignments, I found that they also needed my attention. It made me wonder whether I had ever been truly pushing their thinking or asking them to be in the domain of uncertainty that is often part of learning. I seem to expect that the students in my class who struggle may feel vulnerable as learners. Only recently did I recognize that my top students may never feel this way. I now think I have viewed feeling vulnerable as weak or bad as opposed to a temporary place of discomfort that can truly help learners move on to new ideas, information, and understanding.

Focusing on Strategies

Today's reading instruction places an emphasis on reading strategies. This instructional focus asks even very young children to be aware of what is happening as they read and offers them a variety of ways to identify an unknown word as they come upon it in the printed text they are trying to comprehend. These good reader strategies are explicit. They are talked about during reading instruction and modeled by the teacher. Reminding emergent readers of these strategies is a way to scaffold instruction. We need to make a similar cadre of strategies explicit for use when working with new mathematical content and tasks. Possible strategies, listed in the form of questions, follow. Note that the keywords *connect, try,* and *wonder* are used as cues to aid students as they take on this learning stance. Their use makes the learning process more transparent.

- *Connect:* What do you know about this situation?
- *Connect:* Have you ever solved a problem like this? How might that experience help you now?
- *Connect:* Are there materials in our classroom that can help you?
- *Try:* Can you make a drawing to help you?
- *Try:* Would a list or diagram help?
- *Try:* Will it help if you make an estimate?
- *Try:* Are there numbers you could put together or separate to make it easier?
- *Wonder:* What would you do if the numbers were smaller?
- *Wonder:* What might your friend do to solve this problem?

This morning I heard myself say, "What would a good reader do here?" I paused for a moment and wondered, do I have a similar phrase when a student is stuck solving a math problem?

Asking my students to think about what a good reader does has almost become a mantra in my classroom. I model good reader strategies when tackling a new word or making sense of what is happening in a story, and I have tried to make the process of reading come alive and be more accessible to the students in my class. From the first day of school my goal is to help them become proficient readers and writers and I have found it to be very effective to show them what I mean by being a good reader and writer. They are learning steps that they can rely on every time they come to an unknown word or begin to lose sight of what they are reading about. They are learning to stop, think, reread, give it a go, get their mouths ready to say the sound for the first letter or chunk that they see, read through the word, and much more. They know what I mean by a *strategy* and think about what sounds right, looks right, and, most important, makes sense as they read. But today I stumbled and thought, do I give the same opportunities and models in math?

I see the strategies we use in reading and writing as a way of sharing tips that have been effective for other readers and writers that have come before. It's as though I have now given this newest group of students membership cards in the readers and writers club. Everyone gets a lifetime membership, not just some of us. Have I been this inclusive during math class if I have not made everyone aware of effective learning strategies when they run into trouble like they do in reading?

Making reading strategies a part of learning for all of my students has given all of us a common language that then allows everyone the opportunity to help each other. I love it when I hear one child turn to another and ask, "What's this word?" and the other child responds, "Remember, stop and think, what makes sense?" I'd love to hear this same type of interaction in math class.

Student collaboration

This teacher reminds us that by giving students developmentally appropriate tools and strategies, they have more opportunities to hone their skills both independently and collectively. Further, when we view every member of the classroom as a learner *and* a teacher, there are many more people in the room who can help others learn. Many teachers recognize the powerful possibilities that can arise when peers take on the teacher role. To help students engage in such behavior, teachers strategically structure situations that support peer teaching and learning.

When we engage in think/pair/share debriefings, we are using peer partnerships to scaffold learning. The thinking time may just be a few moments of silence or students might be encouraged to make a drawing, build a model, or jot down some notes before talking with their partners. Talking in pairs can help some students clarify their thinking or gain additional ideas. Sharing can happen between two sets of pairs or as a whole group.

Sometimes a simple "Turn to your neighbor and whisper your prediction" is enough to form partnerships. Direct modeling of how to work in pairs helps more efficacious peer partnerships to develop. Ideally, partners develop a sense of trust, a sense of responsibility to one another, and a commitment to doing their best individual work. Partners also need practice in learning to strike a balance; that is, to be as helpful as possible without becoming overzealous and doing work for someone else.

When more independent work is preferred, teachers might suggest that math partners sit across from one another rather than in the adjacent position usually preferred for reading partners. Materials can be placed between the students. The amount of shared text is much less than when reading a story, and placing written directions between them often is adequate as well. Depending on seating flexibility, you may want students to read tasks side by side first and then assume their working positions.

A variety of strategies can be adapted that foster peer collaboration. In some cases, when children are solving more than one problem, they are given one pencil and trade it between problems so that they take turns being the recorder. Pairs can also alternate recording the work (listing, drawing, or computation) and the explanation. Some teachers prefer students to do the work and write their explanations separately, but then exchange their products for feedback, the same way as they might trade stories they have written. Early in the year, teachers can help students practice how to be helpful to their partners by asking such questions as, "If your partner didn't know if nine or eleven were the greater number, what hint could you give to help?" Over time a list of partner behaviors can be posted on a chart such as:

- Ask questions.
- Don't tell answers.
- Give hints.
- Be helpful.
- Listen well.
- Share the work.

I have been trying to find more effective ways for my kindergartners to develop skills and the right attitudes for working collaboratively by giving them practice in supporting each other while working in pairs or small groups. One way I have chosen to do this is to set out more games that provide practice rather than giving them worksheets to complete independently. I have found that playing a game together naturally elicits conversation, which in turn supports learning.

Just the other day Carmen, Brian, Rachel, and Ezra were playing the commercial board game *Hi Ho! Cherry-O,* produced by Milton Bradley. I wanted to hear their conversation, but I also knew from experience that if I got too close, they would try and pull me into their play. I tried to be unobtrusive, but still hovered nearby.

As I watched and listened I saw them take turns, find ways to reconcile if they did not agree about the rules, and support each other if someone made a counting error. They were also beginning to show more compassion when one child, Ezra, spun the icon of the tipped-over cherry basket three times in a row. This meant that three times he had to return all of his cherries to his tree.

"Why do I always get that?" Ezra bemoaned.

"Any of us could get it, but I think it's not fair that you have it lots of times," Carmen tried to console.

"I think it's better to get it three times together than to get it once, then get more cherries and then spin it again," Rachel added.

I was very impressed by this interaction, and in particular by Rachel's sense that to take away all from none was better in this game than taking away all from some. I'm not sure she realized the mathematical power behind her statement, but I was quite taken with her thinking.

I have also been impressed with the carryover of this type of work. Today I noticed Brian standing by our class survey board. He seemed to have a plan, though he was not really doing anything. "Brian," I asked, "what are you thinking about?" "Oh, I'm waiting for Ezra. He's going to read the survey question for me so I can write my name. I know he's a good reader, and he also won't tell me how to answer. He lets me figure out my own idea." This simple interaction made me realize that children are aware of their own needs as learners and can articulate those needs when they are given the space to do so. This was one more time when I realized the kinds of supports, tangible and intangible, that students need to experience success and feel confident as learners.

Making connections

Making connections is another way to scaffold learning. Students learn more easily when they connect what is to be learned to something they already know. This is one of the reasons that KWL charts are popular. By completing the K or *know* section of the chart, students are establishing their own understanding of the topic. They are also providing their teacher with pre-assessment data. By declaring what they *want to learn* (W), they are providing input into their learning. The final section (L) allows them to summarize what they *have learned* and reconnect to their original knowledge base by comparing the columns. Some teachers add an H, creating a KWHL chart. In section H students identify *how* they want to learn the new information.

Making a connection or an analogy to something that is already known or is within a familiar real-world context helps children make sense of new ideas and gain access to materials that would otherwise be too difficult. Consider the following vignette from a kindergarten class that is struggling a bit with identifying patterns. The class has been working on a unit about patterns for almost three weeks. The students have had many opportunities to copy or add on to existing patterns, and to create their own patterns using a wide variety of math manipulatives and art supplies. The focus of the unit is now shifting to looking at the common structures of repeating patterns.

The students are gathered at the rug area and two patterns are represented on chart paper with stickers of different colors and shapes:

> pattern 1: red, white, blue, red, white, blue, red, white, blue

> pattern 2: square, circle, square, circle, square, circle

The teacher asks, "How are these two patterns the same or different?" Student responses focus on the attributes in the pattern. They identify one as a color pattern and conclude that the other one is different because it is a shape pattern.

The students do not classify the patterns by their core or unit, that is, the part of pattern that repeats. For example the color pattern is said to have an ABC core, while the shape pattern is an AB pattern. Classifying patterns in this manner is a complex skill for kindergartners to attain. Being able to identify how two patterns are the same or different requires logical thinking, an ability to break the pattern into its smallest repeating unit, and language or representation systems for articulating similarities and differences in the underlying structures. As we learn from this teacher reflection, the teacher is surprised that her students have not yet begun to think about patterns in this way.

At this point in the unit, my other kindergarten classes were more ready to take on these ideas. In the past one or two children in the class began to talk about their work by breaking their patterns into the repeating parts, often known as cars in a train. There would then be a ground swelling of energy around this concept and more and more children would begin to talk about their patterns in similar ways. But this year, I don't seem to have anyone setting this direction for our work. I've been trying to figure out what I can put into place that might propel the work in this direction.

I was talking with a colleague about all the connections my students were making between different versions of the same story that we have been focusing on during reading workshop. It is music to my ears when I hear children speak with such command about how two books are the same or different. It made me wonder if I could come up with a poem or story that might help my current students gain that same command when describing patterns.

I got to thinking about where repeating patterns exist in their world. I'd never really thought about patterns in this way. I was looking for ways to describe patterns that might occur in natural conversations; everyday language that five- and six-year-olds can relate to, instead of looking for patterns in wallpaper, clothing, art, and architecture. And then it hit me, every day, children turn on lights and later they turn them off. Putting this predictable, repetitive action into words just might help them make a connection between something they do every day and the more abstract work with repeating patterns.

The next day the children gather in a circle in front of the following "poem" written on large chart paper.

Patterns in Our World

On   Off
On   Off
The light switch has a pattern that goes
On   Off

Green   Yellow   Red
Green   Yellow   Red
The traffic light has a pattern that goes
Green   Yellow   Red

Up   Down
Up   Down
The umbrella has a pattern that goes
Up   Down

Just like with many poems and songs used during shared reading, some children chime in right away. Putting words to repetitive actions jump-starts a whole new way for the children to talk about repeating patterns. On the second day of using the poem the teacher asks the children where else they see patterns like the light switch, the traffic light, or the umbrella. In response, they brainstorm more than twenty ideas. Some of their ideas include:

red and white—the stripes on our flag

open and shut—a door

stop and go—a car

in and out—when you breathe

big, medium, and small—the three bears

The children are excited about their long list, but are beginning to tire from the focused thinking when Larry interjects, "These are like the patterns we make at math workshop."

With that simple statement many children begin to make connections between the familiar words in their list and the patterns they were constructing. In time, AB patterns become known as on-and-off patterns and ABC patterns as ones like the traffic light. For many students in this class, having an opportunity to make connections to everyday actions and observations by putting language to these common events helped them see similarities and differences in the structures of their patterns. It's as though the words helped to organize abstract ideas in new and more powerful ways. By the end of the unit many children had added more stanzas to the pattern poem and had illustrated their examples. The teacher was pleased with their progress. "In some ways," she said, "this class has ended up with a more tangible and internalized concept of patterns than my other classes. I thought they weren't ready for the idea of a core unit, when really, I hadn't yet helped them find an entry point into thinking this way."

Graphic organizers

Graphic organizers—visual representations that provide a prompt or an organizing framework for retrieving, storing, acquiring, or applying knowledge—are also a way to scaffold learning. They can be as simple as using graph paper to help organize and line up numbers or as complex as developing sophisticated structures for organizing conceptual models. Graphic organizers are often used in the teaching of language arts, social studies, and science.

They also have a prominent role in the teaching of mathematics. The more we use both linguistic and nonlinguistic representations in our classrooms, the more we can help our students learn and remember. Graphic organizers often contain both linguistic and nonlinguistic features.

Concept maps or webs are a way to graphically present relationships among ideas. The maps help children develop a framework for what they already know and provide a model that they can make more elaborate as their learning increases. Maps or webs can be developed at the beginning, in the middle, or at the end of units and they can provide important assessment data. The main concept can be written at the top or in the middle of the map. Rays or arrows then span out from that main idea. As the rays fan out, the ideas move from more general to more specific.

Young children can investigate concept maps in a variety of ways. *Kidspiration* is a computer software tool designed for use with K–5 learners. Some teachers provide a physical template for a map, with some of the topics identified. Then real objects, pictures, or words can be added to the diagram. A group of first-grade students who were beginning a unit on money were given a template for a map with some words to position in the headings. Once the words were placed, students chose their own examples to write under the arrows. (See Figure 6–1.)

Webs tend to be more free-flowing than concept maps and can be used to brainstorm what children know. One kindergarten teacher chooses to introduce webs by having students first brainstorm ideas and then look for connections among those ideas. She is careful not to impose her own thoughts or organizational strategies on these young minds, but rather encourages them to think about what they know and where they think their ideas should be recorded.

Figure 6–1 *A concept map for money.*

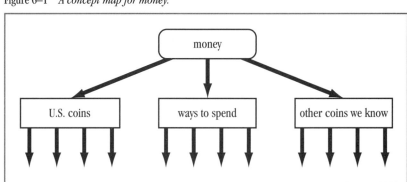

The teacher begins by asking the students to sit in a circle. She has a stack of index cards so that she can document the ideas that the students share. On the top card is the word *calendar*. The teacher informs the class that she is curious about what the children know about the calendar. She reminds them, "We begin our class everyday by checking and changing our calendar. Since we have been in school more than one hundred days, I am curious about what you know about our calendar and how it works. As you share your ideas, I am going to write them down on these cards. I have already printed the word *calendar* right here." As she speaks, she points to the printed word to focus the attention of her students.

The kindergartners are quick to respond. Hands shoot up and before long their teacher has recorded many ideas including:

- We use it every day.
- There are numbers and boxes and words.
- Everyone gets a turn to be the calendar helper.
- [There are] seven days in the week (which is shared by Zara singing the song the class uses at calendar time and followed by Keith giving a list of the seven days and the twelve months of the year).
- [There are] days, months, years.

The children share their ideas spontaneously, but they are listening to each other and building on the ideas that they hear. When Eric suggests, "Rows of boxes, sometimes they have numbers, sometimes they don't." Marianne adds, "There are seven boxes in a row." Next Margo offers, "and some going down," which is followed by Jesse's observation that "some boxes have pictures." When Linc notes that there are "special days like birthdays," students begin to give other examples. Soon Martin Luther King Jr.'s birthday, Hanukkah, Christmas, Kwanzaa, Valentine's Day, Chinese New Year, and the 100th Day are recorded as well.

The teacher records each response and then gives the card to the child who has just shared that idea. Soon everyone has at least one card. Stuart asks, "What are the cards for?" The teacher responds, "I want to keep a record of your ideas. Usually I write on our chart paper, but today I want to try something new." The students are eager to find out what that is, so their teacher asks them to think of their cards as pieces of a puzzle. "I wonder how we might fit them together?" she asks. "Do any of your ideas go together?"

For a few moments there is no response, but a lot of rattling of cards, when finally Tamika says, "Let's put all the special days together." "Yea, like my birthday," Linc suggests loudly while holding up his card. Tamika then stands up, as does Linc, and they walk around the circle in search of other cards they think note special days. This spontaneous response gives the teacher an idea. She suggests, "How about if each of you try and find at least one other person whose card you think goes with your idea? Maybe you can put your cards together in groups in the middle of the rug."

The students in the class are familiar with such directions, and though it might look chaotic to an observer, they are purposeful in their actions. Even though they are a group of predominately nonreaders or emergent readers, they are able to recall responses and work cooperatively to proceed. Before long, questions start to arise about cards belonging to more than one group. For example, the children who had suggested days of the week want to put them in the special days pile, but then they decide to make their own group. Children who had described features of the calendar, such as, "It has numbers," think they should go with the days of the week group and with the "rows and boxes" group. It is clear that the children are identifying conceptual relationships among these ideas and are doing so in a thoughtful manner.

The activity continues until most of the cards are grouped in some way on the rug. To help the children visualize the connections that they have made among these ideas, the teacher takes cut lengths of yarn and tapes each one from her original calendar card to a cluster of other cards. In this way she helps the children model the webbing process.

As the teacher reflects, "This activity was similar to other sorting tasks, something we do often, but the children were much more intense about the ways they negotiated meaning and debated where to put the cards. I was so impressed with how much they knew about our calendar and how they could group their ideas in meaningful ways. Their ideas were numerous. The activity gave the students their first opportunity at thinking about a lot of information and creating a way to organize their own, and their collective thoughts."

As mentioned by this teacher, sorting is a common activity in primary classrooms, particularly in kindergarten where children are just learning to focus on more than one attribute, such as color and shape. Another graphic organizer, Venn diagrams, is often used in the sorting process. In the primary years, the diagrams are usually limited to two rings. Often rings are placed on tables or desktops or drawn on paper. Larger models may also be used. Drawing large intersecting circles on the school's blacktop or putting large rope circles on the playground allows the children to physically sort themselves within the rings. Although the use of Venn diagrams was once limited to mathematics and science, they are now often utilized in literacy and social studies, for example, to compare two stories, characters, or major events. Introducing these graphic organizers during math time and applying them in other subjects can help children view mathematics as a useful tool.

Several graphic organizers can also be designed for use when solving problems. Some teachers use a series of icons to remind students of the steps in problem solving. (See Figure 6–2.) As the teacher explains, "A text we used a few years back had a four-step model of problem solving that was adapted from the ideas of George Polya. My current curriculum does not include this idea and I missed it. I found that it helped organize some of my students, and in particular, helped them remember to check their answers. Now that we put so much emphasis on students explaining their thinking, I added the fifth stage, *explain*."

A scaffold that focuses on mathematical vocabulary, and therefore, supports the explain stage of problem solving, is a word bank or word wall. Some teachers have a mathematical bulletin board in their classrooms where new terms are posted. In some classrooms just the words are displayed, in others, examples and/or illustrations may be shown as well. Students can then refer to the wall when appropriate. Some students may also be given a word bank for a particular task. (See Figure 6–3.)

Another graphic organizer is a vocabulary sheet. One second-grade teacher has students complete a sheet whenever a new term related to geometry or measurement is introduced. Using a blank

Figure 6–2 *Icons for problem-solving steps in a first-grade classroom.*

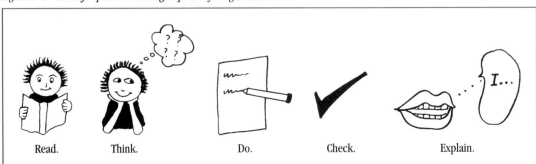

Read.   Think.   Do.   Check.   Explain.

space rather than lines for the example portion of the form allows students to choose to draw pictures or to write words. Students place each new sheet in the back of their mathematics binders and practice their alphabetizing skills by keeping the sheets in order. They can refer to the forms easily whenever they need to be reminded of the meaning of one of the terms. As the teacher explains, "When I went to school, you didn't do geometry until ninth or tenth grade. I remember feeling overwhelmed. There were so many new words to learn. I want my students to be comfortable with the language of geometry and measurement right from the beginning." (See Figure 6–4.)

Some teachers present problems in a way that graphically organizes a student's work. One example is a structured form that requires a number of steps to be completed. (See Figure 6–5.) Sometimes students just need a less-structured form with the problem

Figure 6–3   *A task with accompanying word bank.*

| How would you describe a cube to someone who had never seen one? |

Word Bank:
| box | face | square |
| edge | rectangular prism | three-dimensional |

Figure 6–4   *A graphic organizer used to support the learning of new mathematical terms.*

New word: _____

My definition: _____

_____

_____

_____

Examples:

Used in a sentence: _____

_____

_____

_____

There are some bicycles and tricycles.
There are 7 wheels.
How many bicycles are there?
How many tricycles are there?

Facts:	Drawings:
Computation:	Answer:

Figure 6–5 *A structured scaffold.*

Marcia has 15 pencils.
She gives Brenda some pencils.
Now Marcia has 7 pencils.
How many pencils did Marcia give to Brenda?

Show your work:

Answer: _____ pencils

Figure 6–6 *A less-structured scaffold.*

presented at the top and a clearly designated place to record the answer. (See Figure 6–6.) Such graphics can scaffold students through the problem-solving process, but should not be used with all problems or be implemented for any length of time. It's important that scaffolds, even simple ones, be removed or modified as the student progresses. Remember, the goal is for the problem-solving process to be organized by the student and that the student, not the teacher, take responsibility for deciding if making a drawing would be helpful and for remembering to identify the answer within the work.

Forms with spaces for multiple answers to a word problem allow the child to determine how many answers to provide. For example, if children are asked to identify all the possible combinations of seven, eight response lines can be provided. (See Figure 6–7.) Again, such multiple-response scaffolds should only be used with

There are 7 birds on the fence.
Every bird is either a robin or a sparrow.
How many of each type of bird could there be?

1. _____

2. _____

3. _____

4. _____

5. _____

6. _____

7. _____

8. _____

Figure 6–7   *A scaffold for a problem with multiple responses.*

students who would otherwise be unable to work with a more open-ended presentation. Students can use this problem (without the scaffold) as an opportunity to create their own methods for deciding if they have identified all the correct responses. But for some children this task is too overwhelming at first. The scaffold, or response template, provides a systematic way for them to give the problem a try and the structure can help students who find the empty page, or the requirement to find multiple answers, too intimidating.

The importance of providing only those scaffolds that are needed and to lessen or remove them as soon as possible cannot be overemphasized. It is also important to think critically about why a scaffold would be provided and how it can support students' learning robust concepts. Too often children who experience difficulty with choosing the correct operation to solve a story problem have been told to focus on key words. For example, words such as *take away* and *left* would be viewed as cues for subtraction, while *altogether, in all,* and *total* would cue addition. Teachers sometimes provide further scaffolding by hanging a poster in the classroom identifying key words for each operation and students might be asked to underline these words in story problems.

This approach is problematic for several reasons. For one, no list of key words can be exhaustive. For another, a term such as *total* could indicate addition or multiplication. Also, as our story problems become more realistic and less "canned," such terms may not even appear. Further, this approach assumes that subtraction would be used to solve a story problem such as:

> *There are 8 carrots on the plate.*
> *Kate ate 2 of them.*
> *How many carrots are left?*

Yet some students would determine the answer by counting up from two until they came to eight. Others would think, "What must I add to two to get eight?" For these students, subtraction is not involved. So what would it mean to identify *left* as the key word that maps onto subtraction? Most important, this reductionism asks students to look for specific words, rather than the underlying conceptual meaning of the context.

Educators have identified four categories of addition and subtraction problems: *join, separate, part-part-whole,* and *compare*. Examples of word problems associated with each category include:

Join

> *Marietta has 6 stickers.*
> *Her sister, Sarah, gives her 3 more stickers.*
> *How many stickers does Marietta have now?*

Separate

> *Marietta has 9 stickers.*
> *She gives 3 stickers to her sister, Sarah.*
> *How many stickers does Sarah have now?*

Part-Part-Whole

> *Marietta has 6 animal stickers and 3 smiley stickers.*
> *How many stickers does Marietta have?*

Comparison

> *Marietta has 9 stickers.*
> *Her sister, Sarah, has 6 stickers.*
> *How many more stickers does Marietta have than Sarah?*
> *How many fewer stickers does Sarah have than Marietta?*

Note that these examples all involve the numbers 6, 3, and 9. Often word problems for kindergarten and first-grade students tend to be *join* and *separate* problems. Further, they are often presented in the same manner; that is, the *join* stories ask about the combined total and the *separate* stories ask about the number remaining. In actuality, the questions could involve any one of the three numbers. Examples of join word problems include:

Join with Total Unknown

Marietta has 6 stickers.
Her sister, Sarah, gives her 3 more stickers.
How many stickers does Marietta have now?

Join with Set 2 Unknown

Marietta has 6 stickers.
Her sister, Sarah, gives her some more stickers.
Now Marietta has 9 stickers.
How many stickers did Sarah give her?

Join with Set 1 Unknown

Marietta has some stickers.
Her sister, Sarah, gives her 3 more stickers.
Now Marietta has 9 stickers.
How many stickers did Marietta have before Sarah gave
   her some more?

While limiting initial exposure to similar problem structures may be seen as strategic planning on the part of a teacher and an appropriate scaffold, we must remember to provide appropriate challenges as well. If we don't, we are limiting the conceptual models of joining and separating that our students can build. We prefer to expose our students to a wider array of story problems and use manipulative models, dramatizations, drawings, and peer conversations to support investigations with less familiar structures.

Graphic organizers can also be introduced to connect these problem structures. Note that while the action may vary, each type of join, separate, and part-part-whole story problem shares a similar schema in that there are two distinct sets that make up the whole. (See Figure 6–8.) Arrows can be added to the graphic to show the action of join or separate stories. (See Figure 6–9.) Over time, students can connect problems to this graphic organizer, adding numbers or drawings to make the connection meaningful. Note that as with triangle fact cards (see Chapter 5), any one of the three numbers may be missing.

Ten-frames, hundreds charts, and number lines are graphic organizers of our number system. A ten-frame is a 2-by-5 array with dots or chips placed to show the quantities one through ten. (See Figure 6–10 on page 138.) Note that the numbers are represented in a systematic manner. One more dot or chip is added from left to right in the top row until that row is complete. Then one is added from left

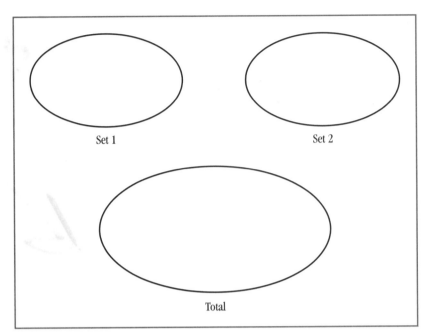

Set 1

Set 2

Total

Figure 6–8   *A graphic organizer for join, separate, and part-part-whole story problem structures.*

to right in the bottom row. This sequence shows that each counting number is one more than the previous number and anchors each of these numbers to five and to ten. Students can order ten-frames, match them to numerals, determine their numbers without actual counting, develop visual images to anchor number quantities and concepts, and respond to questions such as, "How many more than five is this?" "How many more are needed to make ten?" If appropriate, children can be introduced first to a five-frame, which shows only one row and is used for the numbers one through five.

Though many activities can be explored with filled-in ten-frames, some teachers prefer to work with blank arrays or frames. Originally, a child may "show eight" by placing chips one at a time, while counting to keep track. Over time, children might recognize eight as three more than five, two less than ten, or just be able to visualize how eight looks on the frame. While working with a ten-frame, teachers can learn much about their students' number sense. For example, after showing eight, students can be asked to show nine. Some children will remove all of the chips and begin again, while others will recognize the relationship between eight and nine and simply add one more chip to the frame.

Greater numbers can be shown by utilizing two ten-frames. To find 7 + 6, for example, students can show seven and then count on six, beginning by filling in the remaining three places on that frame and then placing the other three chips on a new array. The frames

All: Differentiating Instruction, Grades K–2

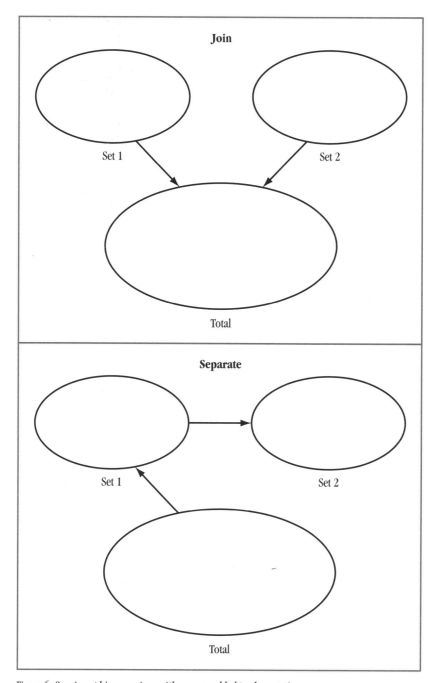

Figure 6–9 *A graphic organizer with arrows added to show action.*

organize the grouping by tens process and help students recognize ten as a benchmark number. Splitting numbers to form ten, for example, recognizing that 8 + 5 is the same as 8 + 2 + 3, can result from work with ten-frames and provide an important conceptual grounding for computation both mentally and with paper and pencil.

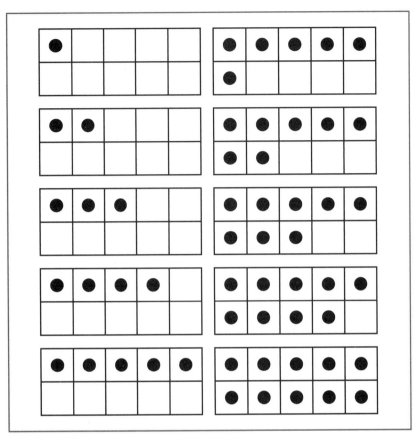

Figure 6–10 *Ten-frames.*

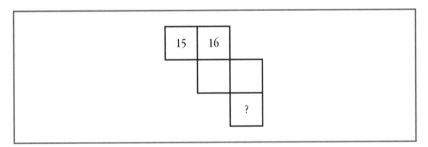

Figure 6–11 *A hundreds chart challenge.*

A hundreds chart also emphasizes the structure of grouping by tens, which is such an important characteristic of our base ten number system. Students recognize the pattern of our counting numbers in both the ones and tens places by using the structure of the hundreds chart. Children can create a hundreds chart with a blank chart and number tiles. Once created, a handful of tiles can be removed and then the missing numbers identified. A similar process could be followed using a pocket chart and index cards. (See Figure 6–11 for an example of a challenging task.)

As with ten-frames, observing how a child uses a hundreds chart can be helpful. For example, when determining 7 + 15, many students will place their fingers on seven and then count up fifteen, touching their fingers to each of the next numbers they encounter as they move to the right and then return sweep to the row below, the same routine they follow when reading in English. Others may recognize that fifteen is composed of one ten and five ones. With this awareness, they may begin on 7, slide their fingers down one row to 17, and then count on five.

Not everyone agrees how a hundreds chart should be organized. (See Figure 6–12 for three different organizations.) In the first chart, the number representing the next decade is shown at the end of each row. The number 34, for example, can be viewed as three complete rows of ten and four more in the next row. Advocates of the second model argue that this placement emphasizes the importance of zero and that the tens digit is the same throughout the row. Further, if a vertical line is drawn down the middle of the chart, numbers on the right side would round up to the next decade (when context is irrelevant) and those on the left, would round down. Critics of this format express concern for the lack of cardinality. That is, the fourth number is three, not four, and thus the starting point for children is confusing. The third model is based on the idea that it is more natural to think of numbers as growing bigger, with the numbers that are less on the bottom and the numbers that are greater on the top. These differences point out the importance of our thinking about the graphic organizers we choose to use.

A number line may emphasize grouping by tens, depending on how it is designed. One way to deepen the connection between a hundreds chart and a number line would be to cut up a chart to make the line or vice versa. Number lines illustrate the continuous nature of our number system, one to which fractions, decimals, and negative numbers can eventually be added. Similar to a ruler, however, children can be confused about starting points and whether they are counting spaces or numbers. (See Figure 6–13.)

Not all number lines show numbers! Open number lines are simply lines, perhaps with one or two numbers identified. They can be an excellent tool for developing a sense of the relative position or size of numbers. Tasks can provide teachers with a glimpse into students' understanding of the relative magnitude of 10 and 100. (See Figure 6–14.)

Number lines can also be shown with hatch marks only. Some tasks help students match a base ten or digital representation of

Beginning with 1

1	2	3	4	5	6	7	8	9	10
11	12	13	14	15	16	17	18	19	20
21	22	23	24	25	26	27	28	29	30
31	32	33	34	35	36	37	38	39	40
41	42	43	44	45	46	47	48	49	50
51	52	53	54	55	56	57	58	59	60
61	62	63	64	65	66	67	68	69	70
71	72	73	74	75	76	77	78	79	80
81	82	83	84	85	86	87	88	89	90
91	92	93	94	95	96	97	98	99	100

Beginning with 0

0	1	2	3	4	5	6	7	8	9
10	11	12	13	14	15	16	17	18	19
20	21	22	23	24	25	26	27	28	29
30	31	32	33	34	35	36	37	38	39
40	41	42	43	44	45	46	47	48	49
50	51	52	53	54	55	56	57	58	59
60	61	62	63	64	65	66	67	68	69
70	71	72	73	74	75	76	77	78	79
80	81	82	83	84	85	86	87	88	89
90	91	92	93	94	95	96	97	98	99

Growing up

91	92	93	94	95	96	97	98	99	100
81	82	83	84	85	86	87	88	89	90
71	72	73	74	75	76	77	78	79	80
61	62	63	64	65	66	67	68	69	70
51	52	53	54	55	56	57	58	59	60
41	42	43	44	45	46	47	48	49	50
31	32	33	34	35	36	37	38	39	40
21	22	23	24	25	26	27	28	29	30
11	12	13	14	15	16	17	18	19	20
1	2	3	4	5	6	7	8	9	10

Figure 6–12 *Three organizational structures for a hundreds chart.*

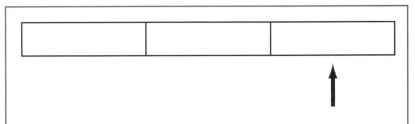

When using a model similar to a ruler or number line, some children place their fingers in the middle of each space while counting, "one, two, three." Thus, they would conclude that the point indicated by the arrow would represent three, rather than two and one-half.

Figure 6–13   *Misconception between spaces and endpoints.*

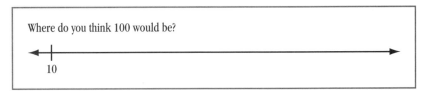

Where do you think 100 would be?

10

Figure 6–14   *A task focused on the relative magnitude of 10 and 100.*

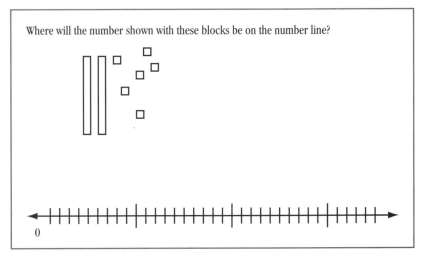

Where will the number shown with these blocks be on the number line?

0

Figure 6–15   *A task with number line that uses hatch marks.*

a number with a ones or linear model. When the longer hatch marks at the tens are included, they can be used to simplify the counting process. Students can use the marks to count ten at once. Such tasks help to support the concept that ten is both one ten and ten ones. (See Figure 6–15.)

As can be seen from the examples of graphic organizers in this chapter, these visual tools can be powerful models for conceptual development or simple ways to illustrate a particular task or process. In the same spirit, asking questions, focusing on strategies, having students collaborate, and making connections are used to support learning by making the work more accessible for all students as they pursue tasks, make choices, and solve problems.

Chapter 7
Supporting Choice

$\mathcal{O}$ur society places value on making choices. Making choices helps us to feel autonomous, confident, and competent. Choice is highly motivating and is one way that students can take responsibility for their own learning. Making a choice involves self-expression, which is a form of creativity. We honor our students as learners by allowing them to make choices. We are also able to differentiate our instruction by providing choice.

Time to make choices is a common practice in preschool and kindergarten classrooms. Often indistinguishable from play to a lay observer, children engage with classroom materials in ways that help them to develop their language, artistic, and social skills as well as motivate them to explore number, space, and scientific ideas. Though having more choices is frequently associated with growing older and being able to handle responsibilities, students often view school as a place where choice diminishes as they advance through the grades. Yet there are teachers committed to maintaining a choice time for students throughout the elementary years. As we learn from the teacher reflection that follows, choice time does not mean that anybody can do anything they want. Rather, students can be given choices among tasks, with each choice designed to support the instructional goals in the classroom.

Teacher Reflection

I make an effort to provide "choice time" for my students. I feel that it gives my second graders a sense of autonomy as learners. I also think it sends a subtle, though powerful, message that I respect them for their individuality and have confidence in the decisions they make.

At the beginning of the school year we spend a lot of time establishing routines and expectations for choice time. There is much to consider for making *good* choices. I emphasize the word *good* for a reason. It sets the tone of accountability and reminds students that the choices they are given to consider are designed to have a positive impact on what they are learning.

By the time students in my school become second graders, having choice time is not a new experience for them. I am grateful for this. I think it is wonderful that children have already been given opportunities to make choices as they learn to read, write, and study topics in math, science, and social studies. I also know that making choices is present in their music, art, and physical education classes. They are used to picking partners and selecting materials and are increasingly more adept at navigating the classroom to find what they need to support their pursuits.

This teacher offers us several ideas to think about when considering choice in our classrooms. Autonomy, decision making, making good choices, selecting materials, and navigating the classroom are ideas that provide us with a framework for thinking about how to design and implement choice in our classrooms. There are managerial implications around time, work habits, disposition for learning, behavior, and ways to monitor student progress that require our attention as well.

Being offered a choice implies the need for reflection and self-direction. Many young children are adept at this, many are not. Childhood is a journey toward independence and self-discovery. Parents and teachers alike recognize that children need predictable structure, clear expectations, and innumerable opportunities to explore, practice, make mistakes, and learn. Teachers (and parents) also recognize that children need the time and room to practice decision making as well as learn how to compromise. In many ways, offering choices requires more preparation than merely directing students, but the gains are worth it. Choice provides powerful opportunities for additional practice and differentiating instruction and also leads to natural extensions for learning.

There are a variety of choices we can offer our students, including:

- which topics to study;
- which tasks to complete;
- what materials to use;
- with whom to partner;
- where to work;
- how long to work;

- the order in which to complete assignments;
- how to represent and present ideas; and/or
- how to demonstrate what is understood.

Letting our students make such choices can have a positive impact on their learning and their self-esteem. The extent to which this potential impact is realized often depends on the ways in which teachers structure and organize choice in the classroom. In this chapter we consider centers, workshop time, menus, Think Tac Toes, RAFTs, and stations as ways to organize and manage classroom choice as we strive to meet individual needs.

Center Choice Time

Most kindergarten classrooms contain a variety of centers: block area, art center, dramatic play area, writing center, classroom library, listening center, sand or water table, and math center are examples. Sometimes a predesigned activity is set up at a particular center. Sometimes the work at centers is entirely open-ended for students. Just the sheer nature of the materials available, or the name of the center, designates the direction of the work. When children are given time to work at the various centers in the room, many teachers refer to this as *choice time*. The word *choice* is used as a signal to students that it is their responsibility to select a center where they will pursue an interest or activity for a sustained period. This feels natural to students and is often met with a flurry of excitement.

Mathematical activities can be pursued in any of these centers. The mathematics center, however, often refers only to the area in the room in which the majority of mathematics materials are stored. This may include a set of shelves where baskets or bins of manipulative materials are arranged. For easy access and return of these materials, labels are put on the bins or baskets, indicating the items, games, or manipulatives found within, and a corresponding label is placed on the shelves. Everything is visible, reachable, and easy to maintain.

In this way the math center is more about storage than actual learning, though we all agree that classrooms need ample space for centers of this sort. Easy access to materials is one of many managerial strategies that support learning. Students should learn early where materials are stored, how to use them, and that keeping them in order is a sign of respect for their fellow students. Clear expectations for use of shared materials are critical in a classroom. As students learn to use mathematical materials and come to expect that such materials are available for their use, they also develop the good work habits and positive behaviors that are indicative of successful, respectful, and independent learners.

When the math center is seen as a place of storage, students learn to come and get the materials they need and then find a more conducive place in the classroom to work. When the math center is more spacious, it can also be a place of learning. Students may find that they rotate into this area to work on a specific project or use a particular set of materials. For example the block area in many primary classes is often considered part of the math center. Students usually stay in the block area rather than moving blocks to another location in the classroom.

Some teachers manage center time with a work board. This graphic organizer uses icons to help establish which centers or activities are available and can also be used to monitor how often students are taking advantage of the choices offered. Students can place their nametag on the board to indicate that they will be starting at a particular center. Many teachers limit the number of children that may work at any one place. Once the maximum number of spaces has been filled, any subsequent students wishing to start with this activity will need to make a different selection. The work board is a visible reminder of what students are expected to do.

Workshop Time

Sometimes materials are taken from the mathematics center and placed at various work areas around the room. Perhaps the students are studying patterns; pattern blocks, color tiles, attribute blocks, and Unifix cubes have been laid out for students to explore. There are a variety of ways to build choice into this workshop experience. Students could be working on the same task (for example, create a pattern) but choose the materials they wish to use to do so, along with the particular patterns they wish to construct. Or teachers can assign specific students to certain materials based on readiness. For example, a teacher may decide that the color tiles and Unifix cubes only differ by color and thus may be more accessible for less-ready students to use. Conversely, as pattern blocks (color and shape) and attribute blocks (size, color, and shape) involve more than one distinguishable characteristic, these materials might provide greater challenge to other students. Once assigned, however, students could still choose a partner with whom to work, the types of patterns to make, and the ways in which the work would be represented.

Menus

Marilyn Burns suggested the use of menus to organize student choice (Burns 1988). Four to six activities are listed in a menu format and, just as if you were in a restaurant, you can choose what to order. A special menu board can be used or the work board can be reorganized to list the menu options. During the span of a week, students may be encouraged to try each item on the menu. A recording sheet can be used to keep track of students' daily choices.

The items on the menu are presented and modeled over time. When first introduced, a game or activity may be explored with the whole class. Familiarity with menu choices may also be developed in small groups or with individual students. These students are then given the responsibility to share their menu experiences with their classmates. It is amazing how quickly an entire class can learn an interesting new game, even if it is only introduced formally to one student.

One kindergarten teacher decides to create a geometry menu for her students so that they will have more opportunities to identify, draw, and describe two- and three-dimensional shapes. She identifies five activities for the menu:

- Create two identical "feely boxes," one for each group of students, filled with four to six three-dimensional shapes. Each box top is labeled with the names of a shape along with its picture. Students work in triads. One student reaches into the box and describes the shape that he or she feels. (Students are reminded not to look, but rather to connect the kinesthetic feedback to what they know about shapes as they describe what they feel.) The other two students listen, discuss their ideas, and then choose a picture on the box to identify the block described.
- Place templates of triangles, squares, rectangles, and circles of different sizes with the art materials; students trace one or two shapes using the templates and integrate these shapes into their drawings.
- Collect appropriate shape books and place them in a milk crate in the library area for the children to explore.

- Collect a variety of pictures of common objects in the shapes of spheres, cylinders, and rectangular prisms (using flyers from grocery and sports stores) for children to sort.
- Include the block area as a menu choice so that students can relate this favorite activity to geometry.

She is confident that the children will readily understand the choices involving the template, book, and block area. She will introduce the feely box during morning meeting on Monday and the sorting activity on Tuesday. She makes a menu chart for each student so that they can remember the various choices and keep track of which ones they have selected to do. (See Figure 7–1).

Figure 7–1   *A menu chart that students can use to record daily choices.*

Make a check mark (✓) to show what you chose.

	Monday	Tuesday	Wednesday	Thursday	Friday
 Feely Box					
Art Project 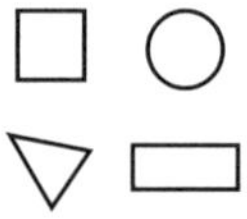					
Books 					
Sorting 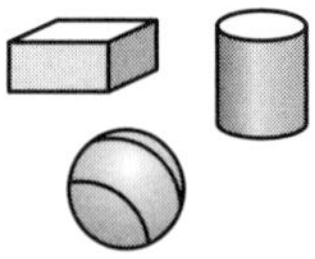					
Block Area 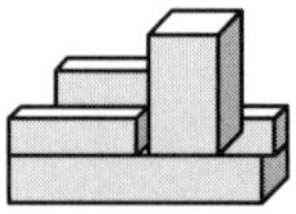					

Students are told that they must make three different choices before returning to an activity explored already.

Some activities on a menu or work board may remain for a significant amount of time. Students, through repetition, are able to explore a certain activity over the course of weeks, months, or the year thereby creating comfort and confidence. Children also like using manipulative materials repeatedly and enjoy the intrigue of finding new uses for familiar items. Having a particular choice available frequently gives more children an opportunity to give it a try, while other activities rotate based on need. Often, teachers focus on a few activities or centers for awhile, and then phase them out gradually. Rotating out some activities leaves room for new and expanded ideas to be developed, while keeping available some of the familiar choices.

How choices are organized is a reflection of a teacher's style and classroom management preferences, coupled with the students' needs. Many teachers add a "have to" element to the choices offered. In this way teachers make certain expectations more explicit for students. In some classes teachers require students to start or complete one or more of the "have to" items before moving on to other choices. In the younger years, these must-make choices are sometimes identified with a star and referred to as "I care" items. This phrase lets children know that the teacher cares that these items are chosen.

Carol Tomlinson (2003a, 2003b) provides menus with required features. Main course listings must be completed, one or two side dishes must be chosen, and desserts are optional choices that students particularly interested in the topic may wish to complete. A first-grade teacher wants to create such a menu. She decides to focus on part-part-whole relationships, a topic that has been the focus of classroom work throughout the year as students explored addition and subtraction concepts. She believes strongly that it is important to view numbers such as three and four as two parts of the whole, seven. She wants her students to move freely among sets of such numbers as they connect these ideas to addition and subtraction sentences (equations). Now that it is March, she is confident that her students are ready for a part-part-whole menu.

To begin, the teacher thinks about her key question for the menu and identifies it as: "How are parts and wholes related?" She then notes the key objectives she has for students:

- Represent part-part-whole relationships by drawing, recording numbers in a table, or through the use of number sentences.

- Identify more than one way to decompose a whole into two parts.
- Apply knowledge of part-part-whole relationships to the solution of story problems.
- Describe ways to find missing parts and wholes.

She then identifies activities that focus on these objectives and includes them within the main course section. She thinks of side dishes as ways to practice part-part-whole relationships, so in this section she lists four practice activities. Finally, she creates three desserts, activities that she thinks her students might enjoy doing.

Her menu explicitly allows choice in activities, numbers, and representations. (See Figure 7–2; see also Blackline Masters.)

Figure 7–2   *A menu that requires completion of main course items, designed for first-grade students.*

Part-Part-Whole Menu

Main Course (You must do each one.)

- Imagine that the children in *Anno's Counting House* move two at a time. Work with a partner to tell this story. Use the teddy bears to model the story as you tell it. After each move, represent the number of children in each house and the number of children in all. Talk about what you notice about your numbers.
- Solve 5 of the problems in the parts-whole story box.
- Imagine 3 numbers: 2 parts, and the whole. Write or tape-record ways to find 1 of these missing numbers when you know the other 2 numbers.

Side Orders (Complete two.)

- Create a puzzle with 10 pieces. On 5 of the pieces write or draw 2 parts. On the other 5 pieces write or draw a whole for each piece with 2 parts. Trade your puzzle with a classmate. Match the pieces in your classmate's puzzle.

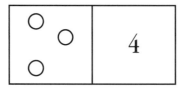 

- Use the *Unifix Software* (Hickey 1997) to make single bars. Then create 2-part bars to match each single bar.
- Get some Unifix cubes and a cup. Play *Cover Up* with a partner.
- Get some red and blue Unifix cubes. Make some towers of 10. How many are red and how many are blue? Make a list.

Desserts (Do one or more if you are interested.)

- Write 2 problems to put in our parts-whole problem box.
- Choose a number as your whole. Make a picture book of your number in parts.
- Make up songs, poems, or raps about parts and wholes.

As needed, the teacher can easily tier the menu for less or more ready students as she strives to provide appropriate practice and challenge for all children. For example, *Anno's Counting House* (Anno 1982), a picture book that shows ten children moving from one house to another and presents opportunities for readers to predict how many children will be at the other house after each move, could be replicated exactly. That is, children would move from one spot to the next one at a time, rather than two at a time. The number of pieces in the puzzle could be increased or decreased, and the explanation example in the main menu could be limited to explaining what to do to find the whole when you know the two parts.

Because the menu format may be problematic for emerging readers, making time to read and describe the menu selections together as a class is important. Another option is to use icons for menu choices, which reduces the reading. This teacher decided to have children work in pairs, with one of the pair having stronger reading skills.

Think Tac Toe

Think Tac Toe and RAFT are two other formats that generally require more reading, and thus, may be more appropriate with second-grade students. A Think Tac Toe board is a 3-by-3 matrix with nine cells, resembling the familiar tic-tac-toe game board. (See Figure 7–3; see also Blackline Masters.) Students may be asked to complete one of the tasks in each row. The tasks in the first row of this example focus on communication about ways to find sums. In the second row are tasks that provide practice with addition and use of the guess-and-check problem-solving strategy. Making connections is the goal of the tasks in the third row. Connections are made to uses of addition in the real world, to a classmate's way of thinking about addition, and to story problems. The tasks in this type of graphic organizer can also be arranged so that students are directed to complete three tasks in one row. Further, it is possible to tier the choices, with each row containing more challenging tasks or offering tasks that are more conducive to particular learning styles and preferences.

RAFT

A RAFT is a strategy for differentiating learning that can also provide choice for students. The acronym stands for **r**ole, **a**udience, **f**ormat, and **t**opic. To complete a RAFT activity, students create a product while being mindful of all four categories. For example,

Addition Think Tac Toe

Choose and complete one activity in each row.

Draw a picture that shows a model of $17 + 15$. Make connections between your drawing and how you find the sum.	Your brother added 18 and 4 and got the answer 23. What could you show and tell your brother to help him understand why his answer is wrong?	Write directions for two different ways to find the sum of $36 + 19$ when you use paper and pencil.
Place the numbers: 10, 20, 30, 40, 50, and 60, so that the sum of each side is 90. ⭕ ⭕ ⭕ ⭕ ⭕ ⭕ Write one more problem like this one and trade it with a classmate.	Place two addition signs to make a number sentence that is true. $$23,915 = 47$$ Write two more problems like this one and trade them with a classmate.	Which two numbers should you exchange so that the sum of the numbers on each card is the same? `12 8 6` `11 3 10` `5 4 13` Write two more problems like this one and trade them with a classmate.
Make a list of ways you use addition outside of school.	Interview a classmate about what he or she knows about addition. Find out as much as you can in three minutes. Write me a report with suggestions for teaching.	Your friend solved a word problem by adding 20 and 7 and then subtracting 3. Write two interesting word problems that your friend could have solved this way.

Figure 7–3 *Addition Think Tac Toe for second-grade students later in the school year.*

as a game designer (role) for children (audience), students might create a game (format) to practice basic facts (topic). As there is a specific purpose for each suggestion within a RAFT, this instructional strategy also helps to emphasize the usefulness of mathematics and offers students an opportunity to think about how mathematics is used beyond the classroom.

A second-grade teacher decides to create a RAFT about telling time. (See Figure 7–4; see also *Blackline Masters.*) She identifies writing times and drawing clocks as key ideas. She tries to think about a variety of roles that might appeal to her students and different products they could create. She pays special attention to thinking about formats that will match a variety of learning styles. She believes that her students who enjoy wordplay will like to create riddles, while her more artistic students will enjoy illustrating a book. Visual learners who are not interested in drawing may wish to make a collage. She thinks the opportunity to reflect on their favorite times of day will appeal to her introspective students.

	RAFT: Time		
Role	**Audience**	**Format**	**Topic**
Teacher	Our class	Riddles (with clues and clock pictures)	What Time Is It?
Writer/Illustrator	Second graders	Illustrated children's book	All About Time
Camp Counselor	Campers	Schedule with activities and times	First Day of Camp
Self	Parents	Analog clock with explanation	This Is the Time I Like the Best!
Self	Classmates	Collage of clocks with written times and activities	How I Spend Saturdays

Figure 7–4 *A RAFT chart about time.*

Making schedules may match her less verbal students and providing an explanation of the advantages of an analog clock may challenge the more able children in the class.

Learning Stations

Learning stations can be used to augment a current unit or to maintain skills from a previous one. They are particularly helpful when there are not enough materials for the whole class to engage with at the same time. For example, a geometry learning station might include photographs of shapes in nature, items that most classrooms would not have in multiple copies. We think of a learning station as a temporary feature in the classroom. We choose to reserve the term *center* for permanent areas in the room, such as a computer or listening center. Many teachers, however, use these terms interchangeably, and that is fine.

In a combination kindergarten and grade 1 class, the teacher designs a new station for her students to use as they work on a measurement unit. She identifies three goals for the focus of the unit:

1. comparing lengths, weights, area, and volume
2. using standard and nonstandard measurements
3. selecting appropriate measurement tools

From previous experience she knows that measurement is an enjoyable, though challenging, unit for this age group. She realizes that students need time and repeated opportunities to make the goals related to measurement salient. Her thought is to have a measurement station where students can explore activities introduced throughout the unit many times. She also recognizes that learning about measurement requires numerous materials that can make some activities difficult to manage with the whole class working at the same time. She wants to design a station where a small group of students can work independently or collaboratively while additional learning opportunities are taking place in other areas of the classroom.

Selecting or designing appropriate tasks is her first step in setting up the measurement station. She wants the station to allow for a variety of measurement activities, but not be overwhelming for her students. She wants the tasks to be somewhat open-ended, but also self-sustaining, as she does not want to be called to the station too frequently while she is working with other groups. She also wants the activities to feel linked, not random to her students, so that they can make connections as they build their understanding of measurement.

She brainstorms a number of options involving length, weight, area, and volume, but while she is excited about all of the ideas she identifies, she believes that she has too many ideas for one station. She decides to identify the following questions as a way to clarify the focus of the station and frame the different tasks that will be included there:

- Why do we measure things?
- What do we use when we measure?
- Do these objects weigh the same?
- How tall is our class?
- Are parts of your body all the same distance around?
- How long is this ribbon?

This teacher often asks questions such as "Why do we measure things?" and "What do we use when we measure?" within an initial KWL (see page 123) brainstorming experience as a whole-class discussion at the beginning of a unit. This teacher decides to have these questions be part of the measurement station as well, so that students can add to a collection of responses over time, connect to classroom experiences, and utilize drawing and writing while learning mathematical content.

The teacher prints all of these questions on sentence strips and posts them on the bulletin board nearest the table where the measurement station will be located. She expects students to draw or write about their ideas. She plans to post their responses on the bulletin board beside each question.

Next she borrows two pan-balances from a colleague and collects common objects from around the classroom that will fit easily on the pans. She wants her students to have a chance to compare the weights of objects that are greater in difference and those that are closer in weight. She makes a note to herself to encourage students to add to the collection of items. The objects include various blocks, a hardbound book and a paperback book, a stapler, a large conch shell, a pinecone, some rocks, and a box of crayons. She thinks about adding instructions and a drawing on the recording sheet to indicate that students are to compare two specific items at a time, but then decides to keep the activity more open-ended. She does add a column that asks students to predict the heavier object before they put the items on the balance.

She also adds a store-bought height chart to the bulletin board. She expects that students will work in pairs to measure each other. She tacks up a string tied to a pencil that students can use to mark their heights with their initials. She also posts a class list nearby so that students can cross off their names when they complete the task. In this way, she can make sure that each child is included.

Since measuring themselves on the height chart is a one-time activity, the teacher includes plastic measuring tapes in the station so that students who are interested can work together to measure each other's height in inches. She also includes an activity using yarn that asks students to compare the girths of different parts of their bodies. On a worksheet she draws an outline of a person with arrows going around the forehead, neck, wrist, knee, and ankle. The children are to find out how long a piece of yarn is needed to go around each of these parts of their bodies. Next they are asked to put these lengths in order from shortest to longest and tape them onto a strip of construction paper. The teacher assembles all of the materials needed to complete this task and lays them out on the table along with the growing collection of other items in the measurement station.

In previous years, the children were asked to estimate the length of strips of tape this teacher had placed on the floor. Then they used Unifix cubes to determine the actual lengths. She still wants students to have more opportunities to estimate, compare, and measure lengths, but this year, she also wants to make the station more mobile, more flexible. So, she cuts twelve pieces of various lengths of one-inch-wide ribbon. She labels each piece (from A to L). Some lengths are short since many of her kindergartners are only comfortable counting to twenty. Other lengths are much longer to provide more challenge for her more able kindergarten and first-grade students. As she wants students to explore measuring these ribbons using both nonstandard and standard units, she sets out containers of craft sticks, paper clips, and Unifix cubes, as well as rulers. Three types of rulers are included, those with demarcations of only an inch, ones with only centimeters, and some more typical rulers from which students can select. She looks forward to seeing how students will use these units to measure the ribbons. Will all students recognize that the same unit must be used when measuring to compare? What will they do if there are not enough of the units they have chosen to cover the length of one of the ribbons? She knows she will have many opportunities to learn about her students' measurement concepts and skills as they work with these tasks. Finally, she provides a corresponding recording sheet that asks students to indicate which ribbon they chose, their estimated length, what they used for measuring, and how many they used.

All items for the ribbon activity are added to the measurement station, along with a sign on the table that reads, *How Many? How Long?* Directions are printed on posters for each activity. For example, the ribbon activity poster lists:

- How can you tell how long a piece of ribbon is?
- Use any of these materials to help you.
- Record your answers on the recording sheet.
- Find the length for at least 3 ribbons.
- You may work with a partner, but you each need to record your own work.

There are now many activities at the station, not to mention materials, and yet the teacher is still thinking about other possibilities. She could add new tasks if the original ones grow tiresome. She thinks about adding a task on time, as children do not think of time as a form of measurement. Maybe she could put out egg timers from a game and ask them how many times they could write their name or maybe the alphabet, or maybe how many numbers they could record before the timer ran out. She also thinks about adding items to the balance activity, or maybe she could find a kitchen scale and ask children to use it to order items from lightest to heaviest. The ideas keep flowing until she realizes that she needs to stop. Though the possibilities seem endless, she knows to focus the station on only some of the goals established for the unit. She wants the station to be interesting, but not too complex. She decides that she can always add activities later, but for now, she believes the station is ready.

During math time the next day, the teacher spends a few minutes introducing the guiding questions for each task and the related materials. She wants her students to be aware of the purpose of the station and the goals for learning. She does not model how to complete the activities, but rather briefly describes each one making a point to show the materials available and to set expectations around working with a partner and how to complete any recording sheets. She takes time for questions and discovers that her students are confused by the activity with the height chart. As a result, she decides that she will model how to complete this task. When that is done, she asks if there are six people who want to open the station. Not everyone is equally interested at first, but she does have to make a selection among the volunteers. She assures the children that they all will get turns and emphasizes that working at the station is an expectation for everyone.

Over the course of the next three weeks the students work diligently on the tasks at the station. The teacher finds that children ask to use the station throughout the day, not just during math time. As the days pass she notices children working together and many ideas being challenged. One day she overhears this exchange.

Malcolm: How come you got so many more? [This is said while he looks at Stephanie's recording sheet for the same ribbon.]

Stephanie: How many did you get?

Malcolm: I got three.

Stephanie: I got eighteen.

Malcolm: But it's three.

Stephanie: What did you use?

Malcolm: What do you mean?

Stephanie: I used the Unifix cubes, did you?

Malcolm: Oh, I used the sticks.

Stephanie: That's why I have more, they are bigger. I mean the cubes are smaller than the sticks so they take more.

On another day she laughs as she sees the drawings on display on the bulletin board. One child has suggested that we measure to find out how big something is, like how big the world is! Another child has written that we measure to see how many more. Malcolm has drawn a picture of the ribbon with his three craft sticks and (presumably) Stephanie's Unifix cubes. He does not show exactly eighteen cubes, but he does add, "eighteen is bigger than three." The teacher thinks to herself, "Math is so confusing." Malcolm's statement is mathematically correct, yet here is a situation where the length of eighteen cubes is in fact equivalent to the length of three craft sticks. "What questions can I ask to help my students understand these complex ideas?" the teacher wonders.

Stations such as this one take time to develop and organize. In the interest of being resourceful, you might consider only making stations for those topics that will be explored in subsequent years. Ideally, station materials can be stored in a plastic tub or folder (without the related manipulatives) so that they are ready to be used again and again. Some teachers also need to store stations in such ways all the time, as they need the station to be portable. This way, it can be used in different parts of the room, or even be put away for a few days, if necessary. Ample space can be a rare commodity in many classrooms. As the following teacher reflection makes clear, making strategic decisions based on availability of space, time, and amount of materials is ongoing as a teacher plans.

Teacher Reflection

I have come to value the need for setting up, maintaining, and rotating learning stations in my classroom. They have helped me be able to offer more choices to my students. In my mind this equates to more opportunities to practice and to learn. Once a station is up and running, my goal is for it to be self-sustaining. I want to be able to engage with other students at their point of need or to have a chance to sit back a bit as an observer. So, I try to design stations that do not require any teacher direction after the initial introduction.

Since I have been teaching for a few years, I have been able to reuse learning stations as a unit comes up for study in later years. Over time I have been able to test out how self-sustaining an activity may be for the majority of my students. I know I always have to be open to different learning styles and preferences. I even have to consider if students are required to read or write to fulfill learning expectations at any given point in the year.

I also need to consider what I use to define the space for the station. Have I given ample room? Have I separated stations from other work areas so that students are not unnecessarily distracted? Have I provided all the necessary materials for success? Do these materials need to be placed at the station or do my students know where to find them when they want them? For example, I do not put pencils and paper at my stations unless the paper is designed for a particular task. I have taught my students where to find resources around our classroom. I have set an expectation that they are the ones who know what they need at any point in time and are encouraged to act responsibly on that need.

Maintaining stations can take a lot of time. In some cases I can store all of the materials for a given activity in one box and when students have completed the work, I can store it away for another time. More typically the manipulatives used at one station are used repeatedly. I cannot store these away. For example, a manipulative like pattern blocks are used in almost every unit we study in math. I have to think about the best ways to juggle all of these things. Sometimes I have more than one station running at the same time. Then I need to think about materials. Do I have enough for my students to meet with success? Sometimes I have to borrow from another teacher or, if need be, redesign a station.

This teacher uses a word in her reflection that sounds familiar to all teachers—*juggle*. Juggling is part of the art and craft of teaching and learning. Determining what is to happen at each station, and feeling confident that the activities are aligned to the curriculum must always be in the forefront of our thoughts. We must also consider the following questions:

- Who decides what materials or activity are available and when?
- Who decides if a student will engage in this work?
- How will time be managed? How long will students be given to complete a task?
- Who initiates what goes on at a center or station?
- How will activities at a center or station be assessed?

These questions are among a host of decisions that may be on our minds as we create and implement learning centers and stations as well as the other instructional strategies for structuring choice presented in this chapter. Let's consider implications for each.

Who decides what materials or activities are available and when?

Once curriculum objectives are agreed on, teachers identify which materials are needed to help students meet those established goals. If the materials are new to students, the students need to learn how they are used and where they are stored. Once the materials are familiar, however, many can be made available to students at all times, to be used whenever needed. Of course some materials, such as thermometers, may be kept in a safe place and made available only under adult supervision. In the spirit of choice, though, we recommend that students choose materials whenever that choice does not hinder safety or greatly reduce the likelihood that learning will be successful.

Who decides if a student will engage in this work?

Often we operate from a mind-set that all students should complete every activity. This stance may stem from the desire to support inclusive and equitable classrooms. We need to balance this desire with the realization that to be equitable, each student must get what he or she needs based on readiness, interest, and learning style. Clearly there will be times when this is not exactly the same thing. All students do not need to complete every activity in order to support a classroom community. Also, we need to open our minds to the possibility that students themselves can participate in making these decisions. In fact, they can often be quite helpful. As one first grader explained to his teacher, "This is really not a good thing for me now. I need to learn more first." Conversely, sometimes a student might select a more difficult task from a RAFT option than the teacher would have assigned. When a student is motivated and supported, they often can achieve and understand more than might be expected.

How will time be managed? How long will students be given to complete a task?

Every teacher has an ongoing battle with the clock in the classroom. We can all agree there is never enough time. Part of this dilemma stems from the fact that no two students seem to work at the same pace or learn at the same rate. Many teachers plan for an average amount of time it will take most students to complete a task and then have to be flexible for those students who finish early and those who require more time. Students who finish early can be encouraged to move on to another activity or station instead of waiting for everyone to be done. Stations can also be kept up for an indefinite amount of time, as they often only require a small percentage of space in the classroom. What is of most value is the recognition that students need different amounts of time at different points of learning.

Who initiates what goes on at a center or station?

This question begs the notion of the teachable moment. Certainly teachers make initial plans for learning stations, but we always want to be open for ideas that students offer us as a direction for learning.

How we finesse these ideas, offer students permission to share their ideas, and give them time, space, and materials to follow their interests is an art. Unfortunately this seems in conflict with some current trends in our educational practices. *Coverage* of material included in curriculum guides and standardized tests seems to be of major concern, and student questions that do not immediately map onto an easily recognizable curriculum objective are sometimes viewed as unnecessary tangents. This concern has increased as school systems have adopted pacing guides teachers are expected to follow.

We do not want our students to think of school as a place where what they want to learn about is disregarded. Often, when we stop and think about how we can relate the topic of study to a current interest, a path can be found. For example, an interest in lost teeth can lead to an investigation on how many teeth different animals have, and a table and related story problems can result.

How will activities at a center or station be assessed?

When an activity results in a product of some kind, teachers often feel that assessment is more manageable and they become more confident in their decision making. The review and reflection of student work samples is an important step in evaluating children's learning. So, too, is taking time to observe students in action and to engage students in conversations as their work is unfolding. Keeping anecdotal records is a natural strategy for capturing these moments. Digital cameras or video can be wonderful ways to document learning as well. Assessments of activities at learning centers or stations come full circle, as do all assessments, to the learning goals that led development of the center or station in the first place. Being mindful of our goals—and letting students know them—helps to focus assessment in any learning environment, whether there is a tangible product or a set of scenarios that tell the story of learning.

Answering the questions posed here can be difficult. They require that we make decisions that can be demanding of our time and our efforts. How to best make any decision is rooted in the context of our own school settings and our students' needs. We must also remember that these decisions are not set in stone. Flexibility is key; as we gather new information or learn new instructional strategies, we can revise our practice to better meet the growing needs of all of our students.

Keeping the Interest Alive

Along with empowering our students, providing choice in our classrooms helps us tap into the interests of our students. But just having choices available does not guarantee interest. Any parent who has heard the lament "There's nothing to do!" understands this well. Part of the excitement of making a choice is that it can lead to something new and exhilarating. Changing the materials made available to students on a regular basis adds a fresh look. Having a familiar material or activity disappear can pique curiosity, or even be a relief. Having it come back again in a few weeks or months can also be a welcome change. As one first grader told his teacher, "I wondered where the attribute blocks went. I like to play with them. I was hoping you didn't lose them."

Changing the format of student work also adds an element of interest that can maintain enthusiasm. Cutting recording sheets so they are in the shape of a rocket or a mailbox breaks the expectation of the $8\frac{1}{2}$-by-11-inch sheet of paper. Engaging new senses, such as smell, can provide unexpected attention. Multimedia presentations can also create new interest. For example, one first-grade teacher created a slideshow on her computer of different architectural styles and famous buildings as a way to illustrate the use of shape and form. Using a computer and asking students to watch in pairs, students could select this station and take a virtual tour while describing elements of shapes they noticed.

Introducing topics in novel ways also piques interest. Treasure maps to find a new activity, a feely box to introduce a new manipulative, or a set of clues to help students make guesses about a new topic adds intrigue to learning. Adding a little surprise to our classrooms can be fun and helps children view mathematics in new ways, even when routines or materials are highly familiar.

There are many ways that teachers can support choice in their classrooms. Recognizing that we have choices about how to do so is also important. Consider this reflection of a kindergarten teacher as she considers how to encourage the block area as a choice for all students.

Teacher Reflection

One focal point for my students is the block area. I know for many students, this is what coming to kindergarten is all about. They cannot wait to dig in and build. I can think of so many students over the years who would have been happy to stay in the block area all day, every day.

I am a staunch advocate of the block area. Here students learn to share, negotiate, and cooperate. Almost hidden from them is the amount and kind of learning that is taking place. They learn about shape, balance, design, height, length, width, weight, symmetry, trial and error, how things take up space, what to do if a block they want is not available, and so much more. The language development alone is awe inspiring. In what they know as play, learning abounds. It is certainly an opportunity I want for all of my students.

This is one reason the block area is also so frustrating to me. Time and time again I see it dominated by the boys in my class. I know I need to address this for the sake of both girls and boys. I want all students to see the block area as a possible choice, but many, mostly girls, do not choose to spend any significant time there.

I asked my fellow kindergarten teachers about this. They were all too familiar with the situation I described. We agreed to set some time at a team meeting to talk about this. During our discussions we realized we ended up talking a lot about the management of choice time. We want our students to make choices, but too often preferences take over and children have a hard time breaking away from favorite centers. Also, some children avoid trying new experiences.

One of my colleagues told me he struggles with this every year. He said he wants to give his students choices, and thus he feels he is not honoring this if he makes them go to another area during choice time. We all acknowledged his feelings, but then went on to say that maybe we are not doing our students any favors if we do not manage this in some way.

In the end we agreed to try an experiment. We thought of a way we could use the block area as part of one of our new math units. We decided to structure an activity in the block area so that all students would have to take a turn. We called them building teams and gave each group of four students a specific task and time limitation for their work. The task was to design a three-story building by using no more than twenty-four of the assorted wooden blocks. We also gave them a 24-inch-by-24-inch paper mat to help organize their building. Their building could not extend beyond this area.

When I set this activity up in my classroom I could not believe the excitement. Some children had a hard time working as a team, but for the most part everyone worked very well. By requiring everyone to work in the block area, I had given permission to girls to become builders and architects. I was thrilled.

Earlier in this chapter another teacher helped us consider making good choices. Helping students self-monitor this criterion is not easy. What does it mean to make a good choice? Did the teachers described in the previous reflection make a good choice about the block area? Who decides? Yet, it is our role as teachers to support our students in their individual decision-making processes. Holding class meetings and individual conversations are strategies frequently used to support students' growth in this area. It is the establishment of expectations, trust, accountability, and security that can support even our youngest students as they make choices in our classrooms. As we get to know them as individuals and they get to know themselves as learners, we can encourage, direct, redirect, and applaud their efforts. All of this must happen within a full and lively classroom that changes in atmosphere and mood throughout the day and over the course of a year. Creating and maintaining learning laboratories like these presents unending questions as to how to balance the needs of the class as a whole with that of individual students. Ways to orchestrate this complex process is a challenge that teachers face every day.

Chapter 8
Managing Differentiated Instruction

*T*he role of a teacher has been compared to that of a coach or a conductor. Both lead a group of individuals with different talents and do not assume that those talents will be nourished in the same manner. Coaches and conductors know how to motivate each member of their group and aim to develop all of the participants' strengths and work on weaknesses. Practices are held with the whole group, identified subgroups, and individuals. Each athlete or musician has slightly different tasks to perfect and yet in the end, the goal is for everyone to work together to produce a unified and masterful performance on the field or in the concert hall.

Teachers also need to develop a sense of a unified classroom while addressing the individual students' strengths and weaknesses. In a differentiated classroom where students are more likely to be engaged in multiple tasks that support their different levels of learning readiness, learning styles, and interests, it can be challenging to also develop a mathematical learning community that comes together to build, discuss, and verify ideas. Yet this is a challenge we must address. Differentiated instruction is not the same thing as individualized instruction. We do not believe that students should learn mathematics in isolation or that they should be deprived of the joy of being an active member of a well-functioning community group.

Teachers must also figure out how to manage different tasks going on at the same time. They need to distribute and collect materials in ways that do not require a lot of time and effort. They are challenged to find ways to have other students engaged in meaningful activities while they work uninterrupted with a small group.

There is a necessity to create classroom spaces for noisy activities and quiet ones. Teachers need to think about the limitations of space, materials, and time as they make their plans. They must take the intricate components of classroom life and the complex needs of young learners and create a masterful learning environment.

While we do not want to promote the idea that a teacher must create a masterpiece each day in the classroom, we do believe that a well-managed classroom that supports students' learning while maintaining a sense of community is a masterpiece, one that begins to be composed the moment students walk in the door on the first day of school. Right from the beginning, values, routines, and expectations need to be established that will develop an environment conducive to learning in a differentiated classroom.

Classroom Space

Ample space can be a rare commodity in many classrooms. Careful decisions need to be made about how the limited space is used so that a variety of groupings and activities can be supported. The following guidelines may be helpful.

- If you only have room for desks or tables, choose tables. In general, tables are more useful because they can accommodate individual or small-group learning and provide additional space for shared materials. Round tables are more conducive to small-group work as they allow each person's face to be seen more easily. If tables are not available, consider arranging desks in clusters to form a similar work space to support collaboration and conversation.

- Without desks, you will need to provide storage bins for students to keep their materials and belongings. Decisions will need to be made about where these bins will be housed. Keeping them in clear sight and easily accessible from the various tables in the room are just two conditions to be considered. Establishing their function and any expectations for use or boundaries around private versus communal space and supplies are also matters of importance when making your plans.

- If you are asking your students to function without desks, think about doing the same yourself. While you also need ample personal storage areas, removing the teacher's desk may allow you to add an extra learning center or private space in the classroom. This may seem out of the question or unrealistic to you at first. Allowing yourself the chance to consider this option may lead to new possibilities for use of space in your classroom. It may also lead to reflecting on how space and arrangement may influence teaching and learning.

- If at all possible, designate an open area for morning meetings and whole-class discussions. A rug is usually placed in the corner of a classroom to create this special space. The rug allows children to sit on the floor, rather than bringing over chairs to a meeting place, and provides two walls for hanging items such as a calendar, attendance record, and number of days in school chart that tend to be part of morning routines. It is important that the meeting area be attractive and inviting and support children's sense of belonging to a community.

- Ample storage space is essential to helping classrooms be organized and efficient. As mentioned in Chapter 7, mathematics materials should be easily accessible for use and labeled to help ensure that they are returned properly. Just as with our drawers and closets at home, too many materials in too little space results in disorganization. Think about storing materials that are used only occasionally or during specific units in a supply closet or in higher cabinets in the room.

- Math manipulatives, games, and puzzles are certainly not the only tools used to learn mathematics. Along with these materials, designating a space for shared pencils, paper, scissors, glue, and a myriad of other art materials such as markers, crayons, and colored pencils also supports mathematical pursuits. Since these materials are used by all students throughout the day and across all subject matters, think about where and how to organize them; this decision is key to classroom efficiency and effectiveness. In many schools students are required to provide their own supplies of this nature. If this is the case where you teach, consider ways to make some or all of these materials more communal.

- Match features in the room to the type of work that will be done there. For example, placing the classroom library near the rug area makes sense as children like to relax when they read and there won't be other groups working in that area. Conversely, art materials should be placed away from the rug area to avoid unnecessary stains. In terms of mathematics, it makes sense to place a table adjacent to the storage area for the math materials. This placement allows one group of students to work with the materials without having to carry them too far. It also allows you and the students to place bins on a nearby tabletop when further organization or distribution of the materials is necessary.

- Consider traffic patterns. Make sure that students can travel easily from one table to another, to and from the classroom door, and to the various centers in the room. Make these pathways wide enough so that you and the students can move back and forth without asking other students to move or interrupting their work.

- Designating space for other vital material such as recording sheets or packets for student work, finished-work baskets, portfolios, or other assessment-related data is an additional consideration. For example, think about the use of hanging file folders. Some teachers use these as a way to organize papers for newly assigned work. Teachers sometimes place all of the activity sheets related to a new unit in an open file box that is labeled so that students can easily get a new sheet without asking. Files of this sort can also be used for collecting student work. Many teachers put a hanging file or open file box beside the place where they do their planning. In this way, teachers can easily access student work as they plan for the next day, prepare for student or parent conferences, or write report cards. They can also easily file students' work in portfolios or other data-type collections.

While these guidelines can help you to think about the arrangement of your room, most teachers need to find creative solutions to provide enough space for both groups and individuals to work. Consider the story of Odessa.

Odessa is a second-grade teacher who just completed her first year of teaching. Over the summer she thought about what worked during the year and what changes she wanted to make for the following year. One of the factors was the layout of the classroom. She realized that she had ample open tables and work areas where children mostly worked together, but few spaces where students could work more privately and be less distracted by what was happening around them. She remembered hearing about a simple concept called a private office where you overlap two manila folders and staple the doubled center panel together to make a trifold. The trifolds could stand up on desks or tables and provide private, separate spaces for students to work.

The following September, Odessa introduces this idea and the children are excited about having their own offices. As Seth explains, "My mom has an office at home, but I don't. Now I have one, too!" The students decorate both the outside and the inside of the folders with things you would find in an office: monthly calendars, plants (made from construction paper), and pictures of families brought from home. One girl writes, "Math is cool!" which reminds Odessa of how she puts inspirational quotes around her desk to keep her motivation high.

Sometimes she asks everyone in the class to get out their private offices. For example, during an assessment task she has the children set up their offices while they write story problems to share. She feels that this approach gives her a more accurate measure of what students are able to produce on their own. It also creates a bit of mystery and the children seem more excited about the problems they share. Spontaneously, some of the students begin to bring their "offices" to a table when they want to work independently without distractions. Over the course of the year she notices more variation in office use. A few of the children seem to use it quite often, while some only do so under direction. She is comfortable with the variety and believes that students are making appropriate choices for their learning styles.

That spring, a staff developer who understands the importance of giving teachers opportunities to share their personal success stories leads a systemwide professional development meeting for elementary teachers. The agenda is "Come share your best idea that has made a difference in how students learned this year." Odessa is excited to share her idea about creating private working spaces in her classroom. When she does so, many of her peers express interest in the idea. Colleagues from first and third grade even ask Odessa if they could visit her classroom to see how the children use their offices.

Courtney decides to plan a visit. She is a first-grade teacher who is struggling with meeting her students' needs this year. The range of the students' ability levels seems broader than usual; she also has more students on individualized education plans (IEPs). She thinks the private office would help her students learn through different models and visual cues. For example, Courtney knows that some of her students really need a number line in front of them to help them visualize the order of the numbers, while some students need domino-type configurations to help them develop better set recognition. In their private offices the students could make decisions about what they want to put in their spaces to support their learning. She can envision helping some students create sequence cards that they could hang in their offices to remind them of specific steps that are required for success. Also, these offices would be portable, allowing the students to easily bring their supportive tools to wherever they were working.

After the visit to Odessa's room, Courtney is even more enthusiastic and decides to implement this idea. Her students are also excited about the opportunity to decorate their own spaces and with some prompting are able to make decisions about what learning tools and models to include as well. Emil draws a picture of a trapezoid and writes, *chrapzoid,* as he tells his neighbor, "I always forget the name of this one." Margo adds a number line saying, "This helps with addition and stuff."

Courtney encourages the students to tape the tools to their folders. She wants them to be attached firmly, but she also wants tools that can be replaced as the students' learning evolves. If they wrote directly on the folders, Courtney believes her students would think of the tools as more permanent, as something they would always need. The offices give the students privacy and encourage them to take ownership of their own learning. They also help Courtney differentiate the scaffolding each student receives.

Respect for Differences

In order for differentiated classrooms to function well, all participants must know that respectful behavior is required. Everyone must respect others' learning needs and styles and realize that everyone has the right to have their needs met. Activities that identify and celebrate differences help students better understand why their classrooms are organized the way that they are. They also help students get to know themselves and each other better. This knowledge allows students to better support each other individually and to feel more connected as a community of learners.

In one kindergarten class, children draw pictures of themselves early in September. Placing these self-portraits up on the bulletin board to be shared helps these new students claim the classroom as their own. Under the title "Our Class," these pictures portray their oneness, while honoring them as individuals. Over the course of the year, portraits are made again and serve as a way for students to compare their drawing skills and update their self-images. In spring, as more literacy skills are emerging, these students also draw themselves doing something. By completing the phrases "I am (who?). I am (doing what?)" kindergartners add words to their portraits.

In one class, the teacher asks the children to think about what they are learning about in math to connect with this literacy and self-discovery activity. The students brainstorm words that describe what they are doing when they learn mathematics. Then they will each record an individual response, for example, working, making a pattern, drawing a shape, playing, reading, adding, counting, building, weighing, comparing, taking a survey, seeing shapes, cooking, matching, concentrating, measuring, seeing how much, and answering. One child added the word *growing*. He said, "I am growing, and when I get measured it shows." (See Figure 8–1.)

A second-grade teacher has students complete a survey form sometime during the first week of school. The form is called *What Matches You?* and provides twenty-five different "I statements" for students to consider. (See Figure 8–2 on page 172; see also Blackline Masters.) Some of the items are general statements about learning, such as "I need quiet when I work." Other statements focus on mathematics, such as "I am better at addition than subtraction."

As we learn from the teacher's reflection on the next page, this form can spark conversations about learning and mathematics.

Figure 8–1   *This child's drawing related mathematics to growing taller.*

What Matches You?

Try to find two classmates to fit each description. Have them write their initials in the box they match. No one may initial more than three boxes on one sheet.

I learn best through hands-on experiences.	I like to solve problems.	I prefer to work alone.	I find it helpful to write about my mathematical ideas.	I sometimes get confused when others explain their thinking.
I like face clocks better than digital ones.	I like to measure things.	I use drawings to understand a problem.	I learn best when the teacher writes on the board.	I find Unifix cubes more helpful than base ten blocks.
I am better at subtraction than addition.	I like building things.	I need quiet when I work.	I find base ten blocks more helpful than Unifix cubes.	I prefer to work with others.
I know my basic facts well.	I like digital clocks better than face clocks.	I am better at addition than subtraction.	I like geometry.	I like to find different ways to solve problems.
I like to brainstorm ideas with a group and then follow up alone.	I like logic games and puzzles.	I want rules for solving problems.	I would like to use a calculator all of the time.	I like collecting data and making graphs.

Figure 8–2 *A survey form for second graders, What Matches You?*

Teacher Reflection

For a couple of years I used a form like this one during the first day or two of school. It got students walking around and talking to each other and learning something about their classmates. I used to put in items such as "I like to play baseball" or "I like chocolate ice cream." This year I decided to focus more on learning. I decided that students would eventually find out about each other's recreational and food preferences, but that they might never talk about how they each learn. Also, I was hoping this activity might help them to gain an intuitive sense of why I strive to provide differentiated learning opportunities in our classroom.

The responses took somewhat longer to be formulated. They used to know right away whether they liked chocolate, but deciding if they wanted rules for solving problems required some reflection. Some students were amazed to find that everybody didn't think a digital clock was better than a face clock and others were pleased to find someone else who preferred to work alone.

After we did this activity, we talked about the differences in our classroom and how it was important to respect these different ways of learning. We made a list of what we learned. Marcus said, "I have to be quiet sometimes so that Billy can think." Jamie said, "I might want to try using base ten blocks." Ellie said, "It's good that we are different. Otherwise, it would be boring." It felt wonderful to hear the students articulate these ideas.

Immediately following this conversation we began our first differentiated learning activity. I introduced it by saying, "Many times in our classroom we will be doing different activities from each other. Why do you think that is so?" Several hands popped up and I called on Ricardo who said, "Because we are different." I couldn't have been more pleased.

Routines

Routines serve several purposes in a classroom. Once students recognize ways to get into groups, distribute assignment papers, put away materials, get in line, and walk in the hallway, these activities will occur quickly and efficiently. Much of the first weeks of school are spent creating these routines and making sure that everyone can follow them. Though considerable time and effort is needed to get them launched, once established they are adhered to with minimal energy and teacher supervision. This is particularly important in a differentiated classroom where students are expected to manage themselves, more frequently and often for longer durations, while the teacher is working with other students.

Routines also instill feelings of safety and security. When the same procedures are followed on a daily or weekly basis, students understand what is expected of them and can predict what will happen next. Such regularity helps students to feel emotionally safe in our schools and thus more able to participate in the learning process. Established routines also create community. As children identify and describe the ways in which their classroom runs, they are forming their understanding of the unique culture of their classroom.

In differentiated mathematics instruction, each group of children may be working with different mathematical materials, but they need to gather and return the materials to the math center in the same manner. The importance of putting them away in the same way you found them is stressed as one of the ways we respect all members of the class.

Figuring out how to share materials is an important aspect of developing respect. What happens when someone else is using a material a child desires or needs? Too often young children grab without asking. This quickly leads to hurt feelings and destroyed work. Role-playing ways to acknowledge these types of conflicts and successful ways of resolving them is critical. Mathematically it can also lead to new learning when a teacher asks, "If all of the hexagons in the pattern block set are being used, what else can you use to fill in the puzzle outline?" Though initially a child may not see selecting different blocks as a viable solution to either the math work or the social conflict, in time, seeing the relationships in the blocks can lead to exciting new opportunities for solving all kinds of problems.

Routines also provide common experiences that help create a sense of community. It seems all teachers, regardless of their students' ages, have some beginning-of-the-day ritual. In many classes morning work, or as one second-grade class calls it, office time, is used to let children transition smoothly into a new day. Such work provides the time to pick up from where students left off the day before, helps frame or launch new challenges for the day, or provides additional practice in areas of need. While students dive right in, the teacher can take care of greeting each student individually and any housekeeping chores such as attendance, lunch count, and communications from home. As teachers are mindful of how best to use every minute of the day, sometimes students take on some of the housekeeping responsibilities. Attendance and lunch counts are wonderful opportunities for utilizing new mathematics concepts such as counting, computation, money, and data collection.

Morning routines can also be customized for differentiation. Each morning one kindergarten class includes two types of calendar activities in its daily routines. One is the familiar community classroom experience in which children gather on the rug near a posted calendar and determine the new date. The other is a more individualized activity.

The community calendar time is often done in song, as children sing the days of the week and then figure out the day and date for today. In some classes the teacher always conducts this part of the morning meeting. In other classes, being the calendar helper rotates each day. Encouraging one child at a time to lead the class in this routine offers many opportunities for the teacher to differentiate the exercise for the calendar helper. For example, Ken is the calendar helper on January fourteenth. His teacher knows he has been working hard to recall the names of all the -teen numbers. After he leads the class in song, Ken's teacher asks him to predict which number he will turn over on the calendar to reveal the number/date for today. Ken begins to hesitate and looks up at his teacher. "How can you figure this out?" she asks. Ken's classmates are familiar with this type of question and do not try to chime in. Waiting is never easy, but it is a sign of respect. Ken points his finger at the 1 on the calendar and begins to count as he moves his finger along in the same manner he would read a book. "Eight, nine, ten, eleven, twelve, thirteen," he pauses. "Thirteen, thirteen, thirteen," he says more silently to himself. Some of Ken's classmates are just on the verge of shouting out, but their teacher puts her palm up in their direction. "Fourteen," Ken exclaims and turns the card over to confirm his prediction.

This class also uses individual calendars as a way to learn more about the calendar and to give children additional opportunities to practice writing numbers. Each student is given a monthly calendar sheet. In September the teacher chooses to have all of the numbers dotted for the dates Monday through Friday; the weekend days are filled in completely. Each day the children trace the new number. As the months go on, fewer numbers are dotted or even shown at all on the grid. This supports the growth the children make in writing numbers and their familiarity with how a calendar works. The teacher can customize these calendars as she deems appropriate.

As children fill in the next number on the calendar they then show their work to their teacher who in turn asks them a calendar question. For this teacher, this additional step makes the learning opportunities even more child centered. She might ask a student such as Ken to count the number of days on the calendar aloud for her. She might ask another student to predict what number will come on a day later in the week or next week. Questions focus on number recognition, patterns, computation skills, and skip-counting; concepts such as *today, tomorrow,* and *yesterday*; or on indicating when a special event might occur. In this way the calendar can also begin to be seen as a representation of time passing. As we learn from the following reflection, taking advantage of learning opportunities such as calendar questions is one teacher's way of trying to maximize learning in her class.

The whole calendar thing grew in my kindergarten class over the course of the winter. I usually have what I call "a morning question" when my students come in the door. Sometimes it's something they can do independently such as responding to a survey question. Sometimes it's an activity like the calendar questions that I use to gather some assessment data. By coincidence two students with very different abilities came in one after the other. The first child, though eventually successful, struggled to identify that the day's date was January 6 when shown a calendar with the numbers 1 through 5 recorded. The next student responded to that question quickly and then added, "I can count by sixes, six, twelve, eighteen, twenty-four, thirty, thirty-six. Oh wait, thirty-six won't be on the calendar." I was struck by how this simple activity met this broad range of abilities and decided to add it to the calendar routines.

Being able to ask a range of questions at a moment's notice is not easy. With practice I have become better at this. Knowing my students and the mathematics that I want them to focus on helps me identify questions. Seeing this in action makes me realize that a lot of ground can be covered in a short amount of time so long as students are familiar with the routine and know how to carry on as I ask similar questions to their classmates.

This routine builds as the year progresses, but it doesn't happen every day. Being patient and flexible are dispositions both students and teachers need to develop!

Grouping Students

Another way to maximize learning is to think critically about group work. Though whole-group teaching can be very powerful and some teachers believe it promotes equality by ensuring that all students are taught the same lessons, it is not always the most effective way to learn. As we have explored throughout this book, differentiation is focused on finding the most effective ways of meeting our students' various needs. Organizing students into groups can promote individual learning.

Grouping for differentiated instruction is different than working in groups. Group work has been long recognized as a way to break up the whole-class instructional pattern, to engage students more actively in their learning, and to provide greater opportunities for communication and social interactions. Traditionally, each group may be completing the same task. The teacher rotates among the groups, supporting their work, and informing their thinking. While a useful instructional strategy, grouping for differentiated instruction is even more intentional.

Within differentiated instruction, grouping is flexible; that is, groups are formed with a specific focus and then reconfigured when a new purpose is identified. The formation of groups may be based on readiness, learning styles, or interests and can be heterogeneous or homogenous. Groups may be formed for a day, a week, or a few weeks. The flexible grouping keeps students from being labeled and allows them to work with a variety of their peers.

It takes time and thought to group students. Thinking about why you are grouping and whether groups will be designed around a specific learning goal, learning style, interest, product, or behavior is all part of the process. Identifying the appropriate size of the groups, the amount of time the group should work together, and the composition of the group are all decisions that need to be made. Teachers also need to think about how groups and their materials will be identified and organized.

Sometimes groups are formed at random. Some teachers keep a deck of cards with stickers on them. If four groups are needed and there are twenty children in the class, five copies of four different kinds of stickers will be used. The deck is shuffled and children randomly select a card. All the like stickers form a new group. Sometimes these stickers correspond to tables or areas of the room and as children pick a card they know right away where to go to meet their new group.

Sometimes students choose their own groups or partnerships. Allowing students to make this choice is one of the ways we can share our classroom authority. Many teachers find that they are most comfortable with this option when groups are formed for a short period of time or on the basis of interest.

More often, differentiated instruction requires teachers to form groups intentionally; that is, teachers match students specifically in ways to best meet learning needs. One second-grade teacher frequently changes student groups in her classroom. She keeps two large magnetic boards resting on the chalk tray to help her organize this process. For each board she has a set of name-tags backed with magnetic tape. When she plans an activity for which new groups are required, she moves the names on the board according to her criteria. As she explains, "I used to do this on paper. When the grouping was obvious, this worked fine. Sometimes, though, I find it challenging to make groups and change my mind several times. With the board, I can try out several formations easily. Then when I am done, the list is already there for my students to see."

Many teachers keep a log of the groups that are formed during the first few weeks of school. The log can serve as a place to keep notes about groups that function particularly well together or partnerships that seem to require more supervision. A teacher can also make sure that everyone has the opportunity to work with all the other classmates during these first weeks of community building. It can also be worthwhile to note how the groups were formed so that over time, students work according to readiness, learning styles, and interests.

Though a child might become upset or feel isolated at any time, forming partners and groups can heighten such feelings. Some children may wonder why they are in one group versus another. Others may worry about being chosen or welcomed. Concern for isolation, safety, comfort, friendships, and working relationships must always be part of the grouping process. Whether in math or any other subject, it is essential to consciously keep children's social-emotional development in mind.

Time with Individual Students

There are times when teachers and students need and want to work one on one. While some may consider this a luxury in a busy classroom, many teachers find such work to be one of the most enlightening aspects of their day. Working with an individual student can be a time for getting to know the child better, to assess a specific skill or competence, or to just dig deeper together on a problem. Sitting side by side can be rewarding and informative to both the student and teacher and can help nourish a supportive, trusting relationship so necessary to teaching and learning.

By building expectations for different learning activities to occur simultaneously, differentiated instruction supports opportunities to work with individual students. Other students do not expect the teacher to always be available to them and their ability to work independently from the teacher has been developed. Teacher-student partnerships become just one of the various configurations within the classroom. Such acceptance also supports longer individual interactions such as when interviews are conducted, some tutoring is needed, or particular follow up to a lesson or task is required.

The image of keeping plates spinning in the air is one to which many teachers can relate. We work tirelessly to keep every child engaged and learning. Sometimes, even in our best attempts, plates fall. In these moments it is important to have time carved out in our day and classroom to work with individual students. Sometimes we can anticipate a falter and a quick spin or adjustment will help the child get back on track. Sometimes more intensive work is needed.

Such was the case at the end of a geometry unit in one kindergarten class. Students had been working for a month on shape recognition, properties of shapes, and composing and decomposing shapes. The teacher was feeling very pleased by all that had been accomplished. She felt confident as she asked the students to work individually to complete one of the unit's assessment tasks. The task asked them to use pattern blocks to fill in two different outlined shapes.

The students had worked repeatedly with pattern blocks during this geometry unit, as well as earlier in the year when working with patterns. It seemed that every day the pattern blocks were a part of math workshop. She knew many of her students had begun to internalize the relationships among the pieces in the set. "I know, two reds make a yellow," she might hear them say. She was excited that during the geometry unit that this fact was translated into "Two trapezoids make a hexagon" or "A diamond is the same as two triangles." She did not expect all her students to see these part-whole relationships, but was excited that many children in the class had an initial grasp of this idea. At the same time, she predicted that everyone would be able to easily complete the first fill-in example because it was the shape of a hexagon. She was interested to see how they would tackle the larger trapezoid.

Directions were given to the whole class initially, but due to a lack of materials, she had set up work areas in four different parts of the room for children to work individually. She directed them to bring their completed work to her and then she would pick the next students to give it a try. As the four children worked, other math activities were soaking up the interests of their classmates. Some children worked with geoboards and shape cards, while others worked with geoblocks, matching like faces. Still others continued to work on tangram and parquetry puzzles and two children worked on the computer with software that had become a class favorite during the geometry unit. The teacher felt she could easily move between the four students doing the assessment task and the other children.

In fact, all went very well, until later that evening when she had time to truly look at the completed work. She did not observe each student completing the task, but was confident that the work matched what she did know about her students' understanding of composing and decomposing shapes. She was very pleased; the papers seemed to document their complete understanding. Then she noticed Vanessa's and Stuart's responses. Vanessa's work showed lots of gaps or holes in four of the five fill-ins. The only example that was filled completely was the hexagon that she had covered with a hexagon. Stuart's work suggested that he disregarded the boundary lines. (See Figure 8–3.) What went wrong? How much she wished she had watched these two students as they worked.

The next day the teacher planned time to be able to meet individually with Vanessa and Stuart. In preparation she thought about what could have been the cause of difficulty for these two students. She wondered if the directions were clear or if fine-motor or visual perception played a factor in their finished work. Did they understand what it meant to "fill in"? She knew that the concept was covered explicitly during the unit. She recalled talking with the class about what it meant to fill in space. They had agreed that everything had to be within the lines of the puzzles they were working with and that no spaces could be left when they were done. Had she noticed Vanessa or Stuart having difficulty with this concept prior to this assessment task?

Figure 8–3 *Stuart's work showed overlaps and unfilled space.*

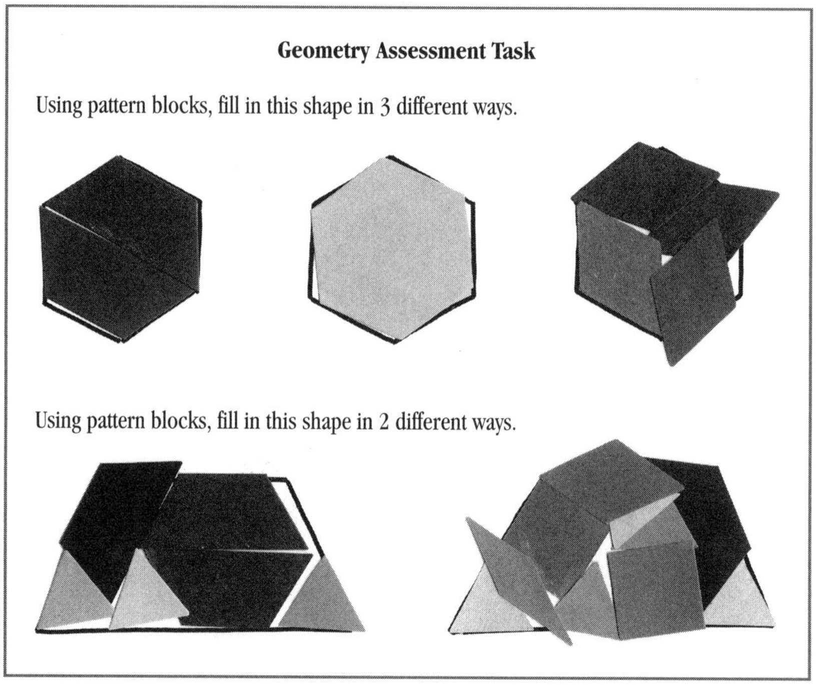

Geometry Assessment Task

Using pattern blocks, fill in this shape in 3 different ways.

Using pattern blocks, fill in this shape in 2 different ways.

She began with Stuart and had the following conversation.

Teacher: Tell me about this work you did yesterday.

Stuart: I filled these shapes [the hexagons and large trapezoids] with two different ways and three different ways.

Teacher: Are they filled in?

Stuart: Yes!

Teacher: How do you know?

Stuart: When I . . . when I put all these shapes in, it filled in. I used two trapezoids [pointing to his work]. I used one big hexagon. I used four diamonds. I used three trapezoids and three triangles. I used one of this shape [pointing to the thin rhombus]. I used five triangles [counting his work as he spoke], two squares, one diamond, and one trapezoid.

Feeling confident that Stuart was pleased with his work the teacher did not want to focus on it too much. She was more curious to see if visual perception was a factor here, as she perceived that Stuart worked extra hard adding more pieces than necessary to make sure it was all filled in completely. To tease this out a bit, she brought over a game board from *The Six Hexagons* game. The game is part of the Investigations in Number, Data, and Space kindergarten curriculum (Economopoulos et al. 1998) and Stuart and his classmates had played it often. She asked Stuart to show her with the blocks, not paper cutouts, how to fill in the hexagons in different ways. As he worked she asked, "How many triangles do you think you need?" Stuart thought it might take five. He got five triangles and put them in his hand. As he worked to place them carefully on the game board, he stopped and announced, "I thought it would take five, but it is six."

Next the teacher asked him about the blue rhombus (diamond). Stuart said he thought it might take three, filled in the hexagon, and got a big smile on his face. Following this success, the teacher thought he was ready to think again about his previous work.

Teacher: Let's look back at your work from yesterday. You used diamonds then, too.

Stuart: I used four [looking at his sheet]. I just wanted to fill one little space in. I did it a different way.

Teacher: Does it matter that part of the diamond is sticking out?

Stuart: It might be OK. . . . It's OK like that.

Teacher: When you fill something in can you go outside the line?

Stuart: It's OK with me.

Teacher: This time I don't want you to go outside the line.

Stuart: OK.

The teacher gives Stuart a blank paper like the one he completed yesterday. Since she would be right there to see his results, she asks him not to glue the paper shapes in place as he did yesterday. Stuart works and completes each fill-in task correctly.

Teacher: Do you have any white space?

Stuart: No. And I stayed in the lines like when I try to color.

This exchange tells us a lot about what can happen when a teacher takes time to analyze work and regroup based on need. After taking the time to work with Stuart she believes that his playful, creative side overruled any sense of constraints about filling in space that was discussed in class. She was pleased that she took the time to sort this out. She is not convinced that Stuart completely grasps the concept of composing and decomposing shapes, but he is further along than the assessment task showed originally.

Ragged Time

When students are involved in different tasks and work at different rates, this creates what some educators refer to as *ragged time*. Helping each student transition to another appropriate activity when the assigned task is completed is not good use of a teacher's time, so it is important to have activities that students go to naturally. Such activities are sometimes known as *sponges*, as they soak up the extra time between early and late finishers. In the literacy curriculum this often translates to free reading or journal writing. It is important to have similar choices within the mathematics curriculum.

A number of options are possible and different choices may be available on different days or within different units. For example, a first-grade teacher begins a miniunit on sorting by having students explore Venn diagrams with the attribute blocks. After a couple of days she introduces the *Guess My Label* game. She first plays the game with the whole class. She draws a large Venn diagram on the board and uses paper replications of the blocks backed with magnetic tape. She also puts magnetic tape on both sides of the label cards. She picks two labels and places one face down by each ring. The students take turns naming a block and she places it in its correct location within the diagram. The children are always excited when she turns over the label cards to confirm that they have guessed the labels correctly.

For a couple of days the students play the game again as a whole class, but she invites student pairs to take her part in leading the game. In this way, students are able to practice this role with support, before doing it alone. Once she is confident that each child knows how to play the game, sets of attribute blocks and rings are available for use when other sorting work is completed. A few days later she reads *The Button Box* by Margarette S. Reid and Sarah Chamberlain (1990), a book about a boy who explores the treasures in his grandmother's button box. Following the story children sort buttons in a variety of ways and boxes of buttons are then placed in the math center as well. Now the students have two unit-based activities between which they may choose when their work is finished.

Some teachers set out a collection of unit-related literature books when beginning a new topic. These books can be placed in a special location and explored when the day's specific math task is completed. Students may also be directed to problem decks, a puzzle table, computer software, menu choices, centers, and stations. All sponge activities don't have to be related to the current topics; in fact, bringing back some favorite choices can be a way to maintain skills. What's important is that students know what to do when they finish their work and that they continue to be involved in mathematical explorations throughout the time designated for mathematics.

Whole-Class Work

Whole-class lessons remain important. Often the notion of all of the students working on the exact same thing at the same time seems contradictory to the notion of differentiated instruction. As we have seen throughout the stories shared from various classrooms, whole-class lessons are vital. They provide common experiences and expose students to a greater array of thinking. They help develop common vocabulary and a sense of community.

They offer an efficient means for introducing new content that can then be continued later working in small groups, in pairs, or individually. There is a time and a place for each form of instruction; knowing your intent and figuring out the best way to meet your goals is what is critical.

Even during the lesson, teachers have ways to support individual needs and strengths. Often a quick think/pair/share time can lead to a more successful whole-class endeavor. Many students prefer being able to stop and reflect or need the support of a partner in a larger group setting. Waiting before responses are given, encouraging several students to respond, and teaching students how to connect their comments to those of the previous speakers are all ways to support whole-class discussions.

Though differentiated instruction emphasizes meeting individual needs, we must not lose sight of the importance of the collective experience in this process. Participation in a learning community is powerful. What we learn together can far exceed what any one individual can learn alone or any single teacher can teach. Finding ways to bring a class of students together to share their experiences is an essential component of differentiated classrooms. Even when students are working on separate tasks, there needs to be designated times for students to gather and share their new knowledge, ideas, and strategies.

Whether in class meetings or debriefing sessions, students require time together to report findings, review ideas, and raise new questions. Within these discussions, students can glimpse how others take on new challenges and make sense of new material. When students have not worked on exactly the same task, sharing can seem less important to them, to some, maybe even irrelevant or confusing. Teachers need to orchestrate these conversations in ways that build commonalities while respecting and celebrating differences.

Looking for common ground is a place to start. That's why we always identify the curriculum goal or standard before we design tasks, form groups, and make other decisions about customizing instruction. Refocusing students on the common threads of their individual learning experiences helps them to see that it makes sense to share. Sometimes simply asking students to describe one new thing they learned today, this week, or during this unit can both honor and link individual experiences. Recording personal responses in a concept web may unearth more similarity and common ground than first perceived.

Class discussions can focus on process as well as content. Sometimes, talking about how we organize our data, visualize a relationship, or represent our thinking may be more informative than sharing an answer or a solution. Further, as children learn more about each other's thinking, they are able to more authentically validate frustrations, make note of growth, and celebrate success.

As teachers gain experience with differentiated instruction, they identify their own ways to organize the classroom space, to build student awareness and respect for differences, to develop classroom routines, to form groups, to work with students individually, to provide interesting activities for students who finish early, and to lead whole-group lessons and discussions. They develop their own methods for supporting the important work of differentiation, for building the masterpiece of a well-functioning classroom that meets individual needs while maintaining classroom community.

Chapter 9

Teaching with the Goal of Differentiation
Ten Ways to Sustain Your Efforts

$\mathcal{H}$opefully, you too believe that it is essential to differentiate mathematical instruction and now have some additional ideas about what that means and how it might look in your classroom. Even with this recognition and vision, however, differentiated instruction is a long-term goal and working toward such a goal is often difficult to sustain. Just as you would require encouragement, reminders, and support to make other significant changes in behavior, you need to find ways to help your differentiation lens stay in focus, to act on your belief that children's readiness, learning styles, and interests should inform the ways in which you teach. So what can you do to keep your spirit for differentiation high? Here are ten suggestions.

1. Identify Where You Already Provide Differentiation.

It's important to remember that differentiation in mathematics is not brand new. You are already grouping students in some ways, working with students individually, and making modifications to meet students' needs. The idea is that now these decisions will be more preplanned and made with more specific needs in mind. Rather than making changes after a lesson has been problematic, you begin to make adjustments in the planning process. Sometimes just tweaking a familiar activity allows the learning experience to be more on target, to be deeper and richer for students.

Some teachers begin by thinking about the students who are the least successful with the curriculum as presented. Perhaps there are three or four students in your class who need much more support or challenge. Putting the effort into making lessons work for these students may take more time in the beginning, but the end result will be well worth it. As one teacher expressed, "Now I work more ahead of time, so I don't have to work so hard when I am teaching."

Don't lose sight of what you can do and, in fact, what you are doing already. Whether you make differentiated instruction in mathematics a priority or not, you still need to assess what students know and align your curriculum to national, state, and local standards. These assessment and alignment processes jump-start your goal of differentiation. It is valuable to do them anyway and they give you a secure foundation on which to base instructional decisions and to build activities that better meet individual needs. Be clear about what new work is needed and what is required already. As we learn from the following teacher reflection, this clarity is not always present.

Teacher Reflection

I spent all day Sunday getting ready for these new mathematics activities I wanted to try. I had been to a workshop on differentiated instruction and decided to do some things differently in the measurement unit we were about to begin. I had given my students a pre-assessment on Friday and spent much of Sunday morning looking at their work and rereading my school's curriculum along with a few other resources. It was a beautiful day and my husband and children were headed out for a hike. I wanted to go with them and I was feeling grouchy that my school work kept me from joining them. I was beginning to wish that I had never started this work. I complained to my husband who said, "But you always spend a Sunday working on stuff before you start a new unit. Is this like the house cleaning?"

I had to laugh at myself then. Just yesterday I had been complaining about how much work it was to have his parents to dinner. At noon we had cleaned the house and gone food shopping and hadn't even started to cook yet. My husband had been clear then, too. He reminded me that we always went food shopping and cleaned the house on Saturday mornings whether his parents were coming to dinner or not. How did I forget that? When I looked at it that way, the additional time wasn't that great and it turned out to be a lovely evening. I sometimes start out new projects with a bit of pessimism. It's important for me to remember why I am doing something and to be clear about what the actual "costs" are.

2. Recognize Where You Are Along the Journey.

Many teachers provide a task in September that students complete again sometime in November or December. The comparison of these work samples provides students and parents with concrete examples of growth. Such evidence can boost morale, particularly for students who struggled initially or who may not realize how their abilities have changed. Just as initial benchmarks help students appreciate what they have gained, teachers also benefit from learning how their teaching abilities have adapted, sharpened, broadened, or transformed. So, before you begin your new commitment to differentiated mathematics instruction, you might want to self-assess your current level of differentiation in mathematics.

We encourage you to make a copy of the "Self Assessment of Differentiation Practices" form. (See Figure 9–1; see also Blackline Masters.) Complete it now and put it in a place where you can find it at a later date. If you keep a personal calendar, mark a date two to three months from now when you will complete this form for a second time. (You may also want to note where you are putting your original response!) Most teachers who do this find that there are significant differences between their responses. For some teachers, just knowing they are going to complete the form again encourages them to try some new instructional strategies.

3. Start Small and Build Up Your Differentiation Muscles.

Once teachers recognize the need for differentiated instruction, they sometimes feel as if they have to differentiate every lesson for every student. This would be an overwhelming task, especially if differentiated mathematics instruction is a new practice for you. Just as if you were starting a new exercise program, it's best to start slowly and extend your goals as you build your skills and experience success. Exercising too much, too soon can result in injuries, frustration, and a sense of failure. These repercussions cause many who make an initial commitment to fitness to conclude that "exercise just isn't right for me." So, begin slowly and increase the differentiation in your mathematics teaching as your skills and confidence grow.

One way to start is to begin with the mathematics strand you believe you know the best or the one that would benefit the most from differentiation strategies. For most teachers these are one and the same: *number* and *operations*. This is the topic that gets the

Rate your agreement with each of the following statements.
1 – disagree strongly 2 – disagree somewhat 3 – agree somewhat 4 – agree strongly

I feel confident in my ability to facilitate the learning of mathematics at my grade level.	1 2 3 4
I can challenge my most mathematically able students.	1 2 3 4
I know how to support my least mathematically able students.	1 2 3 4
I can meet students' individual needs in mathematics as well as or better than I can in literacy.	1 2 3 4
I have enough knowledge of mathematics to support a variety of models, representations, and procedures in my classroom.	1 2 3 4

Rate the likelihood of the following activities occurring within a week of mathematical instruction.
1 – very unlikely 2 – somewhat unlikely 3 – somewhat likely 4 – very likely

I work with students individually.	1 2 3 4
Students are grouped by readiness.	1 2 3 4
Students are grouped by interest.	1 2 3 4
Students are grouped by learning preferences.	1 2 3 4
Different students are working with different materials and tasks.	1 2 3 4

Check off each instructional strategy that you have tried in your teaching of mathematics. Give yourself two points for each checkmark.

☐ Transformation of tasks to make them more open-ended
☐ RAFT
☐ Learning station
☐ Menu
☐ Think Tac Toe
☐ Compacting
☐ Tiered task

Total Score: _____

Scores range from 10 to 54.
Are you comfortable with where you are on this continuum of change? What next step(s) do you want to take?

Figure 9–1 *Self-Assessment of Differentiation Practices.*

greatest attention in the elementary grades, and if you have been teaching for a few years, the one for which you probably have the greatest number of supplementary resources. Once you have selected a strand, you can narrow your focus to a unit, a series of lessons, or a particular outcome, for example developing "strategies for basic addition facts" (NCTM 2006, 13). Work with number and operations often yields the widest range of abilities among students. Perhaps because the skill set is so familiar to most teachers, student abilities are often apparent quickly and can be challenging to address within the same activity. This difficulty is in contrast, for example, to the way student abilities seem to be addressed more easily within the data analysis and probability strand.

Most primary teachers find that all students can easily be engaged with the same task of conducting a survey if choice is given about what data are collected and how the data are organized. Interest will influence the topic chosen. Readiness will impact how the question is stated. For example, *Did you like the school field trip or the school recital best?* is much easier to negotiate than *What did you like best about the school field trip?* Learning preferences may influence how students keep track of the data collected and make sure that everyone has the opportunity to respond. Readiness, learning styles, and interests may inform how the information is displayed and what conclusions are drawn. Most important, these differences occur naturally and do not require much teacher intervention. This is less likely to be the case with number and operations. The following reflection shows how choosing a familiar strategy and topic can be a positive way to begin.

Teacher Reflection

I decided that I would try to incorporate some of the instructional strategies I use in reading in my mathematics program. I often select books with a similar theme that span a wide range of reading levels. In this way I feel like I can place the right book in the hands of every student, books that will challenge their levels of comprehension, while being well within the instructional range of their skill levels for reading. At the same time, we can have a class discussion about themes that emerge in each story and children can be regrouped to share with students who may not have read the same book. There is usually enough commonality to sustain a dynamic conversation. If I have selected nonfiction material, students can compare details and share facts, thus allowing everyone to benefit by the different books read.

Trying to set up a similar dynamic for math has not been as straight-forward, but I wanted to give it a try. Focusing on number and operations I selected a story problem and then created three versions of it. The structure of each problem was the same. I created a story around a set of twins who each earned an allowance for doing chores. Within the three versions of the problem, I differentiated the amount of money each child earned, the difference between their earnings, and how the problem was worded. I predetermined which students would answer each problem. Students initially worked alone and then I paired them with other students who were working on the exact problem. Once I felt as though everyone had solved and compared with at least one other classmate, I grouped children in triads with one student representing each type of problem.

In this new configuration, students were asked to share their problems, answers, and solution strategies. My hope was that each student would act as the expert for the problem they were presenting to the group. Once everyone had familiarized themselves with the three problems, I wanted them to discuss what was the same or different in each problem. This seemed to work well as children made comments such as "In your problem, Tammy and Tommy each made a lot more money." "Tammy saved more money than Tommy in my problem." "We all used take away to get the answers."

This was a small step for me, but it was one that really worked. I could see doing something like this about once a week without too much trouble. The children were successful with their individual problems, but also were exposed to other levels of thinking. Maybe next time I could change problem settings as well, choosing contexts that I knew would appeal to different students' interests.

4. Capitalize on Anticipation.

Teachers are often thinking about what happens next. Sometimes this anticipation can be to our benefit. Sometimes it can lead to trouble. We need to think about how to use anticipation to our best advantage.

On the positive side, being able to anticipate the time and resources a specific activity will require is very helpful. Haven't we all started a lesson only to realize that we had not made enough copies of the activity packet, or that there really wasn't enough time to complete a new lesson because it took much longer to launch than expected and now the students have to be in gym class? Decisions that avoid situations like these come with experience, though even the most seasoned veteran makes similar errors in judgment from time to time. Not having quite the right resources can derail a potentially successful differentiated lesson, so it's important to make sure that manipulatives, worksheets or packets, directions and pieces for games, and any supplies or tools required are readily available. We have to consider purpose and quantity, need for replacement during completion of the task, and the mathematical implications of the types of manipulatives or technology we are offering to students.

Visualizing a future event is part of anticipation. It is important to think about how we envision a lesson unfolding. Keeping in mind our goal(s), where a given lesson falls in the learning progression, and the current levels of our students' understanding, what responses might we anticipate? What leaps in their understanding might occur? What questions might the children ask? What possible errors might they make and what misconceptions might they have? Drawing on our knowledge and past experiences can help us anticipate our responses to new insights, questions, errors, and incomplete understandings that arise. We consider what distractions or diversions may present themselves and identify key questions that we want to ask. We determine ways to scaffold learning and plan groups that will work well together and support the students in their pursuits. Basically, by trying to do as much work up front as possible, teachers reduce potential roadblocks to learning and increase the likelihood that they are available to work with a small group or support individual students once a learning activity has begun.

Establishing blocks of uninterrupted time so that students can truly dig into the task is also helpful. Check your schedule. Many teachers comment that any time they want to start a new unit or are planning a debriefing session, they want all students present. Many students receive support outside of class and it is important to be mindful of what is happening for each student as you prepare new lessons and set a schedule. Also, build in extra time for students to explore any new materials in the lesson. Captivating models and tools such as pattern blocks, handheld clocks, and real coins are distracting when they are first introduced.

As we anticipate, we need to be fresh and ready for new challenges and possibilities. One way that anticipation can lead us into trouble is the overanticipation of behavior. It is only natural for teachers to want to set up the most positive learning environment for students. Keeping everyone's behavior in check can be part of this mind-set. Sadly we can all describe a time in our classrooms when a student's behavior has overshadowed or impeded learning. To avoid this from happening, many teachers overly anticipate how a specific student might respond and then provide unnecessary scaffolding. Though a natural instinct, this form of anticipation can be shortsighted and limit student potential. As we strive for differentiation in our math classrooms, part of our goal is to support students in all areas of their development. Many teachers have found that when they create tailor-made assignments, negative behavior is diminished. So, for example, under new and more comfortable learning conditions, students may no longer need supportive prompts or a separate space to work. Also, even students who have had difficulty working together in the past can learn to appreciate more about each other's strengths.

Many teachers lament about how impossible it is to differentiate mathematics instruction. This attitude and worry can defeat them before they even begin. Part of anticipation is looking forward. Try and visualize how you want your students to succeed, how you want them to develop a rich understanding of and appreciation for mathematics while gaining self-confidence in their abilities. Get excited about the possibilities and visualize yourself as the key ingredient in making this happen. Change is scary, risky, and can be problematic. It also can be exciting, rewarding, and fun.

5. Expect Surprises.

In Chapter 1 we presented a lesson about the Lunar New Year that a kindergarten teacher adapted to try her hand at differentiated learning. There were many surprises in that lesson. Students didn't use the materials in quite the way she expected. This happened even though the experienced teacher took time to plan the lesson carefully and anticipate her students' needs and reactions. But instead of halting the children's work or getting frustrated, the teacher appreciated learning more about her students' thinking.

Sometimes we are surprised to find out that a student knows more than we thought or exhibits a more positive attitude toward mathematics than we believed possible. When choice is involved or mathematics is connected to students' interests, students are often able to make mathematical connections in new ways. For example, as Jalissa, a second-grade student explained, "Once I learned that it takes four quarters to make a dollar, I remember that my music teacher told me about quarter notes and that it's the same. Fractions are everywhere. Even when you bake cookies you need a quarter of a cup."

Parents can also be the source of surprises. Teachers have found that when parents understand how much differentiated instruction helps their children, many ask more questions about mathematics and offer more help. They no longer make statements such as "Well, I wasn't very good at mathematics either; that's just the way it is," and recognize that their children can succeed under the right circumstances.

Teachers tell us that they have been surprised to learn that making plans for differentiated instruction is time consuming at first, but in fact saves time in the long run. Another surprise teachers have expressed is that when they differentiate instruction, they feel more creative and empowered as decision makers. Teachers are also surprised at the amount of mathematics they are learning. For example, when Asa asked, "If a hexagon has six sides and an octagon has eight, what has seven?" his teacher realized she didn't know the name and began to wonder about other vocabulary used for labeling specific shapes.

Surprises are part of the joyful mystery of teaching. They keep us interested and help us learn. They are stimulating and can help sustain our commitment to differentiated instruction.

6. Let Students Help.

Classrooms require significant management of people, paper, and materials. Differentiated instruction often requires even more organization and record-keeping skills. You will be more successful if you let your students take some of the responsibility. Students can:

- organize and distribute materials;
- review one another's work;
- keep track of their own choices and work;
- make sure a partner understands an assigned task;
- lead a routine or familiar game; and
- answer many of each other's questions.

When you encourage your students to take more responsibility for the operation of the classroom, you are fostering their confidence and helping them to be more independent. Their involvement may also increase the likelihood that differentiated activities will succeed.

Sometimes the summer months provide teachers with time to tackle projects that never seem to get accomplished during the year. One summer, Jeanette decided to create a math game library. Every year she recognized that most of her students would benefit from more practice with basic facts and mental arithmetic than she felt she had time for during the week. She decided that offering math games they could play over the weekend would give the students extra practice as well as involve their families in their learning.

Jeanette identified six basic games and then designed three levels of each by changing a few rules or the specific numbers involved. She wrote directions for each of these eighteen game versions and collected the materials such as cards and dice that were needed. She wanted four copies of each game so four children could take home the same activity. She decided to store the games in sealed plastic bags that would protect the games as they traveled back and forth to school. In each bag she put a direction sheet, a materials list, the needed supplies, and a reflection sheet that posed the questions: *How did this game help you? What did you learn while playing this game?*

In the fall she organized a storage area for the games and made additional copies of the directions, materials lists, and reflection forms for replacement. She also stored some extra packs of cards and dice in this area. She had a student teacher that fall who was given responsibility for distributing the games on Friday afternoons and checking them back in on Monday mornings. The morning process involved collecting the reflection slips, following up on any missing materials, inserting new reflection sheets, and putting the games away. Students were eager to get their "weekend game" and Jeanette noted a marked improvement in their skills.

Following the winter break, Jeannette's student teacher returned to his college campus and Jeannette took over support of this activity. She was surprised at how difficult it was to accomplish this process at the same time that so many students seemed to need her. After the second Monday morning she was certain that this ritual would need to end; she just couldn't support it. She shared her disappointment with the school's math coach who responded, "Could your students be assigned the job?"

Jeanette had to admit that she hadn't thought of this and at first didn't believe that it would work. As she thought about it throughout the day though, she decided it was worth a try. To her surprise the students became quite adept at taking over this responsibility. Students assigned to this task were listed on the class chore board along with those for the other jobs. Students were given this task for two weeks. The first week they served as assistants so that they could learn what was expected of them. During the second week they were the "math game librarians" in charge of distributing and checking in the materials, as well as training the new assistants. According to Jeanette, "I am so glad this was suggested to me. Instead of being frustrated with having to give this up, my students have taken over and it really works!"

It's worth thinking about some of the clerical and custodial tasks that you are performing. Could your students take more responsibility for them? Are there more important things you could accomplish with this time?

7. Work with Parents.

As you know, parental support can make the difference between success and failure and so it is important that your students' parents understand how your classroom works. You can begin by asking parents to help you know their children better, perhaps by completing surveys or by talking with you informally before or after school. Most parents support efforts to make sure their children's individual needs are met, once they believe that is really going to be the case. The first back-to-school meeting in the fall is also an opportunity to gain parental understanding and support.

When one teacher was on an errand she started to think about the ways she met her own children's needs. She was buying her three children socks and one child wanted high basketball socks, one wanted tennis socks so low you could hardly see them, and her youngest wanted tube socks because as he explained, "The seams hurt my feet when I have shoes on." She chuckled as she thought about how not having the "right socks" could ruin a morning for the entire family. She decided to share these thoughts at back-to-school night and to ask the parents some additional questions such as: *Do each of your children need the same amount of sleep? Enjoy the same activities? Want to eat the same food? In what ways do you adjust to meet these individual needs and interests?* She found parents enjoyed talking about these differences with others who were also trying to meet children's needs that didn't always match. It was simple to then help the parents understand that these same differences existed in the classroom and must be addressed there as well.

Evidence of their children's growth is often the most persuasive argument. Collect early work so that it can be compared to later samples at the first parent-teacher conference. Help parents see the specific concepts and skills their children have gained. Let them know how differentiated instructional strategies supported this improvement. Conferences can also be a time to address their particular concerns about the way you are teaching. Be prepared to help parents understand that:

- All learning activities are directly tied to curriculum goals and standards.
- Differentiated instruction is not a secret method for tracking the students. Groups change often and for a variety of reasons.
- They are always welcome to visit the classroom and participate in the learning activities.

Then follow up initial meetings with newsletters and notes. Newsletters, in particular, can help parents realize the common instructional threads in the classroom, which tend to lessen parental fears that their children are missing out on something.

Sometimes talking about their child's particular learning strengths and weaknesses reminds parents of their own learning profiles. Parents may also have had their own struggles in school because learning needs weren't met. Many teachers find that when they share observations with parents about their child's learning profiles, the parents sometimes ask questions that suggest they identify with what they have just heard. Comments such as "I wonder what kind of learning disability they might find for me if I were just starting out in school today?" or "I loved math class because I didn't have to read as much. But I'm worried about how much more reading my son needs to do in math class today. It seems to be turning him off."

Parents' feelings are strong and their insights about their child's learning are often profound. It is not always easy for parents to open up about their school experiences, but they often do so once a level of trust has been established with the teacher. About a month after a conference in which a teacher shared with a father that his daughter was struggling to learn the names of numbers and that perhaps this was what was making her development in counting so labored and frustrating for her, he emailed her the following note.

Parent Reflection

I had an interesting conversation with my daughter last night that I think is informative concerning her counting abilities. Lately, while playing games like hide-and-seek with her, I have been trying things such as having her start at fifteen when she counts. Naturally, she tends to hang up at the transitions between twenty to thirty to forty, etc., but she has become very upset at this, which has resulted in several teary and frustrated breakdowns. Last night I asked her how she felt about it and she confided to me that she was ashamed and upset. She went on to say that she experiences a lot of stress at school trying to hide these defects from her peers and teachers. These are my words, but her feelings. I am fairly confident that it is an accurate portrayal.

I also want you to know that I had similar learning difficulties as a child and I still have been unable to memorize half of the multiplication table. Perhaps my little one has inherited some of the same mental weaknesses.

(Continued)

Specific to counting, it is my opinion that Beth conceptually understands our number system, but that she just can't recall the words that represent the numbers in a timely fashion. I'm curious if this fits in with your current understanding of the situation. My game plan has been to integrate counting into as many activities as possible during our free time together to provide repetition, but to downplay the errors so that she doesn't become overly upset. I also have a large repertoire of mental tricks that I have accumulated to help me with these issues and I am trying to pass them on to her. She was visibly relieved the first time I confided to her that I, too, had problems like hers. As I am sure you are aware, she is a terribly proud child and I think her discomfort with needing help has caused her to avoid the very things that need more attention.

The teacher was honored to receive this email and knew that this parent's trust was a wonderful gift, one that would help ensure that his daughter's needs would be better met.

8. Find Sources of Professional Development.

Ideally, you are working with colleagues as you strive to further differentiate your mathematics instruction and your school system has provided you with coaches, consultants, time, and resources. Such circumstances are increasingly rare, however, and so it is more than likely that you will need to find some ways to support your efforts. Sometimes just finding one other teacher that will work with you is sufficient. Here are some activities that other teachers have engaged in with one or more colleagues:

- Use planning time or arrange coverage for your class so you can visit each other's classroom. It will help you understand how things are currently working and the challenges each of you face.
- Attend mathematics conferences in the local area to gain new ideas and connect with a wider group of teachers.
- Contact a local college library to see if they have videos on the teaching of mathematics or the general practice of differentiated instruction that you could watch together.
- Work more closely with any instructional specialists in the system. Many specialists are eager to work with teachers who want to transform their practice.
- See if your school system has a membership in the National Council of Teachers of Mathematics (NCTM) and read its journal, *Teaching Children Mathematics,* if it is available. If not, explore NCTM's website and lesson exemplars.

- Talk with your principal to find out what support might be available and find out if any local grants might support attendance at conferences or purchases of resource materials.
- Engage in instructional debriefing with one another about what is happening during math time.

9. Reflect on Your Journey.

When we reflect on our teaching we take the time to actively deliberate about what is working and what needs further attention. Perhaps in the evening we sift through what happened that day, maybe even replaying conversations with and among our students. Sometimes we uncover something that we didn't know was bothering us; sometimes we develop new insights and ideas. Over time, reflecting on what happens in our classrooms can help us transform as well as reaffirm aspects of our teaching habits and beliefs. Though reflecting on one's teaching is always important, it is particularly helpful when we are adjusting our practice.

Some teachers reflect with others about their teaching, some spend their commuting time mulling over the day. A few teachers reflect more intentionally, by keeping a journal. When we write our reflections, we have a record that we can return to and reread, a record that can help us identify patterns and note our changes over time. One teacher has reserved Wednesday afternoon for journal writing. Her reflection tells us about this tradition.

Teacher Reflection

Early on in my career, I found that by Wednesday, I needed to spend a bit more time working after school. By then plans made over the weekend needed more attention and my desk was a bit unorganized. Also, like many, I think of Wednesday as "hump day" and so working a bit longer on that day made sense to me.

At first, it would take me a while to get started once I returned from walking my students to the bus and pick up area. I'd come back to my desk and collapse in my chair, maybe check my email. Sometimes it would take me an hour to get back up to speed. Then I learned about journaling and how that can give you energy, help you to focus. I decided to try it on Wednesdays and it really worked for me. Now when I return to my desk on Wednesdays, I immediately take out my journal and set the minute timer for fifteen minutes. It might take me a minute or two to start writing, but soon the words just begin to flow and I'm often surprised by what I write. I get so focused that I'm usually surprised when the timer goes off. Maybe it's the quiet, the focus, or the introspection, but after writing I have the energy to tackle the other things I need to do.

Some teachers prefer to take notes rather than write in prose. One teacher has a daily writing practice. She makes notes on a file card about two questions each day: *How did I address individual needs today? What did I learn about my students today that will inform what I do tomorrow?* When she comes in the next morning, she rereads the notes to help her focus on the new day. Some teachers follow a similar process, but record these notes in their plan books so that they are maintained over time. Other questions that help us to think about our practice of differentiation include:

- Did the pace of today's mathematics instruction work? For whom? Why? Why not?
- Are all students being challenged mathematically?
- How did I address students' interests this week? Did I learn anything new about an interest a student has?
- How were different types of learning styles addressed today?
- Are there students I want to meet with individually tomorrow?
- Is there a student I am worried about in terms of mathematics?
- Would some of my students be more successful using different mathematical manipulatives, representations, or recording systems?

10. Keep the Vision.

There will no doubt be times when you question the goal of differentiated mathematics instruction, or at least its viability or sustainability. Perhaps a principal will express reservations about your instructional style, a parent will complain about his or her child not doing the same work as the neighbor's child, or a colleague will suggest that you are making too much work for yourself. At these times it's important to remember the significance of the goal and what good sense it makes. Focus on what is working well in your classroom and what is best for your students. Remember that differentiated instruction is a long quest, a journey that never truly ends. It serves as a lens, however, to remind us to focus on how we can best support the individual differences among our students and provides us with a vision as to how we want our classrooms to be organized and our curriculum to be implemented. It takes courage and passion to sustain our efforts toward the goal of differentiated instruction, and the vision of all of our students becoming successful learners of mathematics.

Blackline Masters

Parent or Guardian Questionnaire

Alternative Parent or Guardian Survey

What Interests You?

Who Are You as a Learner?

What Do You Think About Mathematics?

Sums Investigation: Red

Sums Investigation: Blue

Sums Investigation: Green

Shape Critter Card: Red

Shape Critter Card: Blue

Shape Critter Card: Green

Train Patterns: Red

Train Patterns: Blue

Train Patterns: Green

Ordering Numbers: Red

Ordering Numbers: Blue

Ordering Numbers: Green

Part-Part-Whole Menu

Addition Think Tac Toe

RAFT: Time

What Matches You?

Self-Assessment of Differentiation Practices

Parent or Guardian Questionnaire

Dear Parent or Guardian:

I am always so excited about the start of the school year and a roomful of eager children. I look forward to getting to know each and every one of them, as well as their families. As no one knows your child as well as you do, I am hoping that you will have the time to answer these few questions. There are no right or wrong answers, just responses that will help me to better meet your child's needs when learning math. I am very interested to help children realize that math is an important part of the world, and therefore exciting to learn. I believe by connecting the learning of math to other important aspects of your child's life, I can make it more relevant and exciting. Please feel free to call me if you have any questions. Thank you.

1. What are your child's favorite hobbies, interests, pastimes, books?

2. In what ways is mathematics part of your child's life at home?

3. What, if any, concerns do you have about your child's knowledge of mathematics?

4. What is a mathematical strength that you see in your child?

From *Math for All: Differentiating Instruction, Grades K–2* by Linda Dacey and Rebeka Eston Salemi. © 2007 Math Solutions Publications.

Alternative Parent or Guardian Survey

Dear Parent or Guardian:

This first day has been a wonderful start to the school year. I am excited about getting to know each of my new students. I am hoping that you will help me by completing this questionnaire about mathematics. There are no right or wrong answers! Please feel free to call me if you have any questions. Thank you.

1 = agree
2 = somewhat agree
3 = somewhat disagree
4 = disagree

My child will stick with a math problem, even when it is difficult.	1	2	3	4
My child lacks confidence in mathematics.	1	2	3	4
My child has strong computational skills.	1	2	3	4
My child's favorite subject is mathematics.	1	2	3	4
My child becomes frustrated solving math problems.	1	2	3	4
My child does math homework independently.	1	2	3	4
As a parent, it is my job to help my child with math homework.	1	2	3	4
Math is talked about at home and is part of our everyday life.	1	2	3	4
I do not always understand the way my child thinks about math problems.	1	2	3	4
Math is taught better today than when I was in school.	1	2	3	4

Comments:

From *Math for All: Differentiating Instruction, Grades K–2* by Linda Dacey and Rebeka Eston Salemi. © 2007 Math Solutions Publications.

What Interests You?

1. What activities do you like to do after school?

2. What are your favorite sports or games?

3. What do you like to do at indoor recess?

4. If you could plan a field trip, where would the class go?

5. Who is your favorite character from a book or a video?

6. Which of these things do you like most? Put a 1 there.
   Which of these things do you like second best? Put a 2 there.

   ___ music   ___ reading
   ___ sports   ___ being outside
   ___ acting   ___ drawing
   ___ playing with friends   ___ using blocks

From *Math for All: Differentiating Instruction, Grades K–2* by Linda Dacey and Rebeka Eston Salemi.
© 2007 Math Solutions Publications.

Who Are You as a Learner?

1. If you could learn about anything at school, what would you choose?

2. What do you know a lot about?

3. How do you work best in school?
   __ alone   __ partner   __ small group   __ large group

4. Where do you like to work at school?
   __ desk   __ table   __ rug   __ library area   __ other

5. Do you learn best when your classroom is
   __ quiet   __ somewhat quiet   __ somewhat noisy   __ noisy

6. Do you like schoolwork to be
   __ easy   __ somewhat easy   __ somewhat hard   __ hard

7. What else helps you to learn?

8. What makes it hard for you to learn?

From *Math for All: Differentiating Instruction, Grades K–2* by Linda Dacey and Rebeka Eston Salemi. © 2007 Math Solutions Publications.

What Do You Think About Mathematics?

1. Math is important to learn because . . .

2. When I am learning math I feel . . .

3. One thing I am good at in math is . . .

4. One thing I am not good at yet in math is . . .

5. This year in math I want to learn about . . .

Sums Investigation: Red

Getting Started

- Write the numbers *3, 6, 8,* and *10* on the blank cards clipped to this sheet. Write one number on each card.
- Put your number cards in the bag and shake it.

To Play

- Pull out two cards. Record the numbers and their sum.
- Return the cards to the bag and take another turn.
- Do this at least fifteen times.

Stop and Think

- List all the sums you get.

What Did You Learn?

- Do you think you have all the different sums that can be made by adding two of your numbers at a time?
- Talk together about why you think you have all the possibilities.

From *Math for All: Differentiating Instruction, Grades K–2* by Linda Dacey and Rebeka Eston Salemi. © 2007 Math Solutions Publications.

Sums Investigation: Blue

Getting Started

- Write the numbers *4*, *5*, *11*, and *17* on the blank cards clipped to this sheet. Write one number on each card.
- Put your number cards in the bag and shake it.

To Play

- Pull out two cards. Record the numbers and their sum.
- Return the cards to the bag and take another turn.
- Do this several more times.

Stop and Think

- Make a list all the sums you could get when using these four number cards.
- Continue to play.

What Did You Learn?

- Make a list showing all the sums you made.
- Do you think you have them all?
- Talk together about why you think you have all the possibilities.

From *Math for All: Differentiating Instruction, Grades K–2* by Linda Dacey and Rebeka Eston Salemi.
© 2007 Math Solutions Publications.

Sums Investigation: Green

Getting Started

- Write the numbers *12*, *15*, *19*, and *24* on the blank cards clipped to this sheet.
- Put your number cards in the bag and shake it.

To Play

- Pull out two cards. Record the numbers and their sum.
- Return the cards to the bag and take another turn.
- Do this a few times.

Stop and Think

- How many different sums do you get when you pull two of these number cards from the bag?
- How do you know you have all the possibilities?

What Did You Learn?

- Write about your thinking.

From *Math for All: Differentiating Instruction, Grades K–2* by Linda Dacey and Rebeka Eston Salemi. © 2007 Math Solutions Publications.

Shape Critter Card: Red

Each of these is a whirly do.

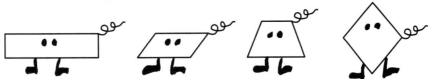

None of these is a whirly do.

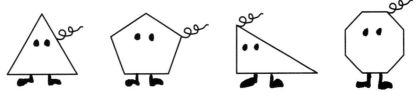

Which of these are whirly dos?

Make up a name for these critters and write it in the blank.

1. Each of these is a _____.

Draw one more critter above. Be sure it fits the rule.

2. None of these is a _____.

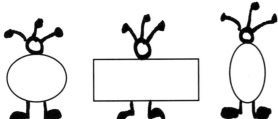

Draw one more critter above. Make sure it does not fit the rule.

From *Math for All: Differentiating Instruction, Grades K–2* by Linda Dacey and Rebeka Eston Salemi.
© 2007 Math Solutions Publications.

Shape Critter Card: Blue

Each of these is a whirly do.

None of these is a whirly do.

Which one of these is a whirly do?

Make up a name for these critters and write it in the blank.

1. Each of these is a _____.

Draw one more critter above. Be sure it fits the rule.

2. None of these is a _____.

Draw one more critter above. Make sure it does not fit the rule.

Shape Critter Card: Green

Each of these is a whirly do.

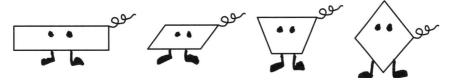

None of these is a whirly do.

Which one of these is a whirly do?

Make up your own critters.

Write their name in each blank.

Draw the pictures.

Write your rule on the back.

Trade cards with a friend and find the rules.

1. Each of these is a _____.

2. None of these is a _____.

3. Which of these are _____?

From *Math for All: Differentiating Instruction, Grades K–2* by Linda Dacey and Rebeka Eston Salemi.
© 2007 Math Solutions Publications.

Train Patterns: Red

Take a look at these trains.
Can you see a pattern?

It takes 2 □, 4 ○, and 1 △ to build a 2-car train.
So, it takes a total of 7 pieces to build a 2-car train.

1-car train   2-car train   3-car train

- Use the □, ○, and △ pieces to build a 4-car train. How many pieces did you use?

- Draw a 5-car train. How many △ did you draw?

- How many □ does it take to build a 6-car train?

- How many ○ does it take to build a 7-car train?

- Write how many of each piece you need to build a 10-car train.

  _____ □   _____ ○   _____ △

From *Math for All: Differentiating Instruction, Grades K–2* by Linda Dacey and Rebeka Eston Salemi.
© 2007 Math Solutions Publications.

Train Patterns: Blue

Take a look at these trains.

Can you see a pattern?

It takes 2 □, 4 ○, and 1 △ to build a 2-car train.

So, it takes a total of 7 pieces to build a 2-car train.

| 1-car train | 2-car train | 3-car train |

How many of each piece will it take to build a 6-car train?

_____ □   _____ ○   _____ △

What is the total number of pieces it will take to build a
10-car train?

Write and draw to show how you know.

From *Math for All: Differentiating Instruction, Grades K–2* by Linda Dacey and Rebeka Eston Salemi.
© 2007 Math Solutions Publications.

Train Patterns: Green

Take a look at these trains.

Can you see a pattern?

It takes 2 □, 4 ○, and 1 △ to build a 2-car train.

So, it takes a total of 7 pieces to build a 2-car train.

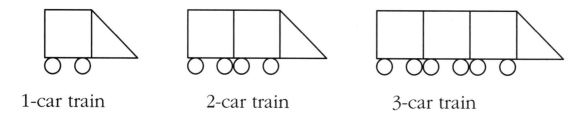

1-car train   2-car train   3-car train

What is the total number of pieces it will take to build a
10-car train?

Janelle used 46 pieces to build a train.

How many cars does Janelle's train have?

Write and draw to show how you know.

Ordering Numbers: Red

Materials: 3 paper plates, counters, and number cards 0–6

Task: Create a specific set of objects based on quantity.

- Turn over a number card and make a set of objects to show how many.

- Keep going until you have made 3 different sets.

- Which set has the most?

Ordering Numbers: Blue

Materials: 6 paper plates, counters, and number cards 0–6

Task: Create a specific set of objects based on quantity.

- Turn over a number card and make a set of objects to show how many.

- Keep going until you have made 6 different sets.

- Put the sets in order.

- Which set has the most?

- Which set has the least?

From *Math for All: Differentiating Instruction, Grades K–2* by Linda Dacey and Rebeka Eston Salemi. © 2007 Math Solutions Publications.

Ordering Numbers: Green

Materials: 6 paper plates, counters, and number cards 0–10

Task: Create a specific set of objects based on quantity.

- Turn over a number card and make a set of objects to show how many.

- Keep going until you have made 6 different sets.

- Put the sets in order.

- Which set has the most?

- Which set has the least?

- Which sets are missing?

Part-Part-Whole Menu

Main Course (You must do each one.)

- Imagine that the children in *Anno's Counting House* move 2 at a time. Work with a partner to tell this story. Use the teddy bears to model the story as you tell it. After each move, represent the number of children in each house and the number of children in all. Talk about what you notice about your numbers.

- Solve 5 of the problems in the parts-whole story box.

- Imagine 3 numbers: 2 parts, and the whole. Write or tape-record ways to find 1 of these missing numbers when you know the other 2 numbers.

Side Orders (Complete two.)

- Create a puzzle with 10 pieces. On 5 of the pieces write or draw 2 parts. On the other 5 pieces write or draw a whole for each piece with 2 parts. Trade your puzzle with a classmate. Match the pieces in your classmate's puzzle.

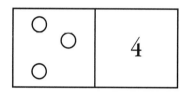 

- Use the *Unifix Software* (Hickey 1996) to make single bars. Then create 2-part bars to match each single bar.

- Get some Unifix cubes and a cup. Play *Cover Up* with a partner.

- Get some red and blue Unifix cubes. Make some towers of 10. How many are red and how many are blue? Make a list.

Desserts (Do one or more if you are interested.)

- Write 2 problems to put in our parts-whole problem box.

- Choose a number as your whole. Make a picture book of your number in parts.

- Make up songs, poems, or raps about parts and wholes.

Addition Think Tac Toe

Choose and complete one activity in each row.

Draw a picture that shows a model of 17 + 15. Make connections between your drawing and how you find the sum.	Your brother added 18 and 4 and got the answer 23. What could you show and tell your brother to help him understand why his answer is wrong?	Write directions for two different ways to find the sum of 36 + 19 when you use paper and pencil.
Place the numbers: 10, 20, 30, 40, 50, and 60, so that the sum of each side is 90. ○ ○　○ ○　○　○ Write one more problem like this one and trade it with a classmate.	Place two addition signs to make a number sentence that is true. 23,915 = 47 Write two more problems like this one and trade them with a classmate.	Which two numbers should you exchange so that the sum of the numbers on each card is the same? 12　11　5 8　3　4 6　10　13 Write two more problems like this one and trade them with a classmate.
Make a list of ways you use addition outside of school.	Interview a classmate about what he or she knows about addition. Find out as much as you can in three minutes. Write me a report with suggestions for teaching.	Your friend solved a word problem by adding 20 and 7 and then subtracting 3. Write two interesting word problems that your friend could have solved this way.

RAFT: Time

Role	Audience	Format	Topic
Teacher	Our class	Riddles (with clues and clock pictures)	What Time Is It?
Writer/ Illustrator	Second graders	Illustrated children's book	All About Time
Camp Counselor	Campers	Schedule with activities and times	First Day of Camp
Self	Parents	Analog clock with explanation	This Is the Time I Like the Best!
Self	Classmates	Collage of clocks with written times and activities	How I Spend Saturdays

From *Math for All: Differentiating Instruction, Grades K–2* by Linda Dacey and Rebeka Eston Salemi. © 2007 Math Solutions Publications.

What Matches You?

Try to find two classmates to fit each description. Have them write their initials in the box they match. No one may initial more than three boxes on one sheet.

I learn best through hands-on experiences.	I like to solve problems.	I prefer to work alone.	I find it helpful to write about my mathematical ideas.	I sometimes get confused when others explain their thinking.
I like face clocks better than digital ones.	I like to measure things.	I use drawings to understand a problem.	I learn best when the teacher writes on the board.	I find Unifix cubes more helpful than base ten blocks.
I am better at subtraction than addition.	I like building things.	I need quiet when I work.	I find base ten blocks more helpful than Unifix cubes.	I prefer to work with others.
I know my basic facts well.	I like digital clocks better than face clocks.	I am better at addition than subtraction.	I like geometry.	I like to find different ways to solve problems.
I like to brainstorm ideas with a group and then follow up alone.	I like logic games and puzzles.	I want rules for solving problems.	I would like to use a calculator all of the time.	I like collecting data and making graphs.

Self-Assessment of Differentiation Practices

Rate your agreement with each of the following statements.

1 – disagree strongly   2 – disagree somewhat   3 – agree somewhat   4 – agree strongly

I feel confident in my ability to facilitate the learning of mathematics at my grade level.	1　2　3　4
I can challenge my most mathematically able students.	1　2　3　4
I know how to support my least mathematically able students.	1　2　3　4
I can meet students' individual needs in mathematics as well as or better than I can in literacy.	1　2　3　4
I have enough knowledge of mathematics to support a variety of models, representations, and procedures in my classroom.	1　2　3　4

Rate the likelihood of the following activities occurring within a week of mathematical instruction.

1 – very unlikely   2 – somewhat unlikely   3 – somewhat likely   4 – very likely

I work with students individually.	1　2　3　4
Students are grouped by readiness.	1　2　3　4
Students are grouped by interest.	1　2　3　4
Students are grouped by learning preferences.	1　2　3　4
Different students are working with different materials and tasks.	1　2　3　4

Check off each instructional strategy that you have tried in your teaching of mathematics. Give yourself two points for each checkmark.

☐ Transformation of tasks to make them more open-ended
☐ RAFT
☐ Learning station
☐ Menu
☐ Think Tac Toe
☐ Compacting
☐ Tiered task

Total Score: _____

Scores range from 10 to 54.

Are you comfortable with where you are on this continuum of change? What next step(s) do you want to take?

From *Math for All: Differentiating Instruction, Grades K–2* by Linda Dacey and Rebeka Eston Salemi. © 2007 Math Solutions Publications.

References

Adams, Thomasenia. 2003. "Reading Mathematics: More Than Words Can Say." *The Reading Teacher* 56 (May): 786–795.

Anno, Mitsumasa. 1982. *Anno's Counting House.* New York: Philomel Books.

Ansell, Ellen, and Helen Doerr. 2000. "NAEP Findings Regarding Gender: Achievement, Affect, and Instructional Experiences." In *Research Results from the Seventh Mathematics Assessment of the National Assessment of Educational Progress,* edited by Edward Silver and Patricia Kenney (73–106). Reston, VA: National Council of Teachers of Mathematics.

Baker, Anne, Kimberly Schirner, and Jo Hoffman. 2006. "Multiage Mathematics: Scaffolding Young Children's Mathematical Learning." *Teaching Children Mathematics* 13 (August): 19–21.

Bessor, Rusty. 2003. "Helping English-Language Learners Develop Computational Fluency." *Teaching Children Mathematics* 9 (February): 294–299.

Bley, Nancy, and Carol Thornton. 1995. *Teaching Mathematics to Students with Learning Disabilities.* 3d ed. Austin, TX: Pro-Ed.

Bloom, Benjamin, ed. 1984. *Taxonomy of Educational Objectives: Book 1 Cognitive Domain.* Reading, MA: Addison-Wesley.

Bracey, Gerald. 1999. "The Demise of the Asian Math Gene." *Phi Delta Kappan* 80 (April): 619–620.

Bray, Wendy. 2005. "Supporting Diverse Learners: Teacher Collaboration in an Inclusive Classroom." *Teaching Children Mathematics* 11 (February): 324–329.

Burns, Marilyn. 1988. *A Collection of Math Lessons: From Grades 1 Through 3.* Sausalito, CA: Math Solutions Publications.

Calkins, Lucy M., with Shelley Harwayne. 1991. *Living Between the Lines.* Portsmouth, NH: Heinemann.

Chipman, Susan, David Krantz, and Rae Silver. 2002. "Mathematics Anxiety and Science Careers Among Able College Women." *Pyschological Science* 3: 292–295.

Cole, Karen, Janet Coffey, and Shelley Goldman. 1999. "Using Assessments to Improve Equity in Mathematics: Assessment That Is Open, Explicit, and Accessible Helps All Students Achieve the Goals of Standards-Based Learning." *Educational Leadership* 56 (March): 56–58.

Colen, Yong. 2006. "A Call for Early Intervention for Mathematically Gifted Elementary Students: A Russian Model." *Teaching Children Mathematics* 13 (December/January): 280–284.

Communications Division for the Office of School Education, Department of Education, Employment and Training. 2001. *Early Numeracy Interview Booklet.* State of Victoria.

Dacey, Linda, and Rebeka Eston. 1999. *Growing Mathematical Ideas in Kindergarten.* Sausalito, CA: Math Solutions Publications.

———. 2002. *Show and Tell: Representing and Communicating Mathematical Ideas in K–2 Classrooms.* Sausalito, CA: Math Solutions Publications.

Economopolous, Karen, Megan Murray, Kim O'Neil, Douglas Clements, Julie Sarama, and Susan Jo Russell. 1998. *Investigations in Number, Data, and Space: Making Shapes and Building Blocks.* White Plains, NY: Dale Seymour.

Educational Development Center. 1995. *Equity in Education Series: Gender Fair Math.* Newton, MA: Educational Development Center.

Edwards, Carol, ed. 1999. *Changing the Faces of Mathematics: Perspectives on Asian Americans and Pacific Islanders.* Reston, VA: National Council of Teachers of Mathematics.

Erwin, Jonathan. 2004. *The Classroom of Choice: Giving Students What They Need and Getting What You Want.* Alexandria, VA: Association for Supervision and Curriculum Development.

Furner, Joseph, and Mary Lou Duffy. 2002. "Equity for All Students in the New Millennium: Disabling Math Anxiety." *Intervention in School & Clinic* 4 (November): 67–74.

Gardner, Howard. 2000. *Intelligence Reframed: Multiple Intelligences for the 21st Century.* New York: Basic.

Garrison, Leslie. 1997. "Making the NCTM's Standards Work for Emergent English Speakers." *Teaching Children Mathematics* 4 (November): 132–138.

Gavin, M. Katherine, and Sally Reis. 2000. "Helping Teachers to Encourage Talented Girls in Mathematics." *Gifted Child Today* 26 (Winter): 32–44.

Gelzheriser, Lynn, Bonnie Giesemer, Robert Pruzek, and Joel Meyers. 2000. "How Are Developmentally Appropriate or Traditional Teaching Practices Related to the Mathematics Achievement of General and Special Education Students?" *Early Childhood and Development* 11 (March): 217–238.

Ginsburg, Herbert. 1997. "Mathematics Learning Disabilities: A View from Developmental Psychology." *Journal of Learning Disabilities* 30 (January/February): 20–33.

Ginsburg, Herbert, and Arthur Baroody. 2003. *Test of Early Mathematics Ability (TEMA3)*. Austin, TX: Pro-Ed.

Gregory, Gayle. 2005. *Differentiating Instruction with Style: Aligning Teacher and Learner Intelligences for Maximum Achievement*. Thousand Oaks, CA: Corwin Press.

Gregory, Gayle, and Carolyn Chapman. 2002. *Differentiated Instructional Strategies: One Size Doesn't Fit All*. Thousand Oaks, CA: Corwin Press.

Guillaume, Andrea. 2005. *Classroom Mathematics Inventory for Grades K–6: An Informal Assessment*. Boston: Pearson.

Heacox, Diane. 2002. *Differentiating Instruction in the Regular Classroom: How to Reach and Teach All Learners, Grades 3–12*. Minneapolis, MN: Free Spirit Press.

Hickey, Ann-Patrice. 1997. *Unifix Software*. Rowley, MA: Didax.

Huinker, DeAnn, ed. 2006. *Mathematics Assessment Sampler*. Series ed. Anne Collins. Reston, VA: National Council of Teachers of Mathematics.

Inspiration Software. 2005. *Kidspiration 2.1*. Beavertown, OR: Inspiration Software.

Isenbarger, Lynn, and Arthur Baroody. 2001. "Fostering the Mathematical Power of Children with Behavioral Difficulties: The Case of Carter." *Teaching Children Mathematics* 7 (April): 468–471.

Jackson, Marjorie. 1999. *Dragon Feet*. Katonah, NY: Richard C. Owen.

Jennings, Lenora, and Lori Likis. 2005. "Meeting a Math Achievement Crisis." *Educational Leadership* 62 (March): 65–68.

Jensen, Eric. 2005. *Teaching with the Brain in Mind*. 2d ed. Alexandria, VA: Association for Supervision and Curriculum Development.

Jitenda, Asha. 2002. "Teaching Students Math Problem-Solving Through Graphic Representations." *Teaching Exceptional Children* 34 (March/April): 34–38.

Jones, Eric, and W. Thomas Southern. 2003. "Balancing Perspectives on Mathematics Instruction." *Focus on Exceptional Children* 35 (May): 1–16.

Kenney, Joan, Euthecia Hancewicz, Loretta Heuer, Diana Metsisto, and Cynthia L. Tuttle. 2005. *Literacy Strategies for Improving Mathematics Instruction*. Alexandria, VA: Association for Supervision and Curriculum Development.

Khisty, Lena. 2002. "Mathematics Learning and the Latino Student: Suggestions from Research for Classroom Practice." *Teaching Children Mathematics* 9 (September): 32–35.

Losq, Christine. 2005. "Number Concepts and Special Needs Students: The Power of Ten-Frame Tiles." *Teaching Children Mathematics* 11 (February): 310–315.

Lubienski, Sarah, and Mack Shelly. 2003. *A Closer Look at U.S. Mathematics Instruction and Achievement: Examinations of Race and SES in a Decade of NAEP Data*. A paper presented at the annual meeting of the American Educational Research Association, Chicago. ERIC Document No. ED476468. Retrieved July 17, 2004 from www.eric.ed.gov/sitemap/html_0900000b8017a624.html.

Malloy, Carol, and Laura Brader-Araje, eds. 1998. *Challenges in the Mathematics Education of African-American Children: Proceedings of the Benjamin Banneker Association Leadership Conference*. Reston, VA: National Council of Teachers of Mathematics.

Marzano, Robert, Debra Pickering, and Jane Pollock. 2001. *Classroom Instruction That Works: Research-Based Strategies for Increasing Student Achievement*. Alexandria, VA: Association for Supervision and Curriculum Development.

Milton Bradley. 1999. *Hi Ho! Cherry-O*. Pawtucket, RI: Hasbro, Inc.

Moon, Jean, and Linda Schulman. 1995. *Finding the Connections: Linking Assessment, Instruction, and Curriculum in Elementary Mathematics*. Portsmouth, NH: Heinemann.

National Council of Teachers of Mathematics. 2000. *Principles and Standards for School Mathematics*. Reston, VA: National Council of Teachers of Mathematics.

———. 2006. *Curriculum Focal Points for Prekindergarten Through Grade 8 Mathematics: A Quest for Coherence*. Reston, VA: National Council of Teachers of Mathematics.

Newstead, Karen. 1998. "Aspects of Children's Mathematics Anxiety." *Educational Studies in Mathematics* 36 (June): 53–71.

Ortiz-Franco, Luis, Norma G. Hernandez, and Yolanda De La Cruz, eds. 1999. *Changing the Faces of Mathematics: Perspectives on Latinos*. Reston, VA: National Council of Teachers of Mathematics.

Parish, Peggy. 1979. *Amelia Bedelia Helps Out*. New York: Greenwillow Books.

Reid, Margarette S. 1990. *The Button Box*. New York: Dutton's Children's Books.

Richardson, Kathy. 2003. *Assessing Math Concepts*. Bellingham, WA: Math Perspectives.

Rotigel, Jennifer, and Susan Fello. 2004. "Mathematically Gifted Students: How Can We Meet Their Needs?" *Gifted Child Today* 27: 46–52.

Silver, Harvey, Richard Strong, and Matthew Perini. 2000. *So Each May Learn: Integrating Learning Styles and Multiple Intelligences*. Alexandria, VA: Association for Supervision and Curriculum Development.

Sliva, Julie. 2004. *Teaching Inclusive Mathematics to Special Learners, K–6*. Thousand Oaks, CA: Corwin Press.

Sloan, Tina, C. J. Daane, and Judy Giesen. 2002. "Mathematics Anxiety and Learning Styles: What Is the Relationship in Elementary Preservice Teachers?" *School Science and Mathematics* 102 (February): 84–87.

Smith, Frank. 2002. *The Glass Wall: Why Mathematics Can Seem Difficult*. New York: Teachers College Press.

Smutny, Joan, and S. E. Fremd. 2004. *Differentiating for the Young Child: Teaching Strategies Across the Content Areas (K–3)*. Thousand Oaks, CA: Corwin Press.

Snow, D. R. 2005. *Classroom Strategies for Helping At-Risk Learners*. Alexandria, VA: Association for Supervision and Curriculum Development.

Sousa, D. A. 2001. *How the Special Needs Brain Works*. Thousand Oaks, CA: Corwin Press.

Sprenger, Marilee. 2002. *Becoming a "Wiz" at Brain-Based Teaching: How to Make Every Year the Best Year*. Thousand Oaks, CA: Corwin Press.

———. 2003. *Differentiation Through Learning Styles and Memory*. Thousand Oaks, CA: Corwin Press.

Strutchens, Marilyn, Martin Johnson, and William Tate, eds. 2000. *Changing the Faces of Mathematics: Perspectives on African Americans*. Reston, VA: National Council of Teachers of Mathematics.

Tate, William. 1997. "Race-Ethnicity, SES, Gender, and Language Proficiency Trends in Mathematics Achievement: An Update." *Journal for Research in Mathematics Education* 28 (December): 652–679.

Thornton, Carol, and Graham Jones. 1996. "Adapting Instruction for Students with Special Needs K–8." *Journal of Education* 178 (2): 59–69.

Tomlinson, Carol. 1999. *The Differentiated Classroom: Responding to the Needs of All Learners*. Alexandria, VA: Association for Supervision and Curriculum Development.

———. 2003a. *Differentiation in Practice: A Resource Guide for Differentiating Curriculum, Grade K–5*. Alexandria, VA: Association for Supervision and Curriculum Development.

———. 2003b. *Fulfilling the Promise of the Differentiated Classroom: Strategies and Tools for Responsive Teaching.* Alexandria, VA: Association for Supervision and Curriculum Development.

Torres-Velasquez, Diane, and Gilberto Lobo. 2004/2005. "Culturally Responsive Mathematics: Teaching and English Language Learners." *Teaching Children Mathematics* 11 (December/January): 249–255.

U.S. Census Bureau. 2003. *Language Use and English Speaking Ability: 2000.* Retrieved January 11, 2006, from www.census.gov/prod/2003pubs/c2kbr-29.pdf.

Van Luit, Johannes, and Esther Schopman. 2000. "Improving Early Numeracy of Young Children with Special Education Needs." *Remedial and Special Education* 21 (January/February): 27–40.

Vygotsky, Lev. 1978. *Mind and Society.* Cambridge, MA: Harvard University Press.

Weaver, Laurie, and Catherine Gaines. 1999. "What to Do When They Don't Speak English: Teaching Mathematics to English-Language Learners." In *Mathematics in the Early Years,* edited by Juanita Copley. Reston, VA: National Council of Teachers of Mathematics.

Wilkins, Michelle Muller, Jesse Wilkins, and Tamra Oliver. 2006. "Differentiating the Curriculum for Elementary Gifted Mathematics Students." *Teaching Children Mathematics* 13 (August): 6–13.

Wolfe, Pat. 2001. *Brain Matters: Translating Research into Classroom Practice.* Alexandria, VA: Association for Supervision and Curriculum Development.

Yatvin, Joanne. 2004. *A Room with a Differentiated View: How to Serve All Children as Individual Learners.* Portsmouth, NH: Heinemann.

Zaslavsky, Claudia. 2002. "Exploring World Cultures in Math Class." *Educational Leadership* 48 (October): 66–69.

Index